The Voyage Perilous

To keep an idea living intact, tinged with all its original feeling, its original mood, preserving in it all the ecstasy which attended its birth, to keep it so all the way from the brain to the hand and transfer it on paper a living thing with color, odor, sound, life all in it, that is what art means, that is the greatest of all the gifts of the gods. And that is the voyage perilous.

Nebraska State Journal, 1 March 1896

SUSAN J. ROSOWSKI

The Voyage Perilous

Willa Cather's Romanticism

University of Nebraska Press   Lincoln & London

Portions of Chapters 8 and 16 have previously been published, in different form, as "Willa Cather's *A Lost Lady:* Art versus the Closing Frontier," *Great Plains Quarterly* 2 (Fall 1982): 239–49, and "Willa Cather's American Gothic: *Sapphira and the Slave Girl,*" *Great Plains Quarterly* 4 (Fall 1984): 220–30, respectively.

The paper in this book meets the minimum requirements of American National Standard for Information Sciences — Permanence of Paper for Printed Library Materials, ANSI Z39.48-1984.

Library of Congress Cataloging-in-Publication Data
Rosowski, Susan J.
   The voyage perilous.
   Bibliography: p.
   Includes index.
   1. Cather, Willa, 1873–1947 — Criticism and interpretation. 2. Romanticism — United States. I. Title.
PS3505.A87Z818   1986   813'.52   86–4341
ISBN 0-8032-3874-6 (alk. paper)

FOR MY MOTHER   AND FOR

AND FATHER   JIM

Contents

Illustrations

Preface

The ultimate truths are never seen through the reason,
but through the imagination.[1]

"Children, the sea, the sun, God himself are all romanticists,"
Willa Cather wrote in 1895.[2] Only twenty-one at the time,
Cather was later to moderate her tone, but never her affinity for
romanticism. This was the tradition of the authors she revered:
Hugo, Dumas père, Daudet, Stevenson, Poe, James, Shelley—
and especially Keats. It was the tradition in which Cather formed
her own principles of art and to which she remained committed
throughout her life.

Unfortunately, "romantic" has long had an effect upon readers
similar to "Nebraska," the very mention of which, Cather once
said, "throws the delicately attuned critic into a clammy shiver of
embarrassment."[3] Unwilling, perhaps, to saddle their subject
with both Nebraska and romanticism, Cather scholars have ap-
plied to her writing a distractingly wide range of critical tags.
"That she was . . . called a classicist, a Jamesian sophisticate, and
the reserved stylist of the novel démeublé may be one of the great
jokes of literary criticism," Bernice Slote noted in 1966, for "the
reality" constant through Cather's work is that she was "primarily
a romantic."[4] Since then, the joke has continued. Other critics
have used other labels—feminist, naturalist, lesbian, realist—yet
there remains no satisfactory interpretation of Willa Cather's writing within the intellectual tradition most important to her.[5]

Tides of criticism change, however, and so has the stock of
romanticism, until we no longer respond to it with a knee-jerk
defensive reflex. Robert Langbaum's argument that romanticism
is a modern tradition is just one of the discussions that stress the
continuity between the English Romantics and ourselves, advanced by Geoffrey Hartman, Northrop Frye, M. H. Abrams, and
Harold Bloom—and more recently extended to romantic impulses in the Victorian and modern novels by Donald D. Stone and

Charles Schug.[6] During this time Cather's reputation too has gone up steadily, until today there is little danger of equating her regionalism with narrow vision or mistaking her lucidity for shallowness. While scholars have concentrated upon collecting materials, critics have focused on interpreting diversity, demonstrating that Cather uses regional subjects for universal themes, conveys complexity beneath apparent simplicity, and has "unusual range and depth of . . . imagination."[7] Now, with basic primary materials available and Cather's major themes and attitudes identified, we are ready to address the broader question of Cather's place in literary tradition and to recognize that through this diversity runs a clear pattern of romanticism.

Before proceeding further, I must make preliminary distinctions among meanings of that most notoriously slippery of terms, *romanticism*. With it, I refer not to a recurring quality of human nature, the sense in which Cather frequently used *romantic* in her letters and essays. Instead, I refer to a historical movement that in literature began in the late eighteenth century in reaction against dehumanizing implications of the scientific world view.[8] The essential characteristic of romanticism concerns a mode of perception by which the imagination is used in its synthesizing or creative powers to transform and give meaning to an alien or meaningless material world. In this sense, the Romantics inaugurated modern literature: moderns and Romantics hold a common view of public official tradition as discredited and of the world as essentially meaningless, and both look to the individual creative imagination to create a new order.

Working from these premises, I only mention Cather's subjects and themes, to note that they include those familiar to the Wordsworthian school of romanticism: love of nature, sympathetic interest in the past, exaltation of youth and the superior individual. Indeed, I would argue that one of the distinguishing features of Cather's romanticism is that she was not nearly so concerned with *what* we see as with the way in which we do so. My thesis is that Willa Cather early took up the romantic challenge to vindicate imaginative thought in a world threatened by materialism and pursued it with remarkable consistency throughout her career. My belief is that by tracing the pattern of romanticism through her canon, especially the novels, we can better understand all her writing as well as her place in literary history. I have written this book accordingly, to be read as a whole, yet so that readers interested primarily in individual novels will find that the discussion of each can stand on its own.

Cather's early essays and stories lay out the terms of her lifelong commitment to vindicating imaginative thought in a world grown material. Her novels, the major subjects of this study, develop that commitment. The initial novels explore the nature of the imagination and celebrate its power; the middle works offer the imagination as a vehicle by which the individual might wrest personal salvation from an increasingly alien world; the late novels are Gothic tales in which the imagination breaks through not to "divine truths" but to darkness.

In her early writing Cather explored the terms of imaginative thought and celebrated creativity. Her first novel, *Alexander's Bridge* (1912), is an allegory about the romantic imagination in its most primitive form, energy flowing between the spiritual world and the physical one. Cather aptly viewed *Alexander's Bridge* as an apprentice work in which she laid out the materials she would later employ; it is a book about the romantic imagination more than an example of it. As such, it prepared the way for *O Pioneers!* (1913), a two-part pastoral charged with the energy of an artist revelling in her new-found imaginative power to create beauty from both triumph and tragedy. In the first part, Cather drew upon Virgilian pastoral tradition to celebrate a communal myth of New World paradise; in the second, she drew upon a modern pastoral tradition to exalt a private paradise within an alien world. With its yoking of classical and romantic materials, *O Pioneers!* serves as a paradigm for Cather's most successful writing, in which she infused a romantic mode with classical myths.

In her next novel Cather again wrote of the imagination, this time in more personal terms. *The Song of the Lark* (1915) is Willa Cather's *Prelude,* in which she used an autobiographical character to trace the growth of an artist's mind. In doing so Cather explored a theme that runs through modern literature, the development of a personal self to serve as a source of value in an otherwise common world, and she made hers the terms of the romantics, with their separation of self and world, private and public.

These are the terms that Cather incorporated into the narrative structure of *My Ántonia* (1918), in which a subject (Jim Burden) writes of an "object" (Ántonia). Here Cather for the first time wrote a fully developed literature of process. The novel is about the capacity of the mind to perceive symbols as self-generating sources of meaning. The narrator, Jim Burden, states a differentia of modern literature inherited from the Romantics when he writes that Ántonia "had always been one to leave images in the mind that did not fade — that grew stronger with time."[9]

In *One of Ours* (1922) Cather wrote of the tragedy of a man who lacks this symbol-making capacity. Here Cather retained the romantic terms of subject and object, but instead of celebrating the reconciliation of the two, she stressed the disparity between them. This book in which Cather explored a character's failure of the imagination preceded that in which she most fully realized its creative potential. *A Lost Lady* (1923) is a carefully modulated romantic prose-poem. In it, as in a Keatsian ode, subject and object engage in dialectic movement, with moments of wholeness followed by separation, of illusion followed by disappointment.

Following *A Lost Lady* Cather asked a question that had run as an undercurrent through her previous writing: what is left when the imagination fades and the world is fallen? In *The Professor's House* (1925) Cather told a romantic version of the Fall by introducing St. Peter as one who has suffered a lapse in perception, from creative imagination to reason, then setting him on a quest for redemption. By casting off ties to the outside world, St. Peter liberates from within himself dreams that contain archetypal truths. In doing so, he reaches an essential unity of symbolic forms. Then, as if preparing for the new key in which she would write, Cather in *My Mortal Enemy* (1926) created characters who reject a romanticism that had deteriorated into sentimentality.

After *My Mortal Enemy,* Cather turned away from the old dichotomy. By creating characters who had denied their personal selves and putting them in the most alien of settings, she revised her literary problem, no longer asking how subject and object meet and instead presenting a unity antecedent to dualism. In *Death Comes to the Archbishop* (1927) two Catholic priests disciplined to erase their individual selves make their way through a desert; in *Shadows on the Rock* (1931) a slight apothecary and his

young daughter lead lives of quiet renunciation on a rock suspended in a Canadian wilderness. Using these most unlikely of
materials, Cather celebrated the harmony of correspondences. No
longer concerned with using language to mediate between self and
other, she embraced possibilities recognized by the symbolist,
who "redefines the whole process of knowing," then deliberately
experiments "with alogical structures of multiple meanings."[10]

Finally, *Lucy Gayheart* (1935) and *Sapphira and the Slave Girl*
(1940) are Gothic novels in which Cather explored the underside of
the romantic imagination. In these, her last books, Cather confronted head-on the threat that runs through her writing, as
through romanticism in general: that the imagination will break
through not to ultimate truths but to evil, chaos, and — worst of
all — nothingness.

In setting for myself a carefully charted path — or at least direction — when I began writing, I recognized that much lay outside
the range of this study. I did not attempt to include a survey of
criticism on Cather, for example. To do so would be quite another
book — a valuable one, for that criticism has now reached impres-
sive proportions in both quantity and quality. But that was not my
purpose here. Nor was my purpose biographical, and though I
have included enough biography to place each novel generally
within Cather's life, my focus remained upon the works themselves.

Nevertheless, much of the pleasure of writing this book has
come from the unexpected. The Gothicism that runs through
Cather's writing is far more important than I had anticipated, the
ambiguity in the middle books more controlled, the use of gender
to heighten tension more extensive. In exploring these ideas and
others, I have come to understand more fully that in all her
novels — *O Pioneers!*, *Death Comes for the Archbishop*, and *Shadows on
the Rock* as well as *The Professor's House* — Cather was profoundly
sensitive to feelings we term modern: a sense of alienation and historical discontinuity, of schism between the individual and the
world, of joylessness. Correspondingly, I have come to feel renewed respect for Cather's lifelong commitment to the saving
power of art.

Acknowledgments

The obvious pleasure in literary criticism lies in coming closer to the writing itself, but one of the unanticipated pleasures concerns working with others interested in that same writer. As a group Cather scholars are remarkably generous with their time and expertise. My book is better by the influence of these people, and my life is richer by knowing them.

I speak for many others when I acknowledge the influence of three people largely responsible for Cather studies today. The scholarship and criticism of Bernice Slote created the foundation upon which Cather studies rest; the vision of Mildred R. Bennett established Red Cloud as a center for Cather scholarship and the Willa Cather Pioneer Memorial and Educational Foundation as its voice; the biography by James Woodress provided the most informed single introduction to Willa Cather's life and art.

I speak more personally when I acknowledge their contributions to this book: Bernice Slote, for reading my first paper on Willa Cather, talking with me about Cather scholarship, and discussing early stages of this book. Mildred Bennett and James Woodress, for reading the manuscript, correcting mistakes, suggesting revisions. Portions of this book were written in direct response to each of these people.

I wish to thank others who read this study and commented upon it. My indebtedness to David Stouck is evident from notes, for his criticism was often a touchstone for my own interpretation. Helen Cather Southwick has provided details of Willa Cather's life, especially of the Pittsburgh years and the Grand Manan sojourns.

I am grateful too to Lucia Woods and Dan Lindley, for reading and commenting upon "*The Professor's House:* A Book of Dreams," and to colleagues at the University of Nebraska–Lincoln, Robert

Knoll and Stephen Behrendt, for providing sound advice about the manuscript in various stages. Viola Borton (president of WCPM) and Carol Petersen (UN–L) are friends with whom I have explored Cather country, and their influence is evident throughout.

For assistance in research, I am indebted to the staffs of the Henry E. Huntington Library, San Marino; the Beinecke Rare Book and Manuscript Library and the Sterling Memorial Library, Yale University, New Haven; the Newberry Library, Chicago; the Houghton Library, Harvard University, Cambridge; the Manuscript Division of the New York Public Library; the Butler Library, Columbia University, New York City; the Pierpont Morgan Library, New York City; and the Nebraska State Historical Society, Lincoln.

I wish to thank especially Joan Crane, Alderman Library, University of Virginia, for providing research materials and for introducing me to the Barrett Library; Joseph Svoboda, Elsie Thomas, and Lynn Porn for ongoing assistance in the Archives and the Faulkner-Slote Collection, University of Nebraska–Lincoln; Scott Stebelman and Eva Sartori for research assistance at Love Library, University of Nebraska–Lincoln; and Ann Billesbach, curator of the Willa Cather Historical Center, Red Cloud, for assistance with materials in those holdings.

Three persons in the English department, University of Nebraska–Lincoln, provided additional research assistance. Carolyn Perry, Babette Kerwin, and Timothy Tostengard helped with innumerable details involved in preparing the manuscript for the Press, and I thank them. I am grateful too to Roma Rector for professional expertise in typing and manuscript form and for unfailing good humor.

Financial support from the Layman Foundation, University of Nebraska–Lincoln, enabled me to travel to libraries with Cather holdings and made possible a research leave during the fall of 1983. The English department of the university provided research assistance, and its chair, Frederick Link, somehow found the means to support this research in innumerable ways. The university Research Council UN–L provided a George Holmes Faculty Summer Research Fellowship in 1983.

All of the Photographs are from the Willa Cather Pioneer Memorial and Educational Foundation Collection at the Nebraska

State Historical Society and are used by courtesy of the Society.

For permission to reprint two essays that appeared originally in their pages, I thank the *Great Plains Quarterly*. I wish to acknowledge also that some ideas developed here appeared originally in my essays published by other journals: *Novel, Genre, Studies in American Fiction, Western American Literature, Prairie Schooner, Women's Studies,* and *The Nebraska Humanist*.

Most important are those who help me remember the realest and truest things: Scott and David Rosowski, Jim Rosowski, Alice and Bill Campbell.

Part I. The Inherited Tradition

In Pittsburgh, ca. 1902

1 Beginnings

Perhaps there are certain advantages for an artist in growing up in an empty country; a country where nothing is made, and everything is to be made.[1]

What were the essential circumstances of Willa Cather's early life? By any account they include three events: she was born in Virginia in 1873; she moved to Nebraska in 1883; she attended the University in Lincoln from 1890 to 1895. Apparently disparate events marking apparently distinct periods, yet they came together to teach the lesson basic to romanticism—that public, inherited traditions of the past are meaningless, or at least discredited, and that the individual must create meaning anew.

Willa Cather was born on December 7, 1873, in Back Creek Valley, Virginia, soon after a Civil War that left the South defeated and the nation disrupted. During the period between 1865 and 1914, from the close of one war to the onset of another (and encompassing the time from Cather's birth to the appearance of O Pioneers!, her first major novel, in 1913), ways of the past were left behind in radical social and economic changes. Economic revolution symbolized by the railroad, enormous industrial growth, urbanization, agricultural revolution—all produced changes so profound that lessons of the past seemed hardly to apply.

A national sense of revolution was made dramatically personal for Cather when at nine years of age she moved with her family to Nebraska, where the Cathers settled first in Webster County, then, the following year, in the frontier town of Red Cloud. Coming from Virginia to the Midwest was an experience Cather later compared to being "thrown out into a country as bare as a piece of sheet iron";[2] her fictional accounts of immigrating to an unsettled land catch the emptiness of a country in which "there was nothing but land; not a country at all, but the material out of which countries are made."[3] It was a new country indeed. When the Cathers came to the Midwest in 1883, Nebraska had been a state only sixteen years; when they moved to Red Cloud in 1884, the town had existed only fourteen years; and when Willa Cather began studies at the University of Nebraska in 1890, it had admitted its first collegiate students, twenty in all, just nineteen years earlier. But perhaps, as Edith Lewis wrote later, "there are certain advantages for an artist in growing up in an empty country; a country where nothing is made, and everything is to be made."[4] Surely such conditions offer advantages for romanticism, with its belief in individual creativity.

While events in America laid the groundwork for individualism, Cather was finding a literary tradition that exalted it. As countless scholars have pointed out, through the American westward tradition of new beginnings runs "a nostalgic tradition," evident in "the ever-present pullback toward modes of culture that lie in our past."[5] This point hardly needs to be elaborated upon in general—or in specific reference to Cather. What does deserve note is that paradoxically this pull back led Cather to the Romantics, with their forward-looking stress on revolution, individualism, and creativity. And that is the point Bernice Slote has made in her ground-breaking essay, "First Principles: The Kingdom of Art."[6]

As Bernice Slote has revealed, Cather's early reading was remarkable for both its diversity and its consistency. Writers Cather read included masters (Homer, Virgil, the Bible, and Shakespeare), and more recent giants (Dumas, Daudet, Poe, Stevenson, Longfellow, Lowell, Carlyle, Ruskin, Pater, Emerson, Sand, Eliot, and Arnold), along with popular writers whose names are no longer familiar (Marie Corelli, Sarah Grand, Oiuda, and Richard Harding Davis, to mention only a few). For the young Willa Cather "explored without logic, and sometimes without discrimination, the remote, the popular, the obscure, the unimportant, the rare, the good, the trashy, even the ludicrous, in anybody's writing" (38). Yet even as she paid tribute to the range of Cather's reading, Professor Slote interpreted the "first principles" that unify it. Cather's "favorites were always nineteenth-century Romantics" (38), and by them she formed her ideas of art. "First Principles: The Kingdom of Art" is a brilliant study that has made it possible for other scholars to concentrate upon other questions— in my case, to look at the ways in which Cather worked out those first principles in her fiction, especially in her novels. When I summarize those principles, then, it is with the expectation that my remarks be read along with Professor Slote's exploration of the strands that make up the larger pattern.

Willa Cather's first premise was the dualism of mind and matter familiar to students of romanticism. Cather wrote of two worlds — the spiritual world and the physical one, an ideal world and an ordinary one — and of two selves in each person — an immortal soul and a mortal body, an artistic self and a common one. The most basic need of the "soul" (Cather lamented "it's too bad we have no word but that to express a man's inner most ego") is to bring the two together.[7] In the past religion did so; when religion seemed discredited by science, the romantic turned to art.

"Art and religion . . . are the same thing in the end," Cather was fond of saying.[8] In developing the idea, she used the artist-priest metaphor common to romanticism, inverting the metaphor to exalt the artist further. Cather replaced the kingdom of heaven with a kingdom of art, and she gave godhead to the Artist. In an 1894 essay, for example, Cather did not make the artist a priestly representative of God so much as she made God a highly effective Artist. "The world was made by an Artist," she wrote, and "God's nature is just a great artistic creation."[9]

The divine faculty by which the artist creates is the imagination, with its power to reconcile the general and the particular. Unlike the reason, which analyzes facts, the imagination formulates or en-visions Truth, the elemental Reality that lies beneath circumstantial realism. Again Cather's early statements recall those of her romantic predecessors; her distinctions between reason and imagination seem audaciously clarified versions of Coleridge's:

There is only one way to see the world truly, and that is to see it in a human way. The scientist who sees the world as a collection of atoms and forces, the political economist who sees it as a set of powers and federations, sees falsely. They see facts, not truths. The only things which are really truths are those which in some degree affect all men. Atoms are not important; the world would be just as happy if we did not know of their existence. The ultimate truths are never seen through the reason, but through the imagination.[10]

As Coleridge distinguished between the primary imagination

common to every person and the secondary imagination held by the artist, so Cather distinguished between seeing the world imaginatively and recreating that experience in art. Only the genius can create life by touching the inert material world with an idea, "can breathe into it a living soul and make it great."[11] In describing how he does so, Cather, like the best of the Romantics, uses science's empiricism to defend imaginative truth against science. If individual experience is the basis for knowledge (and she believed it was), then art must offer that experience; it must live. The idea runs through Cather's early essays. In 1893 she maintained that "the greatest perfection a work of art can ever attain is when it ceases to be a work of art and becomes living fact"; in 1894, "the main requisite [for fictional characters] is that they live"; and in 1896, great art "is all a thing of feeling, you cannot apprehend it intellectually at all." In the same year she expounded upon the principle:

To keep an idea living, intact, tinged with all its original feeling, its original mood, preserving in it all the ecstasy which attended its birth, to keep it so all the way from the brain to the hand and transfer it on paper a living thing with color, odor, sound, life all in it, that is what art means, that is the greatest of all the gifts of the gods. And that is the voyage perilous.[12]

Cather's early principles discussed thus far resemble those common to romanticism of various kinds: a resistance to the dualism which threatens to reduce human experience to passive observations of the material world, an insistence that salvation lies in the imagination's capacity to perceive or create transcendent truths, a belief that the artist-priest can minister to the soul. But distinctions are in order, for romanticism is neither a single nor a simple tradition.

First, I am not concerned with the ornamental romanticism Cather included in some of her early stories, other than to note that she experimented with romanticism in all its varieties. Fortunately, she did not pursue the exoticism of "A Tale of the White Pyramid" (1892) or the orientalism of "The Conversion of Sum Loo" (1900).

Second, I wish to acknowledge Cather's affinities with Continental romanticism and to distinguish those from her ties to an

English brand of romanticism. Cather was widely read in French and German literature (her command of French was good, that of German passing), and she exalted romanticism wherever she found it—in the splendors of Flaubert's Salammbô, the shimmering moods of Verlaine's poetry, the pathos of Dumas père's Camille, the grandeur of Wagner's Ring trilogy. Not unexpectedly, allusions to French and German romantic literature, art, and music run through Cather's writing as surely as do allusions to Virgil.

Yet "the shaping spirit of imagination" which informs Cather's writing is most akin to an English tradition of romanticism, distinguished in various ways from its Continental cousins. The English Romantics were the least self-conscious artists, concerned with creating art rather than theorizing about it, undistracted by the aesthetic theories which dominated German romanticism and the political and religious controversies which characterized French romanticism. The English Romantics excelled in lyric poetry, and they kept the closest ties to the commonplace and to the past: "A sense of belonging to and restoring the native tradition distinguishes the Romantic poets in England, where there was no incisive break in continuity, as in Germany and France." Unlike the French Romantics, who were determined to disprove neoclassical attitudes and form, "the English Romantic movement had evolved slowly and organically out of the native tradition." The result was a literary revolution by which the past was restored to the present: "Whereas the Germans and the French Romantics had to follow and in some way to outdo their glorious immediate predecessors, the English Romantics were strongly conscious of representing a new beginning and upsurge, not a reaction as in France or an over-refinement as in Germany. From this perhaps," writes Lilian R. Furst, "English Romanticism derives its special quality of freshness, freedom, flexibility and grace."[13]

In all these matters Cather wrote in an English tradition of romanticism. She too devoted her energies to creating art rather than to theorizing about it; she too excelled in lyricism, writing her best prose like poetry; and she too saw herself as the first of a new literary tradition, yet one which evolved out of the past and from native traditions rather than in revolt against them.

Third, when Cather stressed that art is "a living thing," with "color, odor, sound" in it, she reminds us of distinctions between the romanticism of her English and American predecessors. Both looked to the imagination as a means to transcendence, yet they prescribed quite different approaches. The English Romantic characteristically wrote a "poetry of experience," beginning with a specific object, then giving himself to it so completely that he reaches, in Blake's phrase, "eternity in a grain of sand." [14] In "This Lime Tree Bower My Prison," for example, Coleridge began by placing himself in time and space: having injured his foot, he remained sitting in his yard beneath a specific tree (he used the demonstrative adjective, "*this* lime tree bower") while his friends departed on a walk. He then moved toward a liberating epiphany by concentrating first upon the tree beneath which he was sitting, then upon a branch, finally upon a single leaf, which he saw ever more closely until he grasped what he elsewhere called "the Eternal through and in the Temporal." [15] The minute observation that leads to Coleridge's epiphany takes the form, finally, of a transformation of personal consciousness (private world) that renders the external universe (public world) vastly altered.

The specifics vary as much as the poets writing of them. Wordsworth wrote of rowing a stolen boat alone at night, Coleridge of sitting in his cottage seeing moonlight shine upon an icicle outside his window, Shelley of hearing a skylark or musing upon Mont Blanc, and Keats of seeing a Grecian urn and hearing a nightingale's song. Such circumstances have the uniqueness of individual lives, yet in them all there is an attempt to affirm imaginative value by "a doctrine of experience, an attempt to salvage on science's own empiric grounds the validity of the individual perception against scientific abstractions." [16] Nowhere is devotion to experience of this world more evident than in the poet Cather most esteemed, Keats. Keats's romanticism is a sensuous, physical experience in which the poet gives himself so passionately to an object that he escapes the limitations of his own ego and reaches illumination in the object — Beauty in the Grecian urn, Happiness in the nightingale's song.

American romanticism has a different flavor, especially as seen in Emerson and Whitman, those American Romantics Cather referred to most often. The transcendentalist Emerson sought a vision of eternity, but he saw "all" by turning his face away from finite nature and gazing into infinite space. In "Nature," his most famous essay, Emerson recorded his own ecstatic epiphany. While "crossing a bare common, in snow puddles, at twilight, under a clouded sky," he felt "a perfect exhilaration" in which he was "uplifted into infinite space; and became "a transparent eyeball." Interpreting the experience, Emerson described himself as "the lover of uncontained and immortal beauty."[17] Unlike the specificity leading to Coleridge's epiphany beneath his lime tree, Emerson provided only a nod to the physical world (he used indefinite articles, "*a* bare common" and "*a* clouded sky," and referred to generalized "snow puddles"), which he left behind as he was uplifted into "infinite space." Similarly, Cather wrote that Whitman celebrated creation in general, venerating physical and material things in "reckless rhapsodies," without grasping the spiritual idea in them. Cather described *Leaves of Grass* as "a sort of dictionary of the English language, and in it is the name of everything in creation set down with great reverence but without any particular connection."[18] In Whitman's writing as in Emerson's, lyric power lies in diffuseness and expansiveness.

Though she praised Whitman's "elemental force" and Emerson's "lofty repose and magnificent tranquillity," Cather's sympathies, if not her practice, were from the first with the British brand of romanticism.[19] The imagination must provide an anchor in the real world; without it, art is empty and effete. Ideally such an anchor results from living one's own life passionately, but one can secure it also by living other lives through "a sympathetic imagination" remarkably like Keats's negative capability. In 1894 Cather asserted that "there are requisites in all arts, and in literature there is one that is inexorable: An author must live, live deeply and richly and generously, live not only his own life, but all lives,"[20] an idea she expanded upon when the next year she wrote that the actor must have "the arts of living and loving":

Into his own art an actor should bring the spoils of every other art on earth, and above all the arts of living and loving. He should give his emotions an anchor that will reach down into the very depth of the very nature of things and hold him to the truth. An actor's imagination is his genius; it should be fed upon whatever is best in science, letters or art. He should know how it felt to be an Egyptian, sunning himself on the marble steps of the temple at Elephantine, how it felt to go up to the Acropolis on a spring morning in old Athens, how it feels to be a thirsty

Bowery boy, hesitating between a free lunch of pork and beans or corned beef and cabbage. He should know how a king ascends the steps of his throne and how a peasant scrapes the mud from his wooden shoes. Potentially he should know all manners, all people, all good and all evil.[21]

Cather was to moderate her tone, but her commitment to the sympathetic imagination remained firm. The idea reappears in her mature explanations of art. Telling how she came to write *O Pioneers!,* she recalled talking to immigrant farm women in Webster County, when "I always felt as if they told me so much more than they said—as if I had actually got inside another person's skin";[22] when speaking of *The Song of the Lark,* she said of Olive Fremstad, the prototype of Thea Kronborg, "Nothing, nothing . . . could equal the bliss of entering into the very skin of another human being."[23] And when she wrote her preface to selected stories of Sarah Orne Jewett, she described the sympathetic imagination as the source of artistic power: "If [a writer] achieves anything noble, anything enduring, it must be by giving himself absolutely to his material. And this gift of sympathy is his great gift; it is the fine thing in him that alone can make his work fine. He fades away into the land and people of his heart, he dies of love only to be born again."[24] These, then, were Cather's first principles—the duality of two worlds and two selves, salvation through the imagination, exaltation of the artist-priest who can create living art, appreciation of the gift of sympathy.

Cather upheld these first principles with remarkable consistency and fervor, qualities possible, perhaps, because circumstances of Cather's life—her Americanism, her southern birth, her western experience, her early reading—all came together to make her romanticism so natural it seemed almost instinctual. And perhaps, too, consistency and fervor were possible because Cather was untroubled by theoretical niceties. She exalted the creative imagination without being concerned with Coleridge's theories of it; she wrote from a premise of dualism without exploring its philosophical antecedents in Descartes; she believed that art must live without tracing empiricism to Locke. Abstract theory simply did not interest Willa Cather; she reserved her probing for her fiction.

Not unexpectedly, the first major literary problem Cather faced involved translating those romantic principles into practice. To do so, she had to overcome both her materials and her method.

The romantic holds that an artist creates most truly when she writes out of her experience, but it must have seemed to the young Willa Cather writing in Nebraska that her life was decidedly unpromising for such creation. Her nature was not the English Lake District, graced with spreading trees, uplifting mountains, and calming streams, all fit subjects for poetic genius. Cather's nature was a flat Nebraska prairie. Then, too, her method seemed unlikely. Though Cather wrote some poetry during those apprentice years, she put her major energies into fiction, a form apparently ill suited to the moments of intense personal, imaginative synthesis she so esteemed.

The dilemma that arises from yoking romantic principles and prosaic materials is evident in Cather's early fiction. Romantic ideas run through her first stories, which characteristically reveal two realities, then trace a character's experiencing the truth of one (imaginative reality) and the falsity of the other (factual reality). The problem Cather faced is what one would expect in romantic fiction: how can a writer present an extraordinary, usually visionary experience of breaking out of time and space within a narrative form suited to circumstantial, ordinary reality?[25]

Cather did so rather artificially at first, by inserting otherworldly characters into ordinary reality or by moving characters from ordinary settings to otherworldly ones. In "The Fear That Walks by Noonday" and "The Affair at Grover Station," ghosts appear, empirically demonstrating that they exist: that of a football player executes extraordinary plays and that of a murdered railway attendant writes messages on a chalkboard. Cather soon left behind the crudity of these stories, but she was to repeat their ideas in other, more sophisticated ones. In "The Treasure of Far Island," Douglass and Margie leave land society and sail to the "far island" of their childhood, an enchanted place of the imagination; in "The Garden Lodge," Caroline Noble falls asleep and is carried off by "the shadows" that show her "the nothingness of time and space"; the narrator-artist of "On the Gulls' Road" is transported on a ship to the southern climes of "a different reality."[26]

The form of revelation varies: in "Jack-a-Boy" and "Eric Hermannson's Soul" divinity appears through otherworldly human beings; in "The Garden Lodge" and "A Wagner Matinee" through music; in "A Resurrection" through the river. Yet beneath differences is the common experience of submitting to a compellingly powerful revelation. To his friends, the child Jack "simply had that divinity in him, that holiness of beauty which the hardest and basest of us must love when we see it," and to Eric, Margaret "represented an entirely new species of humanity" he recognized instinctively as divine.

The terms of romanticism are here, but not yet the method. Cather's early characters are passive recipients of divine visitations; they do not create meaning, but rather record experiences of being carried out of the ordinary and into another, superior world. In them ideas seem inherited rather than chosen. The distinction is one Robert Langbaum has argued is central to romanticism:

It makes no difference whether the romanticist arrives in the end at a new formulation or returns to an old one. It is the process of denial and reaffirmation which distinguishes him both from those who have never denied and those who, having denied, have never reaffirmed. Although many romantic careers look like a working back to what had been originally rejected, it would be a mistake to suppose that the position returned to could ever again be the same as the original position. For the position returned to has been chosen, and that makes it a romantic reconstruction rather than a dogmatic inheritance.[27]

The process of denial and reaffirmation was to lie behind the dialectic pattern of Cather's mature works—*My Ántonia, A Lost Lady,* and *My Mortal Enemy*—in which a narrator approaches a subject in terms of his ideal, withdraws when that ideal is disproved, then returns, his new position a romantic reconstruction. Jim Burden saw Ántonia conventionally as his "Snow White," retreated when she contradicted that ideal, then returned to reaffirm her as a New World Earth Mother. This is the process by which the romantic perceives symbols as sources of meaning. As Keats comes to affirm the Grecian urn as a self-generating symbol of truth and beauty, so Jim Burden comes to affirm Ántonia, an immigrant girl who has matured into a wizened woman, as a symbol of fertility and goodness, both by investing them with transcendent (and transforming) significance.

Cather used symbols in her early stories, of course, but often self-consciously and artificially. She tended to give objects significance, then to position them in the stories as reminders rather than sources of meaning. In "The Treasure of Far Island," trinkets are treasures because Douglass and Margie, the central characters, had endowed them with the rich imaginings of their childhood, then buried them, thereby keeping meanings intact. Uncovered, the objects remind the adult characters of those meanings. As do the sketch by the narrator-artist in "On the Gull's Road" (which reminds him of Alexandra Ebbling) and the canvas by the narrator-artist in "The Namesake" (which reminds him of his uncle), symbols serve to open a door through which characters passively enter a dream world of the imagination.

Yet even in these early stories Cather was experimenting with symbols as sources of meaning. "On the Gulls' Road" (1908), for example, illustrates Cather's working with the symbol as perceived object. This is the story of a narrator's fascination with Alexandra Ebbling, a mysteriously beautiful woman he meets on a voyage. Cather introduced the story by stressing that the narrator is recalling how Alexandra Ebbling *seemed to him*. He is entranced by "her splendid, vigorous hair," which gathers symbolic significance when he compares it to the yellow love vine at his home that "seems to be growing while one looks at it, and it twines and tangles about itself and throws out little tendrils in the wind." The initial distinction between object-as-is and object-as-perceived is lost as the story progresses, however. When their ship carries them "into the abyss" and the narrator "watched her hair grow more alive and irridescent in the moisture," it is as if the hair, quite independent of the narrator's perception, takes on a life of its own. At the conclusion of the story, months after parting from Alexandra Ebbling, the narrator opened a box she gave to him "and lifted out a thick coil, cut where her hair grew thickest and brightest. It was tied firmly at one end, and when it fell over my arm it curled and clung about my sleeve like a living thing set free."

Romantic ideas are here: the voyage resembles Coleridge's "Rime of the Ancient Mariner" in specific verbal echoes as well as in its general movement from ordinary reality to an experience of pure imagination. But while Coleridge consistently presented his mariner's imagination converting his world into symbols, Cather stressed her narrator's perception only briefly, then reveled in the symbol itself. In the end, the hair is treated as a rhetorical device rather than a perceived object: the initial fusion of thought, emotion, and object breaks down, until each has become discrete.

As Cather was experimenting with symbols, so she was experimenting with language, a complementary aspect of the romantic's attempt to vindicate the imagination by freeing meaning from objective reality. Here her models are telling. Of all the English Romantics, Keats — the poet who demonstrated most fully the sensuous potential of imagery and language — held the strongest attraction for Cather. She referred to Keats more frequently in her early essays than to any other writer except Shakespeare, used him as a touchstone in her early stories, and kept his bust, willed to her by Mrs. Fields, in her apartment. Of the French Romantics, Cather admired especially Verlaine. In what could be a description of French symbolist art, she wrote approvingly of Verlaine's fascination with language: "His verses are like music, they are made up on harmony and feeling, they are as indefinite and barren of facts as a nocturne. They tell only of a mood. . . . He created a new verbal art of communicating sensations not only by the meanings of the words, but of their relation, harmony, and sound."[28]

Cather's early stories seem, at times, excuses for little essays on romantic theory. In "The Count of Crow's Nest" (1896), the Jamesian plot (an attempt to obtain private papers that, if revealed, would be damaging to the reputations of famous people) and characters (an elderly gentleman of the old school, his crudely materialistic daughter, and a sympathetic observer) provide the catalyst for a summary of the French symbolist emphasis on language. The narrator laments that in English,

"we haven't the feeling for absolute and specific beauty of diction. We have no sense for the aroma of words as [the French] have. We are never content with the effect of material beauty alone, we are always looking for something else. Of course we lost by this, it is like always thinking about one's dinner when one is invited out."

The Count nodded. "Yes, you look for the definite, whereas the domain of pure art is always the indefinite. You want the fact under the illusion, whereas the illusion is in itself the most wonderful of facts."

Here is the idea that will appear in Cather's later, most famous statements about art. In "The Novel Démeublé," for example, Cather wrote: "Whatever is felt upon the page without being specifically named there — that, one might say, is created. It is the inexplicable presence of the thing not named, of the overtone divined by the ear but not heard by it, the verbal mood, the emotional aura of the fact or the thing or the deed, that gives high quality to the novel or the drama, as well as to poetry itself."[29]

Cather's Jamesian stories reveal her inherited beliefs about art, and as such are sometimes interesting in the same ways her journalistic essays are: for ideas they contain rather than for the art they embody. Her Nebraska stories are another matter. In writing of a land new to literature, Cather faced a challenge analogous to that of the Romantics, who sought to create something new out of a discarded past. In four early stories—"Peter" (1892), "Lou, the Prophet" (1892), "The Clemency of the Court" (1893), and "On the Divide" (1896)—Cather presented the central problem of romanticism—how to see an alien world in a human way—and she did so in the starkest context, where spiritual needs were pitted against a harsh setting and unthinking materialism.[30] "Peter," for example, is the story of the conflict between Peter, once second violinist at Prague but now an old man lost in southwestern Nebraska, and his materialistic son, Antone. The conflict of the action is over Antone's wish to sell his father's violin, the one earthly possession the old man loves. Peter's only defense was to destroy the violin and then himself. He went to the stable, broke his fiddle, then "pulled off his old boot, held the gun between his knees with the muzzle against his forehead, and pressed the trigger with his toe." The concluding paragraph presents the aftermath: "In the morning Antone found him still, frozen fast in a pool of blood. They could not straighten him out enough to fit a coffin, so they buried him in a pine box. Before the funeral Antone carried to town the fiddle-bow which Peter had forgotten to break. Antone was very thrifty, and a better man than his father had been."

The story represents Cather's early Nebraska writing in several ways. The threat of the plains lies not so much in its physical harshness, though that is there, as in the indifference with which obliterating expanses reduce human endeavour to insignificance. In her early stories Cather describes a wasteland, where "there was nothing but sun, and grass, and sky" ("Peter"), a country of "brown, windswept prairies that never lead anywhere" ("The Clemency of the Court"), where "the flat plains rolled to the unbroken horizon vacant and void, forever reaching in empty yearning toward something they never attained" ("El Dorado: A Kansas Recessional"). The challenge Cather perceived in the plains is correspondingly spiritual, not primarily to tame the land in the sense

of breaking sod (in all Cather's fiction the physical action of settling is carried out offstage), but to humanize an alien world.

In 1892, when Cather wrote "Peter," she seemed not to know
what to do with that challenge. She turned to sentiment (before
Peter killed himself, "he held his violin under his wrinkled chin,
his white hair fell over it, and he began to play 'Ave Maria'"), to
heavy-handed irony, and to reversals so artificial they approach
those of a tall tale. To thwart the dehumanizing country and his
insensitive son, Peter broke his violin and committed suicide; but
the final joke was on him, for the weather was so cold it froze his
body too stiff for a coffin, and Antone so materialistic he sold his
dead father's violin bow.

"Peter" is not a tall tale, of course. The essence of the tall tale
lies in the teller's relish of the unexpected, and Cather's impulse is
toward resolution. Yet in these earliest Nebraska stories, Cather
avoided rather than resolved the central conflict of the human
imagination versus an alien world. In "Peter" the major tension is
not between Peter and the land, but between Peter and his son; the
fact that Peter had moved with his family from Bohemia "to the
dreariest part of southwestern Nebraska" intensifies the dilemma
but is not essential to it.

Like "Peter," "Lou, the Prophet" and "The Clemency of the
Court" present characters who are helpless because they are "absent
minded," "weak headed," and "inarticulate." The conflict of each
concerns dehumanizing forces, only one of which is the land. In
"The Clemency of the Court" the orphaned Serge could suffer the
loneliness of one cut off from language in a city as well as on the
plains. In "Lou, the Prophet" the landscape does present an overwhelming threat of desolation, but once Lou begins having visions, Cather shifts her focus from the land to his prophecies.

The fourth of Cather's early Nebraska stories, however, is
another matter. "On the Divide" (1896), often cited as especially
brutal, is in many respects the most positive of the group: in it
Cather presents not the stripping away of her character's defenses,
but the ways in which a man works out responses to an alien landscape. No longer merely a backdrop, the confrontation between
the character and the plains is of primary interest, the melodramatic plot of secondary importance. As important, Cather begins to
use myth to humanize that land.

The setting is again one of obliterating wastes. Canute Canuteson had "first squatted along the banks of Rattlesnake Creek" when "there was not a human being within twenty miles." He was a giant of a man, of such colossal dimensions and legendary strength he was believed to have formed the curved ridge timber of his shanty by bending the log across his knee. Yet even such a man is little in the plains, and Canute's confrontation with this fact is the point of the story. He had come to know the grass "in all the deceitful loveliness of its early summer, in all the bitter barrenness of its autumn. He had seen it smitten by all the plagues of Egypt. He had seen it parched by drought, and sogged by rain, beaten by hail, and swept by fire, and in the grasshopper years he had seen it eaten as bare and clean as bones that the vultures have left. After the great fires he had seen it stretch for miles and miles, black and smoking as the floor of hell.

In defense against the plains, Canute hung up rattlesnake skins that rustled a warning when his door was opened, drank alcohol that deadened him against loneliness, and carved "a series of pictures" in the wide windowsills of his shanty. These pictures, of somber men pursued by laughing demons, are symbols of the death struggle Canute undertook each day:

The strangest things in the shanty were the window sills. At first glance they looked as though they had been ruthlessly hacked and mutilated with a hatchet, but on closer inspection all the notches and holes in the wood took form and shape. There seemed to be a series of pictures. They were, in a rough way, artistic, but the figures were heavy and labored, as though they had been cut very slowly and with very awkward instruments. There were men plowing with little horned imps sitting on their shoulders and on their horses' heads. There were men praying with a skull hanging over their heads and little demons behind them mocking their attitudes. There were men fighting with big serpents, and skeletons dancing together. All about these pictures were blooming vines and foliage such as never grew in this world, and coiled among the branches of the vine there was always the scaly body of a serpent, and behind every flower there was a serpent's head. It was a veritable Dance of Death by one who had felt its sting.

These pictures of men playing, praying, fighting, always pursued by devils that mock their puny efforts, are oddly discordant with the heroic Canute: the discordancy represents, I believe, the problem Cather faced in treating her native materials. She drew upon tradition for Canute Canuteson, a figure legend said would be capable of any physical feat; she then put him on the open plain and posed to him a metaphysical struggle. The conflict was the right one for Cather: I'm hard-pressed to think of a single scene in her mature work in which Cather celebrated physical strength. Her interest always lay elsewhere—in the imaginative power to create a new reality. And this interest is evident in the windowsill carvings in Canute's shanty.[31]

Like the cave drawings of early man, these pictures represent a passage from brute to human sensibility. They occur in a scene symbolic of the immigrant's spiritual confrontation with the plains. Canute's shanty, lost in "a country as flat and gray and naked as the sea," gives him physical protection; but it is the crude drawings on his windowsill that give expression to his spirit, for they translate the alien outside world into a human language.

The ending of the story is melodramatic. Canute abducts Lena Lensen, the daughter in the family on the next eighty, and carries her through blinding snow to his shanty, then abducts a minister to marry them. While Canute returns the minister to his home, the sobbing Lena is left alone in the shanty, consumed by her own misery until, seeing the crudely drawn symbols on the sill, she understands Canute's loneliness. When he returns, she calls him to her. But beyond the melodrama of the story is something most interesting: Cather bases plot reversal on the magical quality of the symbols Canute has carved. For the first time, one of her Nebraska immigrants has created his own art to order and communicate his experience.

Canute's carvings are, of course, a crude form of the symbolic process. Cather places us at a distance from her character and his art, so that we observe in Canute someone who had attempted to use symbols to express his feelings about his struggles with the land. We do not participate in the imaginative creation of a new world, nor will we do so until "The Bohemian Girl" and, especially, *O Pioneers!* In the meantime Cather wrote stories about ordinary people threatened by the temptations of art, the stories she collected in *The Troll Garden.*

2 *The Troll Garden*
and the Dangers of Art

"We must not look at Goblin men,
  We must not buy their fruits."[1]

"In the kingdom of art there is no God, but one God, and his service so exacting that there are few men born of women who are strong enough to take the vows," Willa Cather wrote in 1896.[2] Brave words, ringing with youthful fervor, yet articulating an ideal that Cather was to realize only after a long apprenticeship. For the same year that Cather spoke of the total commitment necessary to the artist, she moved to Pittsburgh, where she worked as editor of the *Home Monthly,* a women's magazine designed for large sales in the popular market. The following year she left the *Home Monthly* to join the staff of the *Pittsburgh Leader,* where she remained until she left in 1900 to do free-lance writing, then to teach high school Latin, algebra, and English until 1906.[3] By then a decade had passed, and though Cather had left Nebraska, she hadn't yet made the commitment necessary to enter the kingdom of art. Instead, she had worked as a journalist, writing about what others were doing, and as a teacher, telling what others had done.

Before this period Cather had written often of two worlds; for her first volume of fiction, *The Troll Garden* (1905), she gathered stories that warned against losing one's soul in the limbo between them.[4] Written by a woman devoted theoretically to the kingdom of art, these stories are paradoxical, for they show the world of the imagination as dangerous. To introduce the volume, Cather used two epigraphs. The first is a quatrain from "Goblin Market," by Christina Rossetti:

"We must not look at Goblin men,
  We must not buy their fruits;
  Who knows upon what soil they fed
  Their hungry, thirsty roots?"[5]

Rossetti's long narrative poem tells of two sisters, Laura and Lizzie, who live in loving harmony until Laura is tempted by goblin men to taste of their fruit, after which she wastes away until she "seemed knocking at Death's door." To save Laura, Lizzie seeks out the goblins. After resisting their temptations to taste their fruit and suffering their anger, scorn, and attacks, Lizzie returns to Laura, who sucks from her the juices of the goblins' fruit, smeared on her body when they attacked her, until she falls unconscious. Lizzie cares for sister through the night, and in the morning Laura awakens, restored to her former innocence. Years pass, and the two, now married, warn their own children against the haunted glen and the wicked goblins. The poem ends by a ritual of forming human bonds to ward off evil:

> Then joining hands to little hands
> Would bid them cling together, —
> "For there is no friend like a sister
> In calm or stormy weather;
> To cheer one on the tedious way,
> To fetch one if one goes astray,
> To lift one if one totters down,
> To strengthen whilst one stands."

For her second epigraph Cather quoted from the parable used by Kingsley to introduce *The Roman and the Teuton:*

A fairy palace, with a fairy garden; . . . . . Inside the trolls dwell,
. . . . . working at their magic forges, making and making always things rare and strange.

The story, which provides the best introduction to *The Troll Garden,* is little known by readers today. The full text from Kingsley is as follows:

Fancy to yourself a great Troll-garden such as our forefathers dreamed of often fifteen hundred years ago; — a fairy palace, with a fairy garden; and all around the primæval wood. Inside the Trolls dwell, cunning and wicked, watching their fairy treasures, working at their magic forges, making and making always things rare and strange; and outside, the forest is full of children; such children as the world had never seen before, but children still: children in frankness, and purity, and affectionateness, and tenderness of conscience, and devout awe of the unseen; and children too in fancy, and silliness, and ignorance, and caprice, and jealousy, and quarrelsomeness, and love of excitement and adventure, and the mere sport of overflowing animal health. They play unharmed among the forest beasts, and conquer them in their play; but the forest is too dull and too poor for them; and they wander to the walls of the Troll-garden and wonder what is inside. One can conceive easily for oneself what from that moment would begin to happen. Some of the more adventurous clamber in. Some, too, the Trolls steal and carry off into the palace. Most never return: but here and there one escapes out again, and tells how the Trolls killed all his comrades: but tells too, of the wonders he has seen inside, of shoes of swiftness, and swords of sharpness, and caps of darkness; of charmed harps, charmed jewels, and above all of the charmed wine: and after all, the Trolls were very kind to him — see what fine clothes they have given him — and he struts about while among his companions; and then returns, and not alone. The Trolls have bewitched him, as they will bewitch more. So the fame of the Troll-garden spreads; and more and more steal in, boys and maidens, and tempt their comrades over the wall, and tell of the jewels, and the dresses, and the wine, the joyous maddening wine, which equals men with gods; and forget to tell how the Trolls have bought them, soul as well as body, and taught them to be vain, and lustful, and slavish; and tempted them, too often, to sins which have no name.

But their better nature flashes out at times. They will not be the slaves and brutes in human form, which the evil Trolls would have them; and they rebel, and escape, and tell of the horrors of that fair foul place. And then rises a noble indignation, and war between the Trolls and the forest-children. But still the Trolls can tempt and bribe the greedier or the more vain; and still the wonders inside haunt their minds; till it becomes a fixed idea among them all, to conquer the garden for themselves and bedizen themselves in the fine clothes, and drink their fill of the wine. Again and again they break in: but the Trolls drive them out, rebuild their walls, keep off those outside by those whom they hold enslaved within; till the boys grow to be youths, and the youths men: and still the Troll-garden is not conquered, and still it shall be. And the Trolls have grown old and weak, and their walls are crumbling away. Perhaps they may succeed this time — perhaps next.

And at last they do succeed — the fairy walls are breached, the fairy palace stormed — and the Trolls are crouching at their feet, and now all will be theirs, gold, jewels, dresses, arms, all that the Troll possesses — except his cunning.

For as each struggles into the charmed ground, the spell of the place falls on him. He drinks the wine, and it maddens him. He fills his arms with precious trumpery, and another snatches it from his grasp. Each envies the youth before him, each cries—Why had I not the luck to enter first? And the Trolls set them against each other, and split them into parties, each mad with excitement, and jealousy, and wine, till, they scarce know how, each falls upon his fellow, and all upon those who are crowding in from the forest, and they fight and fight, up and down the palace halls, till their triumph has become a very feast of the Lapithæ, and the Trolls look on, and laugh a wicked laugh, as they tar them on to the unnatural fight, till the gardens are all trampled, the finery torn, the halls dismantled, and each pavement slippery with brothers' blood. And then, when the wine is gone out of them, the survivors come to their senses, and stare shamefully and sadly round. What an ugly, desolate, tottering ruin the fairy palace has become! Have they spoilt it themselves? or have the Trolls bewitched it? And all the fairy treasure—what has become of it? no man knows. Have they thrown it away in their quarrel? have the cunningest hidden it? have the Trolls flown away with it, to the airy land beyond the Eastern mountains? who can tell? Nothing is left but recrimination and remorse. And they wander back again into the forest, away from the doleful ruin, carrion-strewn, to sulk each apart over some petty spoil which he has saved from the general wreck, hating and dreading each the sound of his neighbour's footstep.

What will become of the forest children, unless some kind saint or hermit comes among them, to bind them in the holy bonds of brotherhood and law?[6]

From these sources Cather took quotations that emphasize a struggle between opposing forces: each quotation presents one side of that struggle—that from Rossetti's poem a warning to resist, that from Kingsley's story a temptation to succumb. Yet both sources in full present the same ideas: both tell of temptations to commit sins of vanity, lust, and idolatry, and both call for a human savior, in Rossetti's poem for Lizzie to save her sister, in Kingsley's story, for "some kind saint or hermit" to come among the forest children and "bind them in the holy bonds of brotherhood and law." These are the ideas of temptation and salvation in *The Troll Garden*. The stories fall into two groups, garden stories and prairie stories. In the first Cather writes of a garden that is false; in the second, of a wilderness that cannot satisfy. What quest exists is not for art but for humanity, a stay against both the lure of the troll garden and the threat of the desert existence outside it.[7] Her heroes, if these stories have heroes, are ordinary people who save their souls by speaking out against falsity.

Cather used different points of view for different aspects of her theme, arranging the stories so they alternate garden with prairie, inside with outside. The first two stories present the contrast. "Flavia and Her Artists" concerns one who tried to enter the world of art falsely, is mocked by those inside, and is saved by her husband. Flavia Hamilton, a woman of neither taste nor talent, has been bewitched by the glitter of success and, like the maidens in Kingsley's story, will bewitch others. She has left her Chicago house on Prairie Avenue and moved outside New York, where she has constructed an "asylum" for artists, to which she entices "the best." There, falsity reigns: guests and hostess, the possessed and the possessor—all are corrupted. In this artificial world, Flavia seems a grotesque imitation of wife, mother, and hostess; her artists seem older and dimmer versions of themselves. Only two guests are still "forest children": Imogen Willard, the scholar daughter of one of Flavia's friends, and Jemima ("Jimmy") Broadwood, a comedian. Together these characters are the Jamesian observers at a house party given by Flavia for her artists.

The central incident of the story is the exposure of Flavia by a novelist who, after visiting at her house, writes a savage satire titled "Roux on Tuft Hunters; The Advanced American Woman As He Sees Her; Aggressive, Superficial and Insincere." But Jimmy Broadwood is most interested in Flavia's husband, Arthur Hamilton, who apparently loves his wife and who protects her from ridicule. Hamilton exposes the writer as a mountebank and snake charmer, in doing so driving away the other guests, who are sensitive to the same charge. In the end the artists have departed, leaving Flavia with her husband, "a pillar of sanity and law in this house of shams and swollen vanities."

The story Cather used to introduce the volume may well be the most personal in it, for Cather apparently used herself and the Canfields as prototypes for her characters. Dorothy Canfield, like Imogen, had studied French language at a university in Paris; Cather, like Jimmy Broadwood, had a hearty laugh, a boyish manner; Flavia Canfield, like Cather's character, "worshipped at the altar of art";[8] and James Canfield, like Hamilton, was a practical, gentle man, temperamentally the opposite of his wife.[9]

"Flavia and Her Artists" complements the second story of *The Troll Garden*. In "The Sculptor's Funeral" Cather wrote of corruption outside the garden fully as ugly as that within it. The story is of those greedy persons who, attracted by the lure of riches, send their children into the world, then corrupt those who return. The sculptor Harvey Merrick's body is returned to the frontier Kansas town of his boyhood, "a desert of newness and ugliness and sordidness." Cather uses a Jamesian observer, Henry Steavens, to describe the horror of the life from which Merrick came. The physical desolation is matched by the pettiness of the town's inhabitants, who scorn the sculptor as a failure in what matters—making money—until Jim Laird, the shrewd town lawyer, "plugs" the truth to the men: he and Harvey went East to school with similar visions of greatness. Laird returned to his hometown, but the townspeople wanted his talents only as a tool for their greed. Harvey Merrick had a soul they couldn't "dirty," however, and that is why the townspeople hate him. After his one moment of defiant truth, Laird returns to alcohol and corrupt law, but that moment, the climax of the story, stands as a testimony that the best in human nature will "flash out at times." Together the two stories present grim alternatives, the corrupting pull of success and a similarly corrupting threat of a wasteland.

In "The Garden Lodge" Cather tells of Caroline Noble, a woman who "held determinedly to the middle course" to overcome her childhood in a shabby house of illusion, set up as "the shrine of idealism" by her father, a vacillating music teacher. She feared worshipping an idol and was determined to see things as they really are. When twenty-four she married Howard Noble, who, as good as his name, rescued her by providing the money, position, and energy she needed to feel safe. All went smoothly until the singer Raymond d'Esquerré visited, staying in the Nobles' garden lodge. Though she recognized that his retinue was composed of grotesques and his successful life covered personal disappointment, Caroline fell under the spell "of the beautiful illusion." The temptation she faced was ambiguous. On the one hand, she was drawn by "an illogical, womanish desire" to comfort d'Esquerré; on the other, she was tempted by the power of dreams within herself, romantically triggered by a stormy night and memories of d'Esquerré's presence and of his music: "It was not enough; this happy, useful, well-ordered life was not enough. It did not satisfy, it was not even real. No, the other things, the shadows—they were the reality." In the morning, however, she recovered her balance and, laughing, told her husband she had decided to tear down the garden lodge and build a summer house. The story ends with relief that by recalling the human bonds of love, Caroline Noble had saved herself.

In "A Death in the Desert," Cather moved again outside the garden, to the seductive power of illusion over mortals who can never enter the rarified realm of great art. While passing through a desert town in Wyoming, Everett Hilgarde, the look-alike brother of the famous composer, Adriance, meets the singer Katharine Gaylord, who had left her family to be educated in art but had then returned to the family she had outgrown to die of consumption. Just as Lizzie keeps watch over Laura in Rossetti's poem, so Everett keeps watch over Katharine. The temptation of art comes by a letter from Adriance, with which he encloses a brilliant sonata he has just composed. The story tells of resistance to that charm. Though he yearns to enter the world of his brother, Everett has the courage to realize he has only talent, not genius; and though she loves Adriance, Katharine has the courage to resist falling victim to that love. In the end the two have the solace of human kindness and the dignity of maintaining themselves against "the madness of art."

Temptation is the theme of the least successful story of the volume, the Jamesian "Marriage of Phaedra." Cather moved from the desert wilderness of her previous story to the garden ruins of a fairy palace and constructed a plot that closely resembles Kingsley's parable. The observer, MacMaster, passes through "a high garden wall" to reach the nearly deserted studio of the deceased artist Hugh Treffinger. Inside he finds Treffinger's man, James, from whom he learns a story of temptation and destruction. Treffinger was an urban version of Kingsley's children, a "London street boy" who almost unawares entered the world of art and who, in turn, persuaded Ellen to join him. Treffinger's courtship of her was unnatural, frenzied, and "theatrical to the point of being ridiculous"; not unexpectedly, their marriage was unhappy, each dissatisfied with the treasure that, when possessed, proved to be empty.

The theme, which concerns temptations to betray human life in the name of art, is represented by Treffinger's most brilliant though unfinished painting, *Marriage of Phaedra*. The painting depicts Phaedra at her marriage to Theseus greeting her husband's son, Hippolytus, with "her first fearsome glance from under the half-lifted veil," like art terrible in its all-consuming passion. Character relationships reveal the human consequences of betraying life, seen most clearly in the marriage between Treffinger and Lady Ellen. It is not enough to say that this is the story of an artist unhappily married to an unsympathetic wife. Cather makes clear that Treffinger's courtship was a charade of which Lady Ellen was a victim: to paint his masterpiece, Treffinger brutally denied both his own human needs and those of his wife.

The temptations continue after Treffinger's death. Betraying her husband, who did not want his painting to leave his studio unfinished, Lady Ellen prepares to sell it to an unscrupulous Australian dealer; to protect it from this "ignominious fate," James steals it from the studio, then turns to MacMaster for help. Saving the painting would mean James and MacMaster would ruin themselves in society, for the evidence would weigh so heavily against them that they would be implicated in, perhaps prosecuted for, theft. In a weak compromise, MacMaster directs that the painting be returned to the studio, half-heartedly pleads for it to remain in England, and finally knows it will be "entombed in a vague continent in the Pacific on the other side of the world." There is some sense that this is the best place for it, for although Cather calls the painting a masterpiece, her plot suggests that such art is a curse against humanity.

The last two stories of *The Troll Garden* are the most successful and best known of the volume. "A Wagner Matinee" and "Paul's Case" present characters who do leave the common world and enter a rarified one, only to find a return unbearably painful. In "A Wagner Matinee" Cather writes of Clark, who grew up in the Midwest, then moved to Boston. There he lived, remote from childhood hardships, until he welcomes to Boston his Aunt Georgiana, the woman who had reared him and to whom he owed most of the good of his boyhood. She had been a music teacher at the Boston Conservatory when, at thirty, she met "a handsome country boy of twenty-one" and eloped with him to the Nebraska frontier, where they lived in the most primitive of conditions. In Boston Clark takes her to a Wagner matinee, to hear music that "broke a silence of thirty years; the inconceivable silence of the plains."

The story can be read as that familiar one in Cather of a sleeping mortal awakening to another world when music carries her past "the happy islands." But it is also the story of the narrator's awakening humanity. As Aunt Georgiana moves from unconsciousness to consciousness, Clark moves from cold objectivity to empathy. When he meets his aunt at the train, his description is as pitiless as the wind that had beaten against her in Nebraska. He describes her bent shoulders, her uneven gown, and her ill-fitting false teeth as if she is a grotesque object he observes from a distance. But once within the concert hall Clark comes to realize "how superficially I had judged her." As the scene assembles below them, Clark describes his perceptions, consciously drawing upon impressionistic art:

We sat at the extreme left of the first balcony, facing the arc of our own and the balcony above us, veritable hanging gardens, brilliant as tulip beds. The matinée audience was made up chiefly of women. One lost the contour of faces and figures, indeed any effect of line whatever, and there was only the colour of bodices past counting, the shimmer of fabrics soft and firm, silky and sheer; red, mauve, pink, blue, lilac, purple, ecru, rose, yellow, cream, and white, all the colours that an impressionist finds in a sunlit landscape, with here and there the dead shadow of a frock coat.

When the musicians come up on the stage, Clark identifies with his aunt, feeling "how all those details sank into her soul" by recalling how they sank into his when he had first come from Nebraska. His description becomes fuller, more sensuous, the colors lovingly moving among the bodies of the instruments: "the beloved shapes of the instruments, the patches of yellow light thrown by the green shaded lamps on the smooth, varnished bellies of the 'cellos and the bass viols in the rear, the restless, wind-tossed forest of fiddle necks and bows." Upon hearing the first strains of the *Tannhäuser* overture, Clark joins his experience to hers so fully he can speak for her, and for all who are powerless to combat "the waste and wear" of living:

There came to me an overwhelming sense of the waste and wear we are so powerless to combat; and I saw again the tall, naked house on the prairie, black and grim as a wooden fortress; the black pond where I had learned to swim, its margin pitted with sun-dried cattle tracks; the rain gullied clay banks about the naked house, the four dwarf ash seedlings where the dish-cloths were always hung to dry before the kitchen door. The world there was the flat world of the ancients; to the east, a cornfield that stretched to daybreak; to the west, a corral that reached to sunset; between, the conquests of peace, dearer bought than those of war.

After the concert, Clark describes the scene before them dissipating as colors deserting a pallet, leaving it as "empty as a winter cornfield." When his aunt cries that she doesn't want to go, Clark replies, "I understand," then concludes the story with their shared emotion: "For her, just outside the door of the concert hall, lay the black pond with the cattle-tracked bluffs; the tall, unpainted house, with weather-curled boards; naked as a tower, the crook-backed ash seedlings where the dish-cloths hung to dry; the gaunt, moulting turkeys picking up refuse about the kitchen door." This scene, repeated here for the third time, has ceased to be a place and has become a symbol of human desolation, conveyed by adjectives ordinarily used for human beings—"naked," "crook-backed," and "gaunt." And Clark, by joining with his aunt in experiencing the pain of that desolation, provides the compassion that is the only stay against it.

In her last story of the volume, "Paul's Case," Cather provides no such comfort. Subtitled "A Study in Temperament," the story tells of Paul, who sought to leave behind the ordinary world of Cordelia Street, where he lives with his father, and to enter "the portal of Romance" at the theater and concert hall where he works as an usher. Paul is an observer of art. Without talent or ambition to perform, he is forever separated from the glittering world he seeks to enter, yet just as separated from the common world he seeks to leave. Taken from school, expelled from the theater, and put to work, Paul rebels. He takes his company's cash deposits and goes to New York, where he rents a suite at the Waldorf and briefly lives the golden days of his dreams. When the world is again closing in upon him, his money exhausted and his father come to retrieve him, Paul escapes forever by committing suicide.

In Paul Cather has created a character who, having looked into Kingsley's troll garden and tasted the fruit of Rossetti's goblin men, has lost his soul. Cordelia Street is ugly indeed, with its vul-

gar art, oppressive smells, and near-sighted people; but the fantasy
Paul attempts to enter is equally inhuman. The story presents the
horror of worshipping a false idol and the tragedy for one who,
having been bewitched by the artificial, has no one to save him.

When considering *The Troll Garden,* one is tempted to stress
promise, to point out that in it certain themes and images
foreshadow Cather's finest writing. [10] But perhaps a more productive question results from the recognition that as a whole the stories are nowhere near Cather's finest writing. What, one asks, distinguishes them from the mature fiction? The first impulse—to
cite technical skill—doesn't take us very far, for Cather's technique in these stories is often quite good. What is missing instead,
I believe, is conviction.

In her essays Cather was remarkably consistent in her allegiance to a romantic creed: imagination, subjectivity, passion,
creativity, and total commitment are prerequisites for entering the
kingdom of art. Yet the stories of *The Troll Garden* present a suspicion of precisely those qualities. Cather's central metaphor reveals
much. She wrote of art made by trolls or hawked by goblins to lure
innocents away from human existence. The point of view in each of
these stories is that of the ordinary person outside the garden who
glimpses the troll magic or hears stories of it but, because unable to
create it, is distrustful. For such persons art is painful or threatening. There are few references to the greatness of art; those that exist
are secondhand reports (a stranger recalls that Harvey Merrick had
sculpted materials into living art), incomplete promises (Hugh
Treffinger died before finishing *The Marriage of Phaedra*), or painfully transitory experiences (the music of Wagner carries Clark and
his Aunt Georgiana only temporarily beyond themselves).

Settings (here as elsewhere in Cather's fiction psychological
projections of characters) are uniformly deceptive. There is not one
that offers security or warmth. The Merricks' home is "a naked,
weather-beaten frame house" which one enters by passing over "an
icy swamp" by "a rickety footbridge." Those places that appear
enticing become threatening: the first floor of Flavia's house is spa-
cious and inviting, but the second floor consists of "cages"
attended by "dim figures . . . lurking in the shadows." Caroline
Noble created a beautiful garden that turns out to be a "maze" in
which she becomes lost. Other settings suggest death: Katharine

Gaylord has created in the desert a music room, a mausoleum of past dreams where she is dying of consumption; and MacMaster enters the dead artist's studio to find it is a coffinlike "long, narrow room, built of smoothed planks . . . cold and damp even on that fine May morning . . . utterly bare . . . windowless." Alternatives are momentary illusions. The concert hall for the Wagner matinee is transformed temporarily into an impressionistic painting, but then the colors fade and the scene becomes blank, leaving Clark and his aunt with the horror that "just outside the door of the concert hall, lay the black pond"; and Paul can escape the desolation of his home only through an illusion obtained by deception.

In these stories art is most often an unholy spell, frequently suggested by imagery of the *Arabian Nights*. Flavia's darkened smoking room has the "suggestion of certain charmers in the Arabian Nights." In her garden Caroline Noble recalls the decadence of her artistic brother, "a Turkish cap upon his head and a cigarette hanging from between his long, tremulous fingers"; shuddering, she thinks of her own experience of art as like "the Arabian fairy tale in which the genii brought the princess of China to the sleeping prince of Damascus, and carried her through the air back to her palace at dawn." The sculptor Harvey Merrick had magic in his fingertips, "like the Arabian prince who fought the enchantress spell for spell," and Adriance Hilgarde writes from Alhambra, enclosing his letter within "the subtleties of Arabic decoration [that] had cast an unholy spell over him."

As threatening as the world of art, the ordinary world is a Browningesque landscape of alienation. The black pond on a Nebraska farm seems not a swimming hole but a symbol of death; a train through the Midwest passes through a wasteland where "the grey and yellow desert was varied only by occasional ruins of deserted towns"; and a Kansas town is reached by passing "long lines of shivering poplars that sentinelled the meadows."

In such a world, Cather's admirable characters are those who see through falsity and possess the courage to speak of what they see—Jimmy Broadwood, Imogen Willard, Jim Laird. These are the "solid" ones who are economically and intellectually independent and who get on with things: Arthur Hamilton, with his money from threshing machines, and Caroline Noble, who earned her way out of shabby dependency. These admirable characters live by a creed of human kindness: Arthur Hamilton protects his wife, Clark shares his aunt's loneliness, and Everett Hilgarde ministers to the dying Katharine Gaylord. They are the ones who resist the temptation of the troll garden.

Cather's progress in her early writing is often interpreted as a matter of coming to terms with her native materials—that is, Nebraska. But the reverse may more accurately be true: she needed to suppress her own world long enough to allow her imagination free rein, to create a vision by which she might transform those materials into art. Her power to do so is first apparent in "The Enchanted Bluff," published in *Harper's Monthly* in 1909. Here Cather turned from action almost entirely: nothing much happens in this story, at least physically. Its interest is entirely imaginative. Through her first-person narrator, Cather tells of one night in which, before leaving their hometown to explore the world, young friends camp on a sandbar in a Nebraska river. Around a "watch fire" they probe first the past and then the future, their imaginations asking questions about a spiritual reality that maps, telling only of a physical one, cannot answer.[11] The narrator builds to an inset story of an enchanted bluff, a place "awful far away" in New Mexico, to children as remote as another planet, where cliff dwellers once lived in a past as distant as that of fairy tales. The enchanted bluff is a magical spot, in a desert yet miraculously lush with water and grass; the telling of it is a magical moment, in time yet removed from it. The story is interrupted by "a scream above our fire," and the boys "jumped up to see a dark, slim bird floating southward far above us—a whooping crane, we knew by her cry and her long neck." The bird "floating" above them is a sign that there is a southern land to which unfettered creatures can travel. In the end the sandbar island, like the enchanted bluff, has become a symbol of such a freedom. Here is the duality of human experience Cather so often described in her early essays: her characters begin in the physical world of everyday existence, momentarily rise above it to a spiritual, imaginative world, then fall back to the world they had left, but forever changed by their dream. Here too is the reassurance of art suggested by the continuity of story telling, which passes the dream of the enchanted bluff from one generation to another, told by an uncle to a boy, then by the boy to his friends, and, later, to his own son.

3 *Alexander's Bridge*:
The Discovered Self

We must be ourselves, but we must be our best selves.[1]

The years 1906–11 were Willa Cather's McClure period. Her 1903 meeting with S. S. McClure had resulted in his company's publishing *The Troll Garden* in 1905, and then in 1906 to the far more important step of her moving from Pittsburgh to New York as an associate editor of *McClure's*, one of the country's most powerful muckraking magazines. By all accounts McClure was a genius—vigorous, eccentric, charming, brilliant, but so erratic and impractical that key members of the magazine had left when he would not turn over to them control of business affairs. The prospect of a suddenly depleted staff presented a crisis, writes Cather biographer James Woodress, and McClure, bounding back, "apparently rushed to Pittsburgh, went to see [Willa Cather] at Judge McClung's house, stayed to dinner, enchanted everyone with his talk, and when he left he had signed a new mate for his disabled ship."[2]

The importance of the move can hardly be overstated. In New York Cather found the city in which she would thereafter maintain her home, and at *McClure's* the woman with whom she would live. Edith Lewis, whom Cather had met in Lincoln, was at *McClure's* as a proofreader. Upon moving to New York Cather took a studio apartment where Lewis also lived, at 60 South Washington Square in Greenwich Village; then in 1908 they took an apartment together. They were to remain companions until 1947, when Cather died. After Lewis died, she was buried near Cather in a Jaffrey, New Hampshire, cemetery.

At *McClure's* Cather found demanding work at which she excelled. Never active in politics and not at all interested in social reform, Cather concentrated upon the literary aspects of the muckraking magazine: she read mounds of unsolicited manuscripts and, when necessary, revised ones to be published, at least once so extensively writing and rewriting copy that the product should be considered part of Cather's canon: the materials for *The Life of Mary Baker Eddy and the History of Christian Science* were collected by Georgine Milmine, but the writing was done almost entirely by Cather, her first extended assignment at McClure's.[3] More important than her writing, however, was the world the magazine opened to her. While at work on *The Life of Mary Baker Eddy*, for example, Cather lived in and traveled about Boston. There she formed the most important literary friendships of her life with Annie Fields, widow of the publisher James T. Fields, and Sarah Orne Jewett.

Because the work was demanding and the life often exhilarating, Cather had neither time nor energy to concentrate upon her own writing. While with *McClure's* she published little: in 1907 four stories she may well have written previously—"The Namesake," "The Profile," "The Willing Muse," and "Eleanor's House." Thereafter Cather's production dropped off sharply: in 1908 only "On the Gulls' Road" appeared; in 1909 only "The Enchanted Bluff"; in 1910 nothing; and in 1911 only "The Joy of Nelly Deane." In a 1908 letter to Sarah Orne Jewett, Cather described the frustrations of this time. She felt as if she were performing on a trapeze, having to catch the right bar at the right moment or fall into the net. She was so exhausted that at times she hated it all, so deadened by reading bad writing that she had come to dread reading anything. S. S. McClure was encouraging her to forget her own writing, saying he felt she would never do much with that and advising her to concentrate on executive work; she too was doubting her own abilities. She was thirty-four years old, she wrote, and acquiring sureness in executive matters, but not in writing. She got no pleasure from the reporter's quick glance at things, yet there was no time to see more closely. As a result she was feeling shallow and superficial, and she knew that another five years of this life would make her fat, bitter, and bad-tempered. One must consider one's immortal soul, she believed, and she quoted Oliver Goldsmith:

And as hare whom hounds and horns pursue,
Pants to the place from which at first she flew.[4]

Cather was not to stay five more years. In 1911, while still working on *McClure's*, she wrote *Alexander's Bridge*, as if a response to advice from Sarah Orne Jewett. Jewett had written to Willa

Cather, "You must find your own quiet center of life and write . . . to the human heart. . . . And to write and work on this level, we must live on it—we must at least recognize it and defer to it at every step. We must be ourselves, but we must be our best selves."[5] *Alexander's Bridge*—with its idea of divided selves and tension over which is the "best self"—followed.

Critics have interpreted *Alexander's Bridge* as the last of Cather's Jamesian period. It concerns cultivated people and settings—Boston and London; its plot presents an internal division within its major character; its characters include a confidante/ficelle who observes and comments on the warring duality within Alexander. Yet, as Bernice Slote has noted, despite these materials *Alexander's Bridge* is anything but Jamesian.[6] In her preface to the 1922 edition of the novel, Cather contrasted stories that form themselves organically (that is, we might add, in a Jamesian way) to "the building of external stories" such as *Alexander's Bridge*.[7] Cather's distinction gets to the heart of the matter: in *Alexander's Bridge* she put together preestablished meanings to build an external story, a tripartite allegory of creativity.

At forty-three, Bartley Alexander is a civil engineer, world-famous for his bridges. When the story opens, he is married to the cultivated, beautiful Winifred Pemberton and at work on the bridge for which he will be remembered—Moorlock Bridge in Canada. Yet material success fails to satisfy; in the public life he is living he has lost the energy of his youth. On a business trip to London, he renews the acquaintance of a woman he had once loved, Hilda Burgoyne, and with her, his youth returns. The rest of the novel dramatizes the effects of strain. Alexander alternates between the two women, or more precisely between his two selves represented by the two women, until he reaches the tormented decision that he will leave his wife for Hilda, though in doing so "he would lose the thing he valued most in the world; he would be destroying himself and his own happiness. There would be nothing for him afterward" (113).[8] Corresponding strain weakens Alexander's bridge, which in the end collapses, carrying with it fifty workmen and Bartley. Bartley had written to his wife, saying he will leave her, but when his body is recovered his letter has been made illegible by the water; his marriage and his reputation seem untouched. In an epilogue Cather presents characters without Alexander. Winifred lives a monastic life devoted to his memory; Hilda and Wilson, his former teacher, live quietly also, for "nothing can happen to one after Bartley" (138).

Certainly the action is conventional and the characters are flat, but to discuss *Alexander's Bridge* as a novel with Cather's other novels is to engage in an exercise in futility. *Alexander's Bridge* is exactly what Cather later said it was—a "studio picture," in which she worked out ideas and experimented with techniques.[9]

In her 1922 preface to *Alexander's Bridge* Willa Cather wrote, "The writer, at the beginning of his career, is often more interested in his discoveries about his art than in the homely truths which have been about him from his cradle."[10] This observation is true not only about style but also about ideas in her first novel. For *Alexander's Bridge* is an allegory about art in which Cather explored relationships among the creative energy of the artist, the spiritual world, and the physical one. In some respects the major characters *are* these ideas: Alexander is energy, a pagan force with the potential for either order cr chaos; Winifred and Hilda are emblems of two worlds of experience, spiritual and physical.[11] Neither woman is comprehensible by human motivation: why do Winifred and, especially, Hilda love Alexander? The question is neither raised nor answered in the fiction; it is the given that as an allegorical idea, each is quite consistent. As spirituality Winifred has the potential for perfect harmony when vitalized by energy, but apart from Bartley she is dim, cold, and inhuman. As physicality, Hilda too requires energy. When Bartley comes to her, she flushes with the color of revived life; when he prepares to leave, she becomes corpselike, "trembling and scarcely breathing, dark shadows growing about her eyes" (81), until she slides to the floor, "as if she were too tired to sit up any longer"(86). Consistent details are associated with each figure. The spirituality of Winifred is conveyed through colors of white and silver, references to the night, moon, and stars, and a cool temper of restraint and stillness; the physicality of Hilda through colors of yellow and gold, references to the day, sun, and fire, and a warm temper of intensity and movement; the energy of Bartley by the bridge that must unite the two.

Settings further link the two worlds necessary to art. Winifred is identified with the interior of the Boston house, a center of calm within a grey world; Hilda is identified with the mummy room of the British Museum, the cold repository of mortality from which she and Alexander emerge to revel in the sun's warmth. The scenes mirror one another: the Boston interior with its life in the midst of death reverses the London interior with death in the midst of life; the Boston interior of peace, quiet, and timelessness complements the London world of excitement, intensity, and change.

Similarly, plot is more accurately described by the creative process than by human relationships. Ideally energy or passion joins the world of spirit and the world of physicality to create art. During that period when he loved Hilda and met Winifred, the young Alexander used his passion to convert matter into art, a bridge that transformed that most inflexible of materials — iron and steel — into a thing of ethereal beauty. This, his first bridge, "is over the wildest river, with mists and clouds always battling about it, and it is as delicate as a cobweb hanging in the sky" (17–18). As Alexander became a middle-aged man, however, he succumbed to the distracting praise of the Philistines, the exhausting demands of public life, the seductive charms of comfort. His last bridge is only "thousands of tons of ironwork" that seem a "great iron carcass" (125, 127), and like it, he is only a carcass of his former self, outwardly the perfect builder but inwardly lifeless.

In writing of an artist who lost his way on the voyage perilous, Cather ingeniously used the most literal meanings of metaphors for art. Art is a linking (or bridging) of two worlds, made possible by energy; as the creator who has lost his creative soul, Alexander has become a literal and therefore debased rendition of that idea. He not only looks "as a tamer of rivers ought to look"; with his head as "hard and powerful as a catapult" and his shoulders as strong as the supports for the spans, he actually looks like a bridge (13). And Bartley's energy has not only become mechanical; it is pounding away in "the engine-room" within the man (13).

As an allegorical statement of Cather's ideas of art, such passages are fascinating; as depictions of character they are often comic. It is bad enough that Cather describes Alexander as a bridge; worse, she identifies him with "the bridges into the future, over which the feet of every one of us will go" — the description calls up a simply impossible picture. Similarly, when Alexander's former tutor, Lucius Wilson, describes strain in Alexander, he suggests a rather confusing cross between a suspension bridge and Mount Rushmore: "'The more dazzling the front you presented, the higher your facade rose, the more I expected to see a big crack zigzagging from top to bottom' he indicated its course in the air with his forefinger, — 'then a crash and clouds of dust. It was curious. I had such a clear picture of it'" (12). Indeed, such pictures are too clear — of Alexander as a bridge spanning from the present into the future, with feet of the multitudes tripping over it (him?); of Alexander as a ship, its (his?) engine room pounding on; of Alexander as a structure rising, then cracking and crashing into clouds of dust.

This, then, is the public Alexander, described by what Dorothy Van Ghent called "finger pointing symbolism."[12] If this were all there is to the novel, I suspect most of us would agree with Cather that the book is disappointingly conventional. But in telling of Alexander's youthful self, Cather used a voice that is another matter altogether, one that gathers in independence and power, until in the end it breaks through as her own.

For this personal, youthful voice Cather initially adopted romantic persona. Like Keats Alexander lingers in the British Museum "to ponder by Lord Elgin's marbles upon the lastingness of some things" (33); like Wordsworth he crosses Westminster Bridge and looks over the city shimmering with its own life. To warn against the dangers of life unfiltered by art, Cather describes a blinding brilliance reminiscent of Tennyson's "The Lady of Shalott." Drawn by his reawakened youth into experience so intense it carries its own curse, Bartley sees "Piccadilly [as] a stream of rapidly moving carriages, from which flashed furs and flowers and bright winter costumes. The metal trappings of the harnesses shown dazzlingly, and the wheels were revolving disks that threw off rays of light" (91).

As this voice gathers in strength, Cather drops the persona and experiments in the manner of the French symbolists, using language rich in synaesthesia to evoke a private mood in which the present moment hangs suspended. One afternoon Alexander walked alone, then sat

to watch the trails of smoke behind the Houses of Parliament catch fire with the sunset. The slender towers were washed by a rain of golden light and licked by little flickering flames; Somerset House and the bleached gray pinnacles about Whitehall were floated in a luminous haze. The yellow light poured through the trees and the leaves seemed to burn with soft fires. There was a smell of acacias in the air everywhere, and the laburnums were dripping gold over the walls of the gardens. (35–36)

Finally, as Alexander rides toward his weakened bridge and his death, he sees a group of boys sitting about a campfire. For this passage, Cather writes in her own voice, with confident, personal, clean prose:

When at last Alexander roused himself, the afternoon had waned to sunset. The train was passing through a gray country and the sky overhead was flushed with a wide flood of clear color. There was a rose-colored light over the gray rocks and hills and meadows. Off to the left, under the approach of a weather-stained wooden bridge, a group of boys were sitting around a little fire. The smell of the wood smoke blew in at the window. Except for an old farmer, jogging along the highroad in his box-wagon, there was not another living creature to be seen. Alexander looked back wistfully at the boys, camped on the edge of a little marsh, crouching under their shelter and looking gravely at their fire. They took his mind back a long way, to a campfire on a sandbar in a Western river, and he wished he could go back and sit down with them. He could remember exactly how the world had looked then. (116)

This is Cather at her best, drawing from her personal experience to write of ordinary objects which, infused with feeling, become symbols. The scene itself is masterful: the aging passenger on a train speeding through the world at sunset, his glimpse of boys about a fire framed beneath the wooden bridge, as if caught in time, so transformed by the light and his own memories that he leaves his middle-aged perspective and sees again through youthful eyes.

The question is, Whose youth is it? I can link Alexander to the young man who loved Hilda, but not to the boy on the sandbar in the western river. The group of children sitting around the little fire, the wood smoke, the old farmer riding in his box-wagon— these memories come directly from Cather's childhood, and they suggest a most interesting shift in focus. It is as if Cather had set out to write sympathetically of a successful professional endangered by an unwanted other self, then found her real sympathies were with neither the middle-aged professional nor the younger self who threatened him, but rather with an identity that, predating either, spoke through a memory of a childhood in an obscure western setting.

Surely Cather infused *Alexander's Bridge* with autobiography, especially of her years at *McClure's*. Like her character she was approaching middle age, apparently successful yet profoundly fatigued; like him she recalled a "second self" when she was newly independent, first working and traveling in Europe. And like Alexander, Cather undoubtedly felt that younger self was threatening to destroy all that she had achieved. In retrospect we might easily underestimate the dilemma, for we know that Cather was on the brink of launching a brilliant career as an American novelist. In 1911, however, she had no such security. She was almost forty years old and working at a job of some importance, and the prospect of leaving it inevitably created uncertainty. Yet the real risk came not with leaving *McClure's* but with devoting herself to writing. In both *Alexander's Bridge* and *The Song of the Lark*, her more overtly autobiographical novel of artistic commitment, Cather tells of the danger of "cutting out all else"; as Alexander recognized, "there would be no going back" (113), and as Thea Kronborg knew, if she "failed . . . she would lose her soul. There was nowhere to fall, after one took that step, except into abysses of wretchedness."[13]

Cather took that step. Late in 1911 she went on leave from the editorial office at *McClure's*, never again to be trapped in office routine. Her writing immediately reflected the renewed creativity she felt: there was "The Bohemian Girl," published separately in 1912, then "Alexandra" and "The White Mulberry Tree," to become part of *O Pioneers!* In these stories Cather returned to her own materials—the Midwest, childhood memories of the land and its people.

The plot of "The Bohemian Girl" is familiar to readers of Cather's early stories: an otherworldly figure (Nils Ericson) reenters the ordinary world (Nebraska) and awakens a mortal (Clara Vavrika Ericson) to imaginative, passionate experience, then departs with her. Two worlds again present alternatives. When Nils visits his mother, he finds a harsh physical world untransformed by ideas. The Ericson homestead resembles settings in Cather's early Nebraska fiction. It is a "grim square house with a tin roof and double porches. Behind the house stretched a row of broken, wind-racked poplars, and down the hill slope to the left straggled the sheds and stables."[14]

Olaf Ericson, Nils's older brother, further represents physical existence unredeemed by ideas. Everything about Olaf is intractable. "His head was large and square, like a block of wood," and his "heavy stubbornness [was] like the unyielding stickiness of wet loam against the plow." Because he is married to Clara, the woman Nils loves, Olaf dramatizes her life in Nebraska. He sits "out on the porch in the dark like a graven image" between her and the world. With him, nothing happens but dinner and threshing, and Clara declares she would "almost be willing to die, just to have a funeral." Her wish is prophetic, for the life in her *is* dying, as her cold hands, her black dress, her rigid expression all testify.

But a second, imaginative world offers salvation, to be reached by escaping from the ordinary or, more importantly, by discovering imaginative possibility within it. Escape from Nebraska is the only happy resolution to the action, for Clara and Nils cannot hope to unite within a community that includes Clara's husband. This action proceeds by a series of highly symbolic meetings between the lovers. Chronology (major scenes occur at sunset, then morning, afternoon, evening, then midnight) symbolizes Nils's reentry into this world from a dream one to claim Clara and then return with her to that dream world. Dress too is symbolic: Clara's severe life is evident in her riding costume and black dress; her softening, apparently in the gradual emergence of white — first in a white muslin dress beneath her riding habit, then in her entirely white figure at the barn dance.

Each of the scenes is a tableau; together they tell of lovers who move from this world to another one. Nils, hiding along a creek bed, first sees Clara when she descends the hill; she suddenly reins in her horse beside him, then mounts the hills again to move along the skyline, silhouetted against the last western color. Clara, imprisoned within her own home, first sees Nils when he appears one morning at her window. One afternoon the lovers meet by chance in Joe Vavrika's idyllic garden, where they recall their childhood play together. After supper they dance in Olaf's new barn, vibrant with life yet already becoming a legend. Finally, at midnight Clara again rides to where Nils waits for her on the plains, this time departing with him, the lovers like shadows disappearing from the mortal world. It all resembles "The Eve of St. Agnes"; when Cather's lovers leave Nebraska for Bergen, they escape to a fairy land as remote as any in Keats's poem.

Yet the finest scenes in "The Bohemian Girl" concern not the lovers at all but the apparently ordinary people about them. When Joe Vavrika raises a bottle of Tokai to his lips, his curly-haired head framed in golden light of the setting sun, he is a Bohemian saloon keeper living in Nebraska who has miraculously become a Bacchus. A dinner following a barn raising is another small miracle. Open barn doors reveal an assembly of women, platters of food, and piles of melons, all apparently ordinary objects, yet described in such detail that they become extraordinary:

Nils leaned against the booth, talking to the excited little girl and watching the people. The barn faced the west, and the sun, pouring in at the big doors, filled the whole interior with a golden light, through which filtered fine particles of dust from the haymow, where the children were romping. There was a great chattering from the stall where Johanna Vavrika exhibited to the admiring women her platters heaped with fried chicken, her roasts of beef, boiled tongues, and baked hams with cloves stuck in the crisp brown fat and garnished with tansy and parsley. The older women, having assured themselves that there were twenty kinds of cake, not counting cookies, and three dozen fat pies, repaired to the corner behind the pile of watermelons, put on their white aprons, and fell to their knitting and fancywork. They were a fine company of old women, and a Dutch painter would have loved to find them there together, where the sun made bright patches on the floor and sent long, quivering shafts of gold through the dusky shade up among the rafters. There were fat, rosy old women who looked hot in their best dresses; spare, alert old women with brown, dark-veined hands; and several of almost heroic frame, not less massive than old Mrs. Ericson herself. Few of them wore glasses, and old Mrs. Svendsen, a Danish woman, who was quite bald, wore the only cap among them. Mrs. Oleson, who had twelve big grandchildren, could still show two braids of yellow hair as thick as her own wrists. Among all these grandmothers there were more brown heads than white. They all had a pleased, prosperous air, as if they were more than satisfied with themselves and with life. Nils, leaning against Hilda's lemonade stand, watched them as they sat chattering in four languages, their fingers, their fingers never lagging behind their tongues.

"Look at them over there," he whispered, detaining Clara as she passed him. "Aren't they the Old Guard? I've just counted thirty hands. I guess they've wrung many a chicken's neck and warmed many a boy's jacket for him in their time."

In reality he fell into amazement when he thought of the Herculean labors those fifteen pairs of hands had performed; of the cows they had milked, the butter they had made, the gardens they had planted, the children and grandchildren they had tended, the brooms they had worn out, the mountains of food they had cooked. It made him dizzy.

The careful composition suggests a painting, with the point of view established by Nils, who directs attention to the central figure, Johanna Vavrika, exhibiting her platters of food. She is set against a background of admiring women brought to life by the detailing of their aprons, veined hands, braided hair, and the single cap. The company of women in the lower corner is balanced by the romping children in the haymow above. Sun pouring in the open barn doors provides warm light. As Cather recognized when she wrote "a Dutch painter would have loved to find them there," the scene is domestic and full in the manner of Dutch genre painting. But Cather has added her own stamp, for this is a scene that is straining against domesticity, the trademark of genre painting, and toward the heroic, with the amassed "mountains" of food, the women who are "of almost heroic frame," and the "Herculean labors" they have performed. It is a scene that celebrates the imagination, which can create from the most ordinary of events—a Nebraska barn scene—a New World heroic.

The problem of "The Bohemian Girl"—if it has a problem—is that while it is ostensibly about two lovers, its best parts are not about them at all, but about the pull of the land and the energy of its inhabitants. The land at night is more seductive and the barn-raising supper more intense than any moment between Nils and Clara. I, for one, willingly release the lovers to Bergen, for I wish to learn more not about them but about Nebraska, in all its contradictions. How is it that a place so apparently lifeless could give rise to such life, that a country so grim could yield such beauty? These are precisely the questions that Cather asked in *O Pioneers!*

Part II. Celebrations

In Red Cloud, ca. 1922

4 *O Pioneers!* Willa Cather's New World Pastoral

[The land] woke up out of its sleep and stretched itself, and it was so big, so rich, that we suddenly found we were rich, just from sitting still.[1]

In her essay "My First Novels [There Were Two]," Willa Cather distinguished between *Alexander's Bridge*, a studio piece that followed "the most conventional pattern," and *O Pioneers!*, a book in which "everything was spontaneous and took its own place, right or wrong." Writing *O Pioneers!*, Cather recalled, "was like taking a ride through a familiar country on a horse that knew the way."[2] The history of the book suggests how it did, indeed, seem to take on a life of its own. In the autumn of 1911, Cather wrote a Swedish story she called "Alexandra," planning it to be approximately the length of *Alexander's Bridge*. Upon completing "Alexandra," she wrote two stories about star-crossed lovers, both set in Nebraska. The first was "The Bohemian Girl"; the second, "The White Mulberry Tree," was to become the Marie-Emil story in *O Pioneers!* Cather conceived the idea for "The White Mulberry Tree" while she was in Nebraska, in a corn field watching the harvest; she returned to Pittsburgh, where she completed it, then read the story with "Alexandra."[3] The result was a sudden inner explosion and enlightenment, and, as Cather later wrote, she realized she "had on her hands a two-part pastoral."[4]

Though the history of *O Pioneers!* is widely known, Cather's reference to it as a two-part pastoral is generally ignored or dismissed.[5] The tendency has been to stress the originality of Cather's subject matter (she was the first to give immigrants heroic stature in serious American literature) and to puzzle over form, especially over the episodic nature and apparent lack of structure of the book. Yet Cather, a student of the classics and especially of Virgil, would have known well the tradition to which she referred, and her conception of her own country in that tradition was as revolutionary as her subject. In Cather's canon, it is not the subject that is new with *O Pioneers!*—she had written of immigrant pioneers in her early, generally bitter Nebraska stories—so much as it is the manner. With the pastoral Cather found the combination she needed for her best work—a rich tradition and great flexibility.

From its earliest appearance the pastoral was loose in form, composed of a series of little pictures, or "eidyllion," with a dream or ideal at its heart. Definitions of the pastoral are as numerous as the critics who have written about it. In pre-Empsonian days, the pastoral was identified by conventions of gardens, shepherds, and lovesick swains. But beginning with Empson's discussion of "the pastoral process of putting the complex into the simple," scholars have recognized varieties of pastoral. Renato Poggioli has interpreted psychological motives behind the pastoral as "a double longing after innocence and happiness, to be recovered . . . through a retreat"; Leo Marx has discussed "the sense of the machine as a sudden, shocking intruder upon a fantasy of idyllic satisfaction" in American literature; Raymond Williams has looked at the transformations of the pastoral mode in the interest "of a developing agrarian capitalism"; and Harold Toliver has stressed the "potential contrasts" seen in "the dialectical, tensive structure characteristic of all worthwhile pastoral."[6]

What these critics have in common is a knowledge that the pastoral celebrates the imaginative capacity to form ideals and to express them in art. Not surprisingly, a number of famous pastorals were written early in their authors' careers, when a writer searches for his or her way. Often, the pastoral was a writer's first major work: Virgil's *Eclogues*, Spenser's *Shepherd's Calendar*, Milton's "Lycidas," Wordworth's "Tintern Abbey," Keats's "Eve of St. Agnes," and Cather's *O Pioneers!* In each the writer celebrates the artistic imagination, with its power to bring order out of disparate materials. For as the garden is a design in nature, so the work is a design in art.

Parallels between *O Pioneers!* and Virgil's *Eclogues* are strong enough to suggest that Cather had not only the pastoral in general but specifically Virgilian pastoral in mind when she revised her stories for *O Pioneers!* The *Eclogues* presented a model of bringing together apparently disparate subjects—farmers and poets, the land and love—as two forms of the human desire for perfection.

Approximately half the eclogues present a primary impulse toward perfect harmony in nature, the other half a primary impulse toward perfect happiness in love.[7] Both follow the tragic pattern characteristic of good pastoral, by which moments of perfection are surrounded by disillusionment and loss.

More specific parallels are striking. Though historical causes differ—Virgil was writing of effects from fighting a civil war, Cather of those from settling a wild land—the disorder described is essentially the same. Each begins with the bewilderment of citizens casting about for moorings where "farms throughout the country are in chaos," and each uses awareness of chaos to intensify the pastoral desire for order. In the initial scene of the *Eclogues* as of *O Pioneers!*, farmers meet to provide the solace of friendship against a background of dispossession. In "The Wild Land," the two meetings of Alexandra and Carl, one destined to stay with the land, the other to leave, closely resemble meetings of farmers in "The Dispossessed" and "The Road to Town." As Virgil's Tityrus and Lycidas remain with the land, so does Alexandra; as Melioboeus and Moerius leave the country for the city after losing their property, so does Carl. The general pastoral contrast of the country versus the city, evident in the pervasive threat of wrenching dispossession, is made specific in scenes of instruction by which artificial city values are cast off and natural ones learned. In Virgil's "Song of Silenus," youths come upon the nature god Silenus in his cave, then implore him to sing to them of nature and of love; in *O Pioneers!* Alexandra, her brothers, and Carl seek out Crazy Ivar in his cave, then hear his biblical verses of creation and love.[8] Similarities are especially strong between the revelations of perfect harmony in nature at the thematic centers of the two works: Cather's description in "Neighboring Fields" of a bountiful nature yielding itself eagerly to the plow echoes the lyrical rhapsody of Virgil's fourth eclogue, "The Golden Age Returns."

The pastoral too, which from its earliest forms brought together farmers and lovers, provided a tradition by which Cather could yoke her love story, "The White Mulberry Tree," with "Alexandra." Again, resemblances to Virgil's *Eclogues* are evident. Like Virgil's passionate shepherd wooing the city-bred Alexis, Emil woos the city-bred Marie. And as Virgil's love eclogues gain in intensity, so Emil—who initially resembles a lovesick swain—

achieves tragic dimensions as he is increasingly ruled by passion. Specific echoes suggest a close relationship. In "Damion and Alphesiboeus," the mortal lovers are pawns of love brought about by magic so potent that the Moon itself participates in casting a spell, creating a desire that builds with Amaryllis's chant, "Bring Daphnis from the town," then culminates when she hears a sound at the gate and asks whether it is a dream or reality. Similarly, the passion of Marie and Emil becomes so strong it resembles witch-craft, and the moon seems to participate in their Midsummer's Eve spell. As Amaryllis desires her lover, so Marie dreams of Emil, then awakens to the sound of someone approaching, her dream of perfect love become reality.

Virgil's pastoral presents also the tragic rhythm Cather was to use in her novel, a means by which she could incorporate into her generally sunny book the loneliness and disillusionment so evident in her early Nebraska stories. Like Virgil's farmers, Cather's meet to provide the solace of friendship on a road that makes dramatically clear that their ways will soon diverge. In Virgil's "The Dispossessed" as in Cather's initial chapter, encroaching shadows surround the farmers as they talk, and when the friends depart, they set off into darkness. As friendship is followed by separation, so a vision of a Golden Age is followed by loss. The ideal harmony in nature of Virgil's "Golden Age Returns" is replaced in the next eclogue, "Daphnis at Heaven's Gate," with natural rhythms that are broken by the death of the ideal leader, Daphnis; and Cather follows her own description of a Golden Age with the death of Amédée, like Daphnis the ideal leader of a race of New World Arcadians. Similarly, desire for perfect happiness in love ends in death and disillusionment. In his last eclogue Virgil writes of Gallus, who, disconsolate when his beloved took another man, bitterly turned from pastoral dreams. Though no Gallus, the poet-friend of Virgil, Frank Shabata too turns bitterly from dreams of love after his wife takes another man.

Parallels suggesting how extensively Cather followed the Virgilian pastoral tradition are interesting in themselves, but Cather's originality lay in the ways she joined her American scene to that tradition. Her initial setting of Hanover, unmistakably her native Nebraska, has a specific reality: "board sidewalks were gray with trampled snow" (4), an "overheated store . . . reeked of pipe smoke, damp woolens, and kerosene" (14), and a "wagon jolted along over the frozen road" (15). The scene is informed with metaphor that moves it from historical reality to pastoral timelessness. Hanover is a Nebraska town that, like a flock left untended, is in danger of perishing. Snowflakes curl and ebb about buildings that, like sheep, are "huddled" together for protection, some looking "as if they were straying off by themselves, headed straight for the open plain" (3). Along the main street two rows of buildings "straggled" (4), and the tracks that extend from the two become fainter as they head into the wilderness. As if separated from the flock, homesteads beyond sight of town are in grave danger: the skeletal evidence of one is "gaunt against the sky"; another is "crouching in a hollow" (15).

The effect is to move a historical reality into a realm that has the potential for the unexpected, even the miraculous. This is a wilderness in which "the wind answered . . . like an echo" (18) and an entire town "vanished as if it had never been" (15). From the outset, Alexandra brings order to chaos. As if a shepherd, she protects those about her, warming her brother against the cold and directing the rescue of a kitten. But she is clearly capable of more—of the "transformations, spells of magic, and unmaskings of obscure divine and demonic forces [that] are recurrent themes of pastoral romances."[9] Alexandra is part of that world of miracles, a noble being disguised as an American immigrant farmer. As if in masquerade she wears "a man's long ulster . . . and a round plush cap, tied down with a thick veil" (6), the cumbersome coat disguising her, but her veil and the plush fabric of her cap suggesting her nobility. Removing her veil to warm her brother, she reveals her hair, shining like a golden crown, and a minor character makes the moment dramatic by paying tribute to her superiority: "A shabby little traveling man . . . stopped and gazed stupidly at the shining mass of hair she bared when she took off her veil; two thick braids, pinned about her head in the German way, with a fringe of reddish-yellow curls blowing out from under her cap" (7–8).

Like the heroine of a fairy tale who must find the key to transformation, Alexandra must learn the secret that will release the land from darkness. She is an initiate who goes through obligatory lessons in farming from her father. In the georgic manner, Mr. Bergson teaches his daughter facts she will need; more importantly, in the manner of romance, he defines her task for her. It is not a physical task (he and his sons have pitted themselves against the land to no avail), but an imaginative one: she must learn the "enigma" of the wild land (21–22). To do so, she goes as if on a pilgrimage to Crazy Ivar, an Americanized nature god who puritanically represses natural desires but who, by singing of creation and speaking of love, instructs Alexandra in natural harmony.

In *O Pioneers!* initiation consists not of action. In a world of miracles, the cause-effect of narrative can be discarded; and as a privileged noble peasant-shepherd, Alexandra is protected from labor by her father, who says she "must not work in the fields any more" (27). Her preparation consists of allowing her own nature to emerge, and it proceeds by a series of scenes in which she is detached and contemplative. As is characteristic of the pastoral, clothing and tools are primarily ornamental rather than useful. Alexandra ordinarily appears motionless and lost in thought with her shawl draped gracefully about her and her sunbonnet or shade hat beside her. She sits, for example, in a rocking chair with an open Bible on her knees, not reading but "looking thoughtfully away," with "her body . . . in an attitude of perfect repose," or stands "leaning against the frame of the mill, looking at the stars" (61, 70). She is never seen with a plow, the major symbol of productive labor in American literature.[10] When she is associated with farming implements, they are as decorative props—a pitchfork upon which she leans as she stands musing in a garden, or a mill against which she rests as she gazes at stars. Similarly, when work is described, it is as a background against which Alexandra is posed. She sits, for example, on the doorstep watching the moon rise above the rim of the prairie while her mother mixes bread in the kitchen behind her. Her brothers do the work of taming the land offstage, while she, untouched by labor and aging, provides the calm center of a noble pioneering spirit. Even in years of drought, Alexandra seems remote from the worry and labor of the barren land, as if she is protected by a magical circle of fertility.

The second of these barren summers was passing. One September afternoon Alexandra had gone over to the garden across the draw to dig sweet potatoes — they had been thriving upon the weather that was fatal to everything else. But when Carl Linstrum came up the garden rows to find her, she was not working. She was standing lost in thought, leaning

upon her pitchfork, her sunbonnet lying beside her on the ground. The
dry garden patch smelled of drying vines and was strewn with yellow
seed-cucumbers and pumpkins and citrons. At one end, next the rhu-
barb, grew feathery asparagus, with red berries. Down the middle of the
garden was a row of gooseberry and currant bushes. A few tough zenias
and marigolds and a row of scarlet sage [were there]. . . . Carl came
quietly and slowly up the garden path, looking intently at Alexandra.
She did not hear him. She was standing perfectly still, with that serious
ease so characteristic of her. Her thick, reddish braids, twisted about her
head, fairly burned in the sunlight. (48–49)

Such moments—contemplative, solitary, and spiritual—prepare
Alexandra for illumination, the moment on the Divide when she
realizes her love for the land and "felt the future stirring" (7 1).
   Alexandra's vision is the climax of her story. In the opening
paragraphs of the next section, "Neighboring Fields," the narrator
presents that vision made real. By love, the miracle that in fairy
tales breaks spells and enables transformations, Alexandra has released the sleeping country from darkness. The old country "has
vanished forever," and nature, freed from chaos, revels in its new
life:

It is sixteen years since John Bergson died. His wife now lies beside
him, and the white shaft that marks their graves gleams across the
wheat-fields. Could he rise from beneath it, he would not know the
country under which he has been asleep. The shaggy coat of the prairie,
which they lifted to make him a bed, has vanished forever. From the
Norwegian graveyard one looks out over a vast checker-board, marked
off in squares of wheat and corn; light and dark, dark and light. Telephone wires hum along the white roads, which always run at right
angles. From the graveyard gate one can count a dozen gayly painted
farmhouses; the gilded weather-vanes on the big red barns wink at each
other across the green and brown and yellow fields. The light steel windmills tremble throughout their frames and tug at their moorings, as they
vibrate in the wind that often blows from one week's end to another
across that high, active, resolute stretch of country.
   The Divide is now thickly populated. The rich soil yields heavy har-
vests; the dry, bracing climate and the smoothness of the land make
labor easy for men and beasts. There are few scenes more gratifying than
a spring plowing in that country, where the furrows of a single field often

lie a mile in length, and the brown earth, with such a strong, clean smell, and such a power of growth and fertility in it, yields itself eagerly to the plow; rolls away from the shear, not even dimming the brightness of the metal, with a soft, deep sigh of happiness. The wheatcutting sometimes goes on all night as well as all day, and in good seasons there are scarcely men and horses enough to do the harvesting. The grain is so heavy that it bends toward the blade and cuts like velvet.

There is something frank and joyous and young in the open face of the country. It gives itself ungrudgingly to the moods of the seasons, holding nothing back. Like the plains of Lombardy, it seems to rise a little to meet the sun. The air and the earth are curiously mated and intermingled, as if the one were the breath of the other. You feel in the atmosphere the same tonic, puissant quality that is in the tilth, the same strength and resoluteness. (75–77)

In this scene, the imaginative center of the book, Cather makes no pretense at realism or naturalism. Describing an archetypal paradise transplanted to America, she celebrates that her own neighborhood has joined the myth of the Golden Age. "The country insisted on being the Hero" of her book, she recalled after completing it, and she "did not interfere."[11] In its frank, joyous youth combined with its "strength and resoluteness," the land far more than any character has heroic qualities. As Alexandra tells Carl, the land did it by itself; it woke up and stretched, and she and the other farmers became rich just by sitting there.

But inherent in the idea of a Golden Age is loss and separation, for the self-sufficiency that makes the garden so desirable also makes its human inhabitants strangely irrelevant. Freed from the burden of work, Cather's farmers seem Americanized shepherds whiling away their time in idle pleasure. Alexandra keeps three pretty young Swedish girls in her house, not to work but "to hear them giggle" (85), and she keeps Ivar, now "too old to work in the fields," and sometimes "calls him into the sitting-room to read the Bible aloud to her" (87). When Alexandra and her brothers gather, they play: Lou and Oscar go to the orchard to pick cherries; Alexandra takes the young girls into the flower garden; Annie, Alexandra's sister-in-law, goes to the kitchen "to gossip with Alexandra's kitchen girls" (104).

Cather has skipped over sixteen years of change so radical it seems fantastic, of transformation from a wild land and an unde-

veloped, crude society to one of the world's most productive re-
gions. It would, as Leo Marx states, "be difficult to imagine more
profound contradictions of value or meaning than those made
manifest by this circumstance."[12] Social and class conflicts are inevitable between city and country, first- and second-generation
immigrants, old and new ways. These are the social actualities that
would in a Victorian novel provide the basis for treatment of status, class, and property; but American authors tend to turn from
social verisimilitude—and so does Cather, who is interested primarily in the idealizing imagination.

Cather turns aside social questions in several ways. She pasto-
ralizes harsh realities: death is gentle, a sleep beneath a prairie
blanket, and industry is part of the harmonious idyl—"telephone
wires hum" and "light steel windmills tremble throughout their
frames and tug at their moorings." She uses comedy to treat the
contradictions inherent in the transformation from a wild land to a
settled society. Lou, Oscar, and their families are clowns, country
bumpkins in whom reside serious questions of change. Displacement from rural to urban life is seen in Annie's determination "to
rent the place and move into town as soon as the girls are old
enough to go out into company" (111), political questions in Lou's
belief that the solution to class war is to blow up Wall Street, conflict between old and new ways in Mrs. Lee's fondness for nightcaps
and distrust of bathtubs.

More basically, Cather sets aside questions of social and class
conflict by turning her attention to the Marie and Emil love story.
Nowhere does Cather demonstrate her romantic sympathies more
clearly than in this so-called break in her novel: in 1912, as always,
she was far more interested in the implications of the idealizing
imagination than in social themes. Alexandra's pastoral vision was
a private experience of the wild land; following it, she is estranged
from the community that thrives upon the awakened earth.

With the Marie-Emil action, Cather explores the idea of
estrangement through characters who seek a personal paradise in
defiance of their communities. As if signaling the shift, Marie describes the same fields, land, and seasons that Alexandra and the
narrator celebrated in their pastoral visions, but turns them
around, seeing them not as life-giving but as deadening: "The
years seemed to stretch before her like the land; spring, summer,

autumn, winter, spring; always the same patient fields, the patient little trees, the patient lives; always the same yearning, the same pulling at the chain—until the instinct to live had torn itself and bled and weakened for the last time, until the chain secured a dead woman, who might cautiously be released" (248).

For the love action, Cather draws upon an expanded pastoral tradition and gives it distinctly modern implications. Of the three major antecedent myths Cather uses, two are pastoral. The biblical Garden of Eden is evoked in the general setting of the Shabata orchard, where Maria and Emil play in apparent childlike innocence and where danger takes the form of a snake. The more specific setting for their love recalls Ovid's *Metamorphosis*. Like Pyramis and Thisbe, Emil and Marie meet and die beneath a mulberry tree, their blood staining the white berries dark. But here, as elsewhere, Cather's closest emotional ties are to Keats, and her love story recalls most of all his romantic pastoral, "The Eve of St. Agnes." The passionate individuality of Emil and Marie, quite unlike Ovid's stylized figures, makes them close kin to Porphyro and Madeline.

Specific parallels are so close it is as if Cather has placed Keatsian lovers beneath Ovid's mulberry tree. As Keats wrote of love that combines sacred and profane passion on the eve of St. Agnes day, so Cather tells of the love of Emil and Marie under the shadow of the Church of Sainte-Agnes. In both stories the idealizing imagination transforms the world until the ordinary fades and dream becomes reality; and in both weather signals this movement. The winter cold framing the love episodes is so intense that Keats's "hare limped trembling through the frozen grass" and Cather's "rabbits run shivering from one frozen garden patch to another" (187). As Porphyro moves first inside the castle, then to the bedroom where Madeline is sleeping, details become increasingly warm and sensuous; similarly, Emil passes from the cold of winter to the warmth of spring, then to summer and the orchard, a natural bedroom where Marie is asleep.

The yearning music of the ball builds Porphyro's ardor and prepares for the contrasting stillness of the bedroom, where delicacies magically appear to fill the air with perfumes and where the light through a stained glass window transforms the setting into an enchanted lovers' paradise. In Cather's story, Gounod's "Ave

Maria" begins the climatic movement toward ecstasy, triggering in Emil the combination of sacred and profane passion that transforms reality, until the world "passed him like pleasant things in a dream" (258). In the quiet orchard, nature participates in courtship. As if by magic it supplies the delicacies Emil offers to Marie when, in an early scene, "he reached up among the branches and began to pick the sweet, insipid fruit, —long ivory-colored berries, tipped with faint pink, like white coral. . . . He dropped a handful into her lap" (153). Natural perfumes become increasingly seductive as courtship becomes more intense: "the fresh, salty scent of the wild roses" in early summer gives way to "this more powerful perfume of midsummer," when in the consummation scene the wild cotton has reached the bursting point, and "wherever those ashes-of-rose balls hung on their milky stalks, the air about them was saturated with their breath" (247).

As light in Madeline's bedroom passes through the stained glass of a window, so in the orchard "long fingers of light reached through the apple branches as through a net; the orchard was riddled and shot with gold; light was the reality, the trees were merely interferences that reflected and refracted light" (258). As Porphyro kneels beside Madeline, who awakens to see the subject of her dream, then with him fuses reality and dream in "solution sweet," so "Emil threw himself down beside [Marie] and took her in his arms. The blood came back to her cheeks, her amber eyes opened slowly, and in them Emil saw his own face and the orchard and the sun. 'I was dreaming this,' she whispered, hiding her face against him, 'don't take my dream away!' " (259).

Because the pastoral transformation in romantic literature is so intensely personal, the return to reality is characteristically abrupt and painful. With Frank Shabata's appearance, as with the sharp sleet against the windowpanes of Madeline's bedroom, the external world resumes, breaking the spell of a suspended paradise. Cather intensifies the break by placing the reader with Frank outside the orchard, voyeuristically peering through the mulberry hedge at the lovers, who are touchingly vulnerable in their oblivion. As if they have already left the mortal world, Marie and Emil blend with nature: their voices seem the murmuring of a stream, and their bodies are dark figures among shadows of the mulberry tree beneath which they lie.

Frank's response encapsulates the suffering of the mortal world the lovers have left behind: he shoots automatically, recoils in horror, and finally feels a wrenching sympathy for Marie. When he sobs, "Maria, . . . Maria," the love song that began with Emil's thoughts of Maria Shabata, then blended with Gounod's "Ave Maria," ends in an echo of loss and betrayal. As in Keats's poem, the movement from the secular to the sacred is completed by a return to the worldly.

This movement—of preparation for illumination, illumination, and return—is characteristic of pastoral, as is open-endedness with the return, for good pastoral asks questions rather than answers them. But the kind of question differs through the history of pastoral. Classical and biblical myths follow through, to tell of Pyramis and Thisbe's metamorphosis and of Adam and Eve's expulsion from the Garden. These are public myths of vision and loss; the questions they evoke concern the consequences of disobedience rather than the validity of the experience. In romantic literature, the return to the worldly is accompanied by doubts and disorientation as well as by loss. The emptiness at the end of "The Eve of St. Agnes" is so complete it is as if the lovers never existed; at the end of the later "Ode to a Nightingale," the poet returns to his "sole self," his vision fades, and with no way to validate his experience, he is left with the question "Was it a vision, or a waking dream?" Recent pastorals—Nathanael West's *Miss Lonelyhearts* and James Leo Herlihy's *Midnight Cowboy*—extend doubt to skepticism by showing individuals caught in myths that are seductive and false. [13]

Even while Willa Cather recalls the oldest pastorals, she shares the doubts of the Romantics and the scepticism of the moderns. Like the Romantics, Cather makes pastoral moments personal revelations by which the creative imagination transforms the world, with subsequent returns to public reality abrupt and difficult. Like the moderns, Cather places her characters within myths that are inadequate or that disintegrate, leaving them helpless. Emil and Marie in the orchard recall Adam and Eve in the Garden, but with enormous differences: by making the orchard lapsed and Marie a married woman, Cather makes a "fit" between characters and myth impossible, then presents the consequences of that distortion.

The Shabata orchard was once part of the original New World Eden, planted by the Linstrums with that vision in mind, then tended by Alexandra, and finally sold to the young Shabatas. Ironically, it is because the awakened land is so fertile ("it was almost more than Shabata and his man could do to keep up with the corn" [151]) that the orchard has fallen into "a neglected wilderness." In this, her version of a Fortunate Fall, Cather suggests that the lapse is also a liberation, for it has freed this spot of earth for magical possibilities lost in the symmetrical order of Alexandra's land.

Unlike the tamed world outside it, that within the orchard holds the potential for both the bliss and horror of primitive magic. The comforting patterns of Catholicism, with its suppers, weddings, confirmations, and funerals, give way to ancient practices of tree worship. The rites of the church seem inadequate for the primitivism of the forest, and Marie tells of her attraction to superstition: "The old people in the mountains plant lindens to purify the forest, and to do away with the spells that come from the old trees they say have lasted from heathen times" (152).

From the beginning, tensions against pastoral myths suggest dangers. The "merry sound" that calls Marie to the orchard is not that of pipes playing but that of a whetstone sharpening a scythe, and Marie dresses to run to the orchard by putting on a short skirt and, incongruously, her husband's boots (149). Cather's description of the growth in the orchard recalls a flower passage, a topos common to pastoral tradition; but instead of presenting harmonious nature, it threatens chaos: "All sorts of weeds and herbs and flowers had grown up there; splotches of wild larkspur, pale green-and-white spikes of hoarhound, plantations of wild cotton, tangles of foxtail and wild wheat." (151).

As the scene unfolds, apparently innocent play becomes dangerously deceptive, and Cather uses the pastoral mode, which evokes expectations of a visionary ideal, to tell of blindness. When Marie tells Emil she will call him if she sees a snake, she reveals little about the danger of snakes but much about her own inability to see the danger of Emil. Similarly, Marie tells Emil if he "had any eyes" he would see Alexandra's fondness for Carl—true enough, but Marie fails to see the more immediate truth of Emil's love for her (154). And when Emil accuses Marie of refusing to understand his feelings for her, he reveals his own blindness to the dangers of their love. Tensions build against an ideal that glorifies childhood innocence and denies full human experience. Presciently Marie declares she doesn't want to live to be more than thirty; and Emil threatens, "I can't play with you like a little boy any more" (156). Ultimately the illusion of pastoral play is broken, and Marie, bitterly crying, leaves Emil angrily mowing the orchard.

More than any other factor, Marie's status as a married woman sets her story apart from its predecessors and gives it ironic dimensions. As Marie loved Frank, so now she loves Emil, a youthful version of Frank. Both men are related to rich women who pamper them; both, released by these women from the need to work, seem dandies to their communities. Frank "was a sight to see, with his silk hat and tucked shirt and blue frock-coat, wearing gloves and carrying a little wisp of a yellow cane" (143); Emil was "a strikingly exotic figure in a tall Mexican hat, a silk sash, and a black velvet jacket sewn with silver buttons" (212). Both are restless and rash; both are romantic in a Byronic sense—brooding, soulful, dramatic, self-absorbed; both have had the power "to take the blood from [Marie's] cheeks" (225).

Against the background of Marie's love for Frank, Marie and Emil's story is ironic. Characters follow roles that are outdated and distorted. Saying to Emil that she will call him if she sees a snake, Marie suggests Eve in the biblical story; and crying that he would rather be eaten by wild beasts than have seen his wife harmed, Frank echoes Pyramis in Ovid's tale. But parts have shifted, so that Emil has the role not of Adam but of the snake, and Frank not that of Pyramis but of the lion.

With repetition Cather adds also a moral dimension missing from antecedent tales. Pyramis and Thisbe, like Porphyro and Madeline, love with an intensity that creates their own code of truth to one another. Cather allows her lovers no such justification. A romantic code of mutual devotion would demand that Marie be true to Frank, and as she recognizes, "when a girl had loved one man, and then loved another while that man was still alive, everybody knew what to think of her" (249). Nor have they the support of religion. The strongly Catholic Marie prays for deliverance from an adulterous love, and Ivar believes the dead lovers are eternally damned. Unlike her proud secret love for Frank, Marie's love for Emil is a guilty thing which she cannot admit even to herself.

Emil's love for Marie is similarly dark. Because of it, he compares his life to the grain that "lay still in the earth and rotted" (164), and Marie, who once suggested to Frank that they run away together, views Emil's similar suggestion to her as wicked (231).

Without a social or personal code from which to act, Marie and Emil reveal a passivity quite unlike their literary predecessors. Pyramis and Thisbe, Porphyro and Madeline, are just two in a long line of romantic lovers who act resolutely to acknowledge and protect their love. Indeed, the story of Marie's first love follows this convention far more closely than that of her second: Marie and Frank defied their elders, took their fate into their own hands, fled their families and homes. But then, as if Pyramis and Thisbe or Porphyro and Madeline had returned to set up housekeeping in the suburbs, so Frank and Marie returned to a Nebraska farm, where their love gave way to disappointment and bitterness.

Cather has given to Marie and Emil, then, the distinctly modern quality of characters in parts they do not understand, motivated not by a commitment to a code, even one of defiance, so much as by the desperation of entrapment—Marie in a disappointing marriage, Emil by an uncertain future. They follow their impulses rather than their resolve, and they rely upon blindness to protect them. At no point do they seize control of their own destinies: they meet only by a combination of chance and self-deception, and they die not by their own but by another's action.

With their deaths there is a return from the private, suspended world created by their love, and it is in the return, as much a part of the pastoral as the vision of an ideal, that the pastoral must be evaluated. Cather placed the Emil-Marie story within Alexandra's story, titling the last section of the book "Alexandra" and focusing on paradises lost. As the lovers vanish into death, Alexandra confronts a world of pain and separation. Balancing her ecstasy of a visionary future, Alexandra now faces death in a dark night of the soul. She goes to the graveyard, where she gets "so near the dead, they seem more real than the living" (281). In doing so, she comes full circle, where endings join with beginnings:

I think it has done me good to get cold clear through like this once. I don't believe I shall suffer so much any more. When you get so near the dead, they seem more real than the living. Worldly thoughts leave one. Ever since Emil died, I've suffered so when it rained. Now that I've been

out in it with him, I shan't dread it. After you once get cold clear
through, the feeling of the rain on you is sweet. It seems to bring back
feelings you had when you were a baby. It carries you back into the dark,
before you were born; you can't see things, but they come to you, somehow, and you know them and aren't afraid of them. Maybe it's like that
with the dead. If they feel anything at all, it's the old things, before they
were born, that comfort people like the feeling of their own bed does
when they are little. (280–81)

With her newly gained knowledge, Alexandra is able to rejoin
the human community. She goes first to Lincoln, where she talks
with Frank in prison, then rejoins Carl, who has returned from
Alaska. Alexandra takes off her black mourning clothes and puts
on a white dress to walk with Carl through the sunny fields and sit
talking with him until shadows announce evening. The scene is
classically pastoral, and it balances their first, similarly classically
pastoral meetings. But unlike the overwhelming sense of loss in
those initial scenes, the final ones combine light and dark, youth
and age: "The straw-stacks were throwing long shadows, the owls
were flying home to the prairie-dog town. When they came to the
corner where the pasture joined, Alexandra's twelve young colts
were galloping in a drove over the brow of the hills" (306). The
anxiety and ecstasy of the inital scene have been replaced by "exalted serenity" (308), for Alexandra has reconciled a human relationship to pastoral vision. She accepts that possession is impossible, of people and of the land. Others have an integrity of their
own—Marie is not just a married woman and Emil not simply her
brother—and we may possess nature only by loving it, for we live
in it as a sojourner: "We come and go, but the land is always here.
And the people who love it and understand it are the people who
own it—for a little while" (308).

The overwhelming effect of the concluding scene is of timelessness. The narrator, drawing back, joins age and youth, life and
death, the present and the universal: "They went into the house
together, leaving the Divide behind them, under the evening star.
Fortunate country, that is one day to receive hearts like Alexandra's into its bosom, to give them out again in the yellow wheat, in
the rustling corn, in the shining eyes of youth!" (309).

Here the narrator brings together the two parts of Cather's pastoral, much as Virgil's poet unifies the parts of the *Eclogues*. Both

narrators are sophisticated artists, distinct from the relatively simple characters they speak of. Unlike Alexandra, who has little imagination and less verbal skill, Cather's narrator writes with full imaginative and poetic power; and unlike Marie and Emil, who vibrate with youthful passion, the narrator is calm, orderly, and wise. While the characters present specific responses—Alexandra, a love for the land, and Marie and Emil, a sexual, romantic love for each other—the narrator is universal and shows how art unifies. She luxuriates in the triumph of a New World Golden Age as she luxuriates in the tragedy of the Marie-Emil love; both are beautiful when ordered by art. Appropriately, it is this narrator who tells of the marriage of Alexandra and Carl. Like the ritual unions of pastoral romance, theirs is a highly stylized resolution made effective by the narrator's calm, contemplative tone. "This tone, characteristic of Virgilian pastoral, is a way of saying that the episode belongs to a timeless, recurrent pattern of human affairs. It falls easily into a conventional design because it has occurred often before."[14] As Carl tells Alexandra, "There are only two or three human stories, and they go on repeating themselves as fiercely as if they had never happened before; like the larks in this country, that have been singing the same five notes over for thousands of years" (119).

5 *The Song of the Lark*: The Growth of an Artist's Mind

Thea Kronborg learned the thing that old Dumas meant when he told the Romanticists that to make a drama he needed but one passion and four walls.[1]

O Pioneers! was unlike anything Cather had written before—more spontaneous, natural, inevitable. Here there was no sense a writer had prepared an outline of her story, then mechanically followed it, as in *Alexander's Bridge*.[2] Instead, *O Pioneers!* seemed to have written itself, with the country and the people telling their own story.[3] As though Cather had erased her individual self, the book has an impersonal quality. The narrator speaks with a universal voice, and Alexandra, one of Cather's few major characters not based on an identified model, seems more mythic than human. It was as if in writing this book Cather had become the impersonal, godlike creator she had long been writing about.

In her next book, *The Song of the Lark*, Cather explored what led to that experience. She returned the creative act to time and the artist to the real world—her world. Moonstone, Colorado, *is* Red Cloud, Nebraska. Cather reproduced her hometown so precisely that one could map the stores, churches, houses, and streets of one and find her way in the other. Moreover, Thea Kronborg is Willa Cather in essentials, though Olive Fremstad was her external prototype. Cather's experiences in her small midwestern hometown live again in Thea's: the attic room Cather covered with rose-patterned wallpaper appears as Thea's room, G. E. McKeeby, the doctor who befriended Willa and cared for her when she was ill, appears as Dr. Archie, and Professor Schindelmeisser, a wandering musician who taught music lessons to Willa, as Herr Wunsch.[4] Willa Cather's strong-minded personality became Thea Kronborg's, and Cather's struggles to find her way as a writer became her character's to do so as a singer. In short, Cather made her character personal in a way unprecedented in her earlier writing. It was as if before writing *O Pioneers!* Cather had not dared to ask whether there was an artist inside her, for "the reality, one cannot uncover *that* until one is sure" (266).

Autobiography as preparation for a life's work of creation—it is the romantic's way, seen in its classic form in *The Prelude*. When the self is the source of value in an otherwise meaningless world, the prerequisite for the artist is to know that self. As Wordsworth explained in his 1814 Preface, he prepared to write "a literary Work that might live" by recording "the origin and progress of his own powers," reviewing their growth until "his faculties were sufficiently mature for entering upon the arduous labor which he had proposed to himself."[5] In *The Song of the Lark*, her "Prelude," Cather used her own experiences to trace the growth of the artist's mind. She followed Thea until she "came into full possession" of her creative faculties, as Cather herself had at a similar age "hit the home pasture" in *O Pioneers!*[6]

Because *The Song of the Lark* is, as Cather described it, a "full-blooded" narrative, filled with details, readers often have overlooked how selective Cather was with that action. She focused on the psychology of her artist, the forces within and outside her that propelled her to greatness. In doing so, she ignored or telescoped experiences conventionally considered essential to a life story. Thea's education, for example, is a romantic one, ministered by nature or by individuals at odds with society—the drunken minstrel Herr Wunsch and the weary artist Harsanyi. Except for Thea's music lessons, Cather omits formal schooling in Moonstone; she includes Thea's Chicago voice lessons as an example of false art, uninspired by love, and she gives only the briefest nod to Thea's mandatory European training. Similarly, Cather provides the most perfunctory reference to Thea's marriage and nothing at all about the possibility of her having children, those essentials of other women's lives.

What Cather does explore is Thea's imaginative life. The novel begins with the birth of a child to the Kronborg family; simultaneously, an older child, Thea, has pneumonia and struggles to survive. The scene announces Cather's concern with double birth: a biological one is an accidental thing and highly overrated, the narrator says, while the far more important "second self" necessary for creative life is ignored. The book is about that second self, its gestation, birth, and passion.

In the early scenes the child Thea outwardly conforms to the public roles dictated by her family and community, but inwardly carries about a secret or second self, which she nourishes by drinking in sensations: seeing the sandhills glittering in the distance as she walks to the Kohlers' house for her music lessons, smelling the linden bloom in the Kohlers' garden, hearing Ray Kennedy's stories of adventure, watching rabbits in the moonlight. Unlike Ray Kennedy, who believed expression was obligatory and laboriously recorded his impressions in a notebook, only to admit "the material you were so full of vanished mysteriously under your striving hand" (146), Thea instinctively refuses to explain her feelings, for "it spoils things to ask questions" (98). When it comes, knowledge will occur not by reasoning but in a flash of insight.

Thea's education is remarkably similar to Wordsworth's, a combination of associationism and divine insight. She records experiences as fragments until she has a revelation — the epiphany of creative imagination — that enables her to put them together. As her teachers realize, Thea is talented but not quick: "She could not think a thing out in passages. Until she saw it as a whole, she wandered like a blind man surrounded by torments. After she once had her 'revelation,' after she got the idea that to her . . . explained everything, then she went forward rapidly" (241). But Thea is the superior individual to whom such knowledge will come: she herself is aware of a special destiny, as are those closest to her — her mother, Dr. Archie, Professor Wunsch, Ray Kennedy.

Thea's "soul crisis," that staple of romantic development in which a person becomes aware of herself as an individual, occurs in Chicago, where she has gone to study music. Her formal lessons are mechanical and disappointing: she struggles with the piano, which she is not by nature suited for; then she wears herself out in voice lessons with a talented but soulless teacher. But the strongest need of Thea's nature is not to learn technique but to find herself, and her real education, appropriately, occurs alone. Indeed, the lesson is that she *is* alone. While listening to Dvorak's Symphony in E minor, *From the New World*, Thea feels the ecstasy of art; following it she confronts the barrenness of the world outside the concert hall. Unthinking ways of the past are discarded, and Thea for the first time is conscious of her self as separate from her world. The crisis that ensues recalls similar moments recorded by Wordsworth, John Stuart Mill, and Carlyle. Like Carlyle, whose Professor Teufelsdröckh recognized a mechanical, soulless universe as his enemy, "one huge, dead, immeasurable Steam-engine, rolling on, in its dead indifference, to grind me limb from limb,"[7] so Thea "for almost the first time . . . was conscious of the city itself, of the congestion of life all about her, of the brutality and power of those streams that flowed in the streets, threatening to drive one under" (252–53). Teufelsdröckh responded defiantly to the Everlasting No, Carlyle's term for negative forces that would deny meaning to life: "*I* am not thine, but Free, and forever hate thee!"[8] Similarly, Thea confronts the world as her enemy and by her defiance begins her spiritual newbirth: "All these things and people were no longer remote and negligible; they had to be met, they were lined up against her, they were there to take something from her. Very well; they should never have it" (254).

The superior individual pitted against a common world—it is a familiar stance of negative romanticism, the necessary discarding of outmoded beliefs before one can affirm new ones. Carlyle's Teufelsdröckh entered a "Center of Indifference," seeing through and despising the wretchedness of a world in which mortals are "Shadow-hunters or Shadow-hunted"; similarly, Thea Kronborg, her eyes newly unsealed, comes to feel contempt for the complacency of second-rate singers, the wretchedly conducted boarding houses, the "stupid faces" of common people in a common world. Unable to find value outside herself and not yet able to create it from within, she falls into a period of emotional sterility. She is "a moving figure of discouragement" (363), listless, dull, "frozen up" (324).

The turning point for the romantic comes when, usually alone in nature, he affirms his own feelings as a source of value. Following his despair over excesses of the French Revolution, Wordsworth returned to Nature, where his imagination was restored; Mill recovered his ability to feel while reading Wordsworth's poetry; Carlyle's Teufelsdröckh recognized the "Everlasting Yea" while sitting alone on a hill, seeing at a distance smoke from a cottage. Thea Kronborg is in this tradition when she leaves the superficial life she had lived in Chicago and literally goes into the earth, into Panther Canyon, where she lives alone during part of one summer. There, "completely released from the enslaving desire to get on in the world" (369), she opens herself to those things in the world which were for her. She ceases to struggle with music and experiences it as "sensuous form" by which "she could become a mere receptacle for heat, or become a colour, like the bright lizards that darted about on the hot stones outside her door; or she could become a continuous repetition of sound, like the cicadas" (373).[9] Recollections from childhood surface, to become part of her art. The narrator, interpreting the experience, describes the sensuous relationship of a romantic artist to her past, her world, and her art:

The faculty of observation was never highly developed in Thea Kronborg. A great deal escaped her eye as she passed through the world. But the things which were for her, she saw; she experienced them physically and remembered them as if they had once been a part of herself. The roses she used to see in the florists' shops in Chicago were merely roses. But when she thought of the moonflowers that grew over Mrs. Tellamantez's door, it was as if she had been that vine and had opened up in white flowers every night. There were memories of light on the sand hills, of masses of prickly-pear blossoms she had found in the desert in early childhood, of the late afternoon sun pouring through the grape leaves and the mint bed in Mrs. Kohler's garden, which she would never lose. These recollections were a part of her mind and personality. In Chicago she had got almost nothing that went into her subconscious self and took root there. But here, in Panther Cañon, there were again things which seemed destined for her. (374)

Thea's revelation resembles the foresplendors of divine Truth that fell mysteriously over Teufelsdröckh's soul; even more so, it resembles Wordsworth's newly awakened sense of artistic power. The climax of the Panther Canyon scenes — indeed of the novel — occurs when Thea receives this knowledge. As a "plastic power" takes possession of Wordsworth at Hawkshead, enabling him to see his own imagination as a divinely granted intuitive force corresponding in the individual to the creative imagination of God in the universe, so a divine creative knowledge is granted to Thea. Ideas recorded upon her come together in a sudden revelation of her relation to art. She recognizes that as an artist she can intuit the abiding in the stream of life, and by holding it, can create universal truths. The revelation profoundly alters her response to life, imaged throughout the novel as a stream. In Chicago Thea had seen it as a chaotic one of disorderly people outside the concert hall; in Panther Canyon she still sees it as a stream, but now positively, as "the shining, elusive element" caught by a painting or sculpture or song "in a flash of arrested motion" (378).

The revelation is the essential experience; what follows involves a necessary but, for the romantic, not particularly interesting working out of its implications. When Thea emerges from the canyon and returns to the real world, she must refine "the sense of truthfulness" (571) she now holds. She and her mentor chart a worldly education in Germany, but Cather omits this European training. When Thea next appears, she is transformed, so hardened that her old friend, Dr. Archie, feels estranged from her: a "woman he had never known had somehow devoured his little friend" (500). But though she has sacrificed her personal life, Thea's artistic life is, as Cather wrote in her 1932 preface, happy, free, and real. She realizes her potential when, as Sieglinde, "the closed roads opened, the gates dropped," and she enters the kingdom of art. Like Michelangelo's God giving life, "she had only to touch an idea to make it live" (571). Cutting through commonplaces about her performance, Harsayni says Thea's "secret . . . is every artist's secret . . . passion. That is all" (570–71).

Thea's development has been a working out of this idea — the passion, the container, and the drama. In Moonstone a young Thea was uncontained passion. Lying on her bedroom floor in the moonlight, she responded with excitement to the life she believed was rushing in upon her; the narrator, explaining that it actually comes from within, uses the metaphor central to her subsequent development: "On such nights . . . Thea Kronborg learned the thing that old Dumas meant when he told the Romanticists that to make a drama he needed but one passion and four walls" (177). In Panther Canyon Thea realized that the artist makes herself a vessel, like the Indian women's pottery to hold water or Dumas's four walls to hold the drama. And in New York Thea was refined passion, "entirely illuminated, or wholly present," only when performing, otherwise — and again Cather uses Dumas's metaphor of four walls — she was "a little cold and empty, like a big room with no people in it" (533). As Sieglinde she brings the metaphor together — the passion contained within the vessel that can make a drama.

For Cather such passion combines the sacred and the profane in an experience akin to religious ecstasy — boundless, intense, consuming. She frequently gave it a connotation of martyrdom, the complete giving up of oneself as illustrated by Thea in the final scenes of *The Song of the Lark*. Yet in doing so, Cather never turned from the things of this world. Art and religion are, as Godfrey St. Peter will later remark, the same thing in the end. It was a yoking Cather defined in her earliest writing:

It is peculiar, this idea people have of everything colorless and spiritless being sacred. It is strange how we object to giving beautiful things to God. He must be very fond of beauty Himself. He never made an unlovely thing any more than He ever made a "moral" thing. In nature God does not teach morals. He never limits or interferes with beauty. His laws are the laws of beauty and all the natural forces work together to produce it. The nightingale's song is not moral; it is perfectly pagan in its unrestrained passion. . . . The world was made by an Artist, by the divinity and godhead of art, an Artist of such insatiate love of beauty that He takes all forces, all space, all time to fill them with His universes of beauty; an Artist whose dreams are so intense and real that they, too, love and suffer and have dreams of their own. [10]

Thea Kronborg has become such an artist—pure energy or passion, so emptied of a personal self that she can take into herself others' desires and convert them into song: the vague sentimental longings of Tillie Kronborg and the romantic dreams of Ray Kennedy, the sensitivity of Herr Wunsch, the searching of Dr. Archie, the generosity of Harsanyi, the madness of Spanish Johnny, the cynicism of Madison Bowers. Desire extends from the past: the Indian women who made and painted the clay pots Thea finds in Panther Canyon, "bits of their frail clay vessels, fragments of their desire" (399), and from the country, "the immeasurable yearning of all flat lands" (251). This is the longing of the finite for the infinite, of mortality for immortality.

The Song of the Lark ends with a short epilogue set in Moonstone, "twenty years after Thea Kronborg left it for the last time" (575). Thea does not appear as herself, but only as the dream enjoyed by her queer old aunt, Tillie Kronborg. The girl who became the woman, then the artist, has passed altogether from the ordinary world, returning in Tillie's stories as a legend to awaken others' imaginations: "So, into all the little settlements of quiet people, tidings of what their boys and girls are doing in the world bring refreshment; bring to the old, memories and to the young, dreams" (581).

In its narrative, then, *The Song of the Lark* is a romantic Künstlerroman, a *Bildungsroman* or novel of development which treats artistic growth as the growth of the imagination.[11] The central relationship is between the major character's mind and art; secondary characters, setting, and action support that development. What is unusual with the narrative is that the artist is a woman. I know of few novels in which a female character so clearly follows conventionally male narrative patterns.[12] By giving to Thea talent, ambition, hard-headedness, egocentricity, and a certain ruthlessness, Cather distinguishes her from the usual female *Bildungsroman* character, who defines herself by other people. She further protects Thea by plot manipulation. Cather uses Herr Wunsch to introduce Thea to music, then disposes of him by having him leave Moonstone, apparently to end his days in an alcoholic haze. She creates Ray Kennedy to introduce the young Thea to the world beyond Moonstone, then when an older Thea needs money to study in Chicago, kills Kennedy in a railway accident, thus providing to Thea insurance money with the stipulation that she use it to study in Chicago.

Moreover, Cather protects Thea by reversals of conventional sex roles. Thea's two suitors, Ray Kennedy and Fred Ottenberg, assume roles complementary women ordinarily play: the older woman who provides money, the younger who initiates the hero into sexual passion, both prevented by plot manipulation from complicating the hero's development. In Samuel Butler's *The Way of All Flesh,* for example, Althea Pontifex, like Ray Kennedy, dies, leaving the hero an inheritance, and Ellen, like Fred Ottenberg, initiates the hero into sexual experience, the complications of which are avoided by the discovery of a previous marriage. Fred Ottenberg assumes traditionally female roles of nurturing. When he joins Thea in Panther Canyon, he cooks for her, covers her against the rain, remains behind while she explores the higher trail. His major qualification for loving Thea is that he recognizes her special mission and wishes to be an instrument in furthering it. As worldly female characters have done for countless male ones, Fred supplies Thea with experience in culture and sex, preparing her to take her place in the world.

At the same time that Cather structured the narrative of *The Song of the Lark* along traditionally male patterns, she made Thea Kronborg's imaginative growth intensely female.[13] Imaginative growth involves the capacity to forge a relationship between one-self and the world, to create connections between or metaphors of the idea and the thing. Cather, within the romantic tradition, stresses that the mind is an active (though not always self-conscious) agent of perception. Wordsworth's poet learned to love nature when a babe-in-arms, combining love he felt in his mother's arms with perceptions of nature:

> For feeling has to him imparted power
> That through the growing faculties of sense
> Doth like an agent of the one great Mind
> Creates, creator, and receiver both,
> Working but in alliance with the works
> Which it beholds. —Such, verily, is the first
> Poetic spirit of our human life.[14]

Cather too specifies the active reciprocity between the receiving mind and the world. Like the familiar romantic aeolian harp, a young Thea at night vibrates with excitement before her open window: "Life rushed in upon her through that window—or so it seemed. In reality, of course, life rushes from within, not from without" (177). For that active, creative power of the imagination, which is "creator, and receiver both," Cather uses metaphors that reveal Thea Kronborg's developing consciousness, a nature perceived as hers in such richly personal terms it was called by the late Ellen Moers "the most thoroughly elaborated female landscape in literature."[15]

Initially, Thea's world extends no farther than the cradlelike oasis in the desert, Moonstone, Colorado, where she passes her childhood. Gradually, she becomes aware of a larger world, one metaphorically linked with the female sexuality that underlies a woman's creative passion. Beyond Moonstone are the sand hills, "a constant tantalization" with their "lines of deep violet where the clefts and valleys were" (58). When twelve, Thea goes into the sand hills, a rite of passage into womanhood that foreshadows her Panther Canyon passage into the kingdom of art. With her mother she travels to Pedro's Cup, "a great amphitheatre, cut out in the hills, its floor smooth and packed hard, dotted with sagebrush and greasewood." From it, as blood flows from a woman's body during her menses, flows "soft sand which drained down from the crumbling banks. On the surface of this fluid sand, one could find bits of brilliant stone, crystals and agates and onyx, and petrified wood as red as blood" (60). As significant as the metaphor that links Thea's growth to her world is the beauty of the description, by which Cather affirms her character's growth in terms of her developing female body.

Subsequent action extends the metaphorical pattern of female sexuality. Returning to Moonstone, Thea feels awakening desire. Lying awake in the moonlight beside her window, she pulses "with ardour and anticipation." Yearning intensifies when, after Thea moves from Moonstone to Chicago, she listens to Dvorak's Symphony in E minor and identifies as hers "the sand hills . . . the reaching and reaching of high plains, the immeasurable yearning of all flat lands" (251).

Thea's awakening desire anticipates consummation in the Panther Canyon scenes. From a distance, Panther Canyon seems "like a thousand others — one of those abrupt fissures with which the earth in the Southwest is riddled" (369). Moving point of view into the canyon, Cather creates an effect of moving into a secret personal landscape, into "a gentler cañon within a wilder one," to "the dead city [that] lay at the point where the perpendicular outer wall ceased and the V-shaped inner gorge began." Within this inner landscape are evidences of ancient life that remain as if in a primal womb: "There a stratum of rock, softer than those above, had been hollowed out by the action of time until it was like a deep groove running along the sides of the cañon. In this hollow (like a great fold in the rock) the Ancient People had built their houses of yellowish stone and mortar" (370).

In the protected recess of Panther Canyon, Thea prepares to receive the creative impulse "in that sensuous form" (373), much as Alexandra met "the Genius of the Divide." After ritualistically bathing, Thea climbs to her rock chamber in Panther Canyon's hollow groove, where "she drew herself out long upon the rugs . . . as if she were waiting for something to catch up with her" (372–73).

Receptivity culminates when, bathing in a sunny pool at the canyon's bottom, Thea participates in creative union. Setting metaphorically suggests this union. When she enters the pool, the stream seems a lover, a "glittering thread of current [that] had a kind of lightly worn, loosely knit personality, graceful and laughing" (378). In the pool "splashing water between her shoulder-blades," Thea meets "something [that] flashed through her mind," the idea of how art and life join, how she and the world fuse. Again, the metaphor is of female sexuality: "What was any art but an effort to make a sheath, a mould in which to imprison for a moment the shining, elusive element which is life itself—life hurrying past us and running away, too strong to stop, too sweet to lose. . . . In singing, one made a vessel of one's throat and nostrils and held it on one's breath, caught the stream in a scale of natural intervals" (378). Thus conception occurs "in this crack in the world, so far back in the night of the past" (379).

Outward movement follows immediately, as creative life begins: "Down here at the beginning, that painful thing was already stirring; the seed of sorrow, and of so much delight" (379), and "everything seemed suddenly to take the form of a desire for action" (382). Thea rejoins the human community. Her lover, Fred Ottenberg, arrives, a human correlative for the stream's maleness. The previously embracing canyon with its womblike security becomes confining, and imagery of movement suggests the generative powers that exert themselves from its depths: "The yuccas were in blossom now. Out of each clump of sharp bayonet leaves rose a tall stalk hung with greenish-white bells with thick, fleshy petals. The niggerhead cactus was thrusting its crimson blooms up out of every crevice in the rocks" (383). Previously separated male and female imagery, now combined as opposites working together, anticipates the final stage of Cather's metaphor of imaginative growth, that of androgyny.

From Panther Canyon, Thea carries within herself the seed of artistic life until in her role as Sieglinde she "came into full possession of things she had been refining and perfecting for so long." Until now Cather had presented Thea fitting herself to and accommodating metaphor; at this point, metaphor proceeds from her: "Her body was absolutely the instrument of her idea. . . . All that deep-rooted vitality flowered in her voice, her face, in her very finger-tips. She felt like a tree bursting into bloom" (571). As Sieglinde, Thea Kronborg fulfills Cather's definition of art, "to keep an idea living, intact, tinged with all its original feeling . . . and transfer it on paper a living thing with color, odor, sound, life all in it."[16]

When *The Song of the Lark* is considered with other *Bildungsroman* and *Künstlerroman,* it is exceptional in Cather's use of a female character as artist, capable of absorbing into herself her world, then converting it by passion into art. That world is Moonstone, and Cather's treatment of it is exceptional too. In a 1916 letter to Dorothy Canfield Fisher, Cather specified that the novel is about Moonstone—what Thea received from Moonstone and what she returned to it. In writing it Cather kept herself so firmly planted there that, although she had written much of the German part, she deleted it because she did not want to leave the Moonstone point of view. [17] In her early draft Cather used quotation marks for her narrator's Moonstone voice, until her manuscript became so cluttered that she removed them. Yet even without quotation marks, the narrator clearly speaks "Moonstone speech"; no one could confuse her with the universal poet of *O Pioneers!*

Cather establishes her narrator's point of view in the opening section, "Friends of Childhood," set in Moonstone. Diction is both colloquial and regional (Thea uses money she earns teaching music lessons "to fit up a little room for herself upstairs in the half storey" [71]), and imagery is familiar, even homey ("the town looked as if it had just been washed" [26–27]). Speech rhythms are conversational: "What with the pain of the tooth . . . Thea was fairly worn out" (76–77); "there is hardly a German family . . . but has its oleander trees" (32); "people were dug up, as it were" (27). The narrator often speaks with the gossipy tone of a small town: Belle White Archie had a "harum-scarum spirit" (44), Lily Fisher is "the most stuck up doll in the world" (76), and "Uncle Billy had been one of the most worthless old drunkards who sat on a store box and told filthy stories"(47).

When Thea leaves, she takes Moonstone with her in nonessentials that she changes—her clothes, manners, and speech—and also in the essential values that she doesn't change. She always measures "high buildings by the Moonstone standpipe. There are standards we can't get away from" (548), and these values protect her. She recognizes the distinction between being married and not being married and knows that without marriage Fred Ottenberg would be "keeping" her. Even when famous and wealthy, she measures money by Moonstone values and the six hundred dollars left her by Ray Kennedy's death insurance, the price of a man's life that enabled her to get her start.

We have long accepted the view that Cather returned to her native materials in *O Pioneers!*, and in some sense that is true, of course. But she did so by moving those materials out of time, with them celebrating a pastoral dream. In many respects it was not until *The Song of the Lark* that Cather came to terms with her heritage. For the first time she used a midwestern point of view and spoke with a midwestern narrative voice. This highly particularized, personal point of view combined with the detailed narrative is the aspect of the novel most criticized; Cather herself believed she had "taken the wrong road" with her "full blooded method."[18] Yet perhaps that fullness was what Cather needed to make her materials her own. Robert Langbaum writes of the romanticist's essential concreteness in poetry; we need only change the genre to the novel to realize how apt it is for Cather's *Song of the Lark:* "The emphasis on particularity (the autobiographical connection being one of the means of achieving it) is a guarantee that the [novel] is an authentic experience which gives birth to an idea rather than the illustration of a ready-made idea."[19]

In *The Song of the Lark* Cather confronted the paradoxical feelings she had about Nebraska, the happiness and curse of her life. Thea Kronborg escapes "from a smug, domestic, self-satisfied provincial world of utter ignorance,"[20] but when she leaves, she carries with her "the essentials" of all she will ever do. As she tells Dr. Archie, "When I set out from Moonstone with you, I had had a rich, romantic past. I had lived a long, eventful life, and an artist's life, every hour of it" (552). These are paradoxes Cather would use for her greatest plains novels, *My Ántonia* and *A Lost Lady*. With *My Ántonia* Cather returned to the manner of *O Pioneers!* but with a difference. While *O Pioneers!* soars with an artist's joy at transforming her materials into a pastoral vision, *My Ántonia* has the depth of lived experience.

6 *My Ántonia*: The Closing
of the Circle

She . . . had that something which fires the imagination, could . . . stop one's breath for a moment by a look or gesture that somehow revealed the meaning in common things.[1]

It was as if everything Cather had written until now had been in preparation for *My Ántonia*. In her early essays and short stories she had told of imaginatively fusing two worlds—that of ideas and that of experience, of the general and the particular. She allegorically described the need to do so in *Alexander's Bridge*, then focused sequentially on each world, in *O Pioneers!* so celebrating the idea that she seemed to leave physical realities behind, and in *The Song of the Lark* so involved with particulars that they sometimes seem all there is. In *My Ántonia* she put the two together. The result was the single work that would insure Cather's place in literature.

One sign of Cather's achievement is that *My Ántonia* defies analysis, a quality critics often note when beginning a discussion of it. In 1918 W. C. Brownell said he did not "mind being incoherent" in writing of Cather's new book if he could "convey his notion in the least by [his] flounderings," compared its air to that of Homer, who lifted his subject "somehow," then concluded, "I don't know any art more essentially elusive."[2] Half a century later James Woodress wrote of the same quality in different terms. *My Ántonia* has passion, and though "one knows when he is in the presence of it, . . . the identification of it is somewhat intuitive. . . . it is difficult to explain."[3] More specific readings differ dramatically—David Stouck interprets it as a pastoral and Paul A. Olson as an epic; James E. Miller, Jr., as a commentary on the American dream and Blanche H. Gelfant as a drama of distorted sexuality—until one wonders how a single work can mean so many things to so many people.[4] Yet the greatness of the book lies in precisely this capacity. With *My Ántonia* Cather introduced into American fiction what Wordsworth had introduced to English poetry a century earlier—the continuously changing work.

By creating a narrator, Jim Burden, to recall Ántonia, a girl he knew while growing up in Nebraska, Cather for the first time in a novel used the narrative structure ideally suited to the romantic. She made the reacting mind a structural feature of her book. She then provided what E. K. Brown called a "very curious preface," in which she instructed her reader about what was to follow.[5] In that preface Cather anticipated major questions raised by critics. Is *My Ántonia* about Jim or about Ántonia? The question assumes mutually exclusive alternatives Cather rejected. Jim originally titled his story simply "Ántonia," then frowned, added "my," and seemed satisfied. As his title indicates, *My Ántonia* is about neither Jim nor Ántonia per se, but how the two, mind and object, come together, so "this girl seemed to mean to us the country, the conditions, the whole adventure of our childhood."[6]

Is it a novel, and has it any form? The impetus for Jim's story was his desire to recollect his emotions, so that he might understand the pattern that emerges from them. To speak Ántonia's name "was to call up pictures of people and places, to set a quiet drama going in one's brain," and in writing, Jim was true to his experience of remembering (xii). He didn't make notes, didn't arrange or rearrange, but "simply wrote down what of herself and myself and other people Ántonia's name recalls to me" (xiv). Thus his story is not structured by situation, as novels usually are, but by one person's feelings, in the manner of a lyric. Its meaning is as personal as its form; Jim specifies that his story won't be his reader's. When he presents his manuscript to Cather (and implicitly to each reader), he asks, "Now what about yours?" then cautions, "Don't let it influence your own story" (xiii, xiv). This is a book, then, that hasn't a settled form, but instead that sets in motion an ever-changing, expanding process of symbolic experience, "a quiet drama" in the mind of each reader.

That is not to say *My Ántonia* is formless. From the apparently episodic looseness of Jim's recollections emerges the classic romantic pattern of a dialectic between subject and object, momentarily resolved as a symbol. It consists of two major movements, followed by fusion: first, awakening to experience (Part I) and moving outward by its physicality (Part II), then awakening to ideas (Part III) and returning by them (Part IV); finally, fusing the two as symbol (Part V). By turning back upon itself, the pattern forms circles of expanding meaning. As Jim returned to scenes of his childhood, so the story returns the reader to the beginning, to recognize as symbols particulars once seen discretely. This is precisely the process Jim articulates at the conclusion (a misnomer, for here there is no conclusion; meaning is open-ended and ongoing), when he walks again along the first road over which he and Ántonia came together and realizes that man's experience is "a little circle" (372).[7]

That circle begins in and returns to childhood, "the fair seed-time" of the soul.[8] Part I, "The Shimerdas," tells of a child's awakening to nature. When he came to Nebraska as a ten-year-old orphan, Jim Burden felt he had entered a prairie that at night seemed the void predating creation. Awakening the next morning, Jim found himself in the beginning of a new world. It was a pastoral, Edenic world, in which his grandmother's garden seemed nature's womb. There Jim was warmed by the earth, nourished by fruit within arm's reach, entertained by acrobatic feats of giant grasshoppers, and comforted by the wind humming a tune. His was the unconscious sensation of "something that lay under the sun and felt it, like the pumpkins, and . . . [he] did not want to be anything more." As if one with the mother who holds him within her body, he feels the happiness of being "dissolved into something complete and great" (18).

The scene anticipates point of view throughout this section, in which Cather describes geographical and imaginative expanses from carefully defined vantage points, usually nestled within the earth. Jim is characteristically stationary, securely protected within a bed of one kind or another—a womblike garden, a prairie nest, a hay bed in Peter's wagon, his own bed beside the open window, even his grandmother's kitchen, "tucked away so snugly underground" (101). And Ántonia too is associated with a bed within the earth, dug into the wall of her family's cave and "warm like the badger hole" (75).

Stationary themselves, Jim and Ántonia are witness to the miraculous activity of nature. From it flowers grow as big as trees and cottonwoods shimmer with colors of a fairy tale; from it too come animal forms, astonishing in their variety. When Jim watched the Shimerdas emerge from a hole in the bank, it was as if the earth was giving birth to life itself. First appeared a woman with "an alert and lively" face and "a sharp chin and shrewd little eyes," then a girl of fourteen with eyes "full of light, like the sun shining on brown pools in the wood" and wild-looking brown hair. Following them came a foxlike son of nineteen, with sly, suspicious little hazel eyes, which "fairly snapped at the food" Jim's grandmother brought, and following him a little sister, mild, fair, and obedient. From behind the barn appeared another Shimerda son, unexpectedly with webbed hands and the speech of a rooster. Finally, most surprising of all, the father emerges, neatly dressed in a vest and a silk scarf, carefully crossed and held by a red coral pin. When he bends over Mrs. Burden's hand, he could be greeting her in the most formal of drawing rooms rather than on a wild prairie in an unsettled land (22–24).

The effect of a miracle recalls *O Pioneers!* Yet unlike that first Nebraska novel, where characters often seem more mythic than human, in *My Ántonia* the miraculous resides within the ordinary. The prairie Jim entered is the one a nine-year-old Cather had entered, and it has the depth of lived experience—the smells, textures, sounds, sights of the land itself. Autobiographical particularity continues throughout the book. In Black Hawk (Red Cloud transformed into art) Cather's childhood friends appear: the Miner family, neighbors to the Cathers, as the Harlings; Mrs. Holland, the hotel keeper, as Mrs. Gardener; two musicians—Blind Boone and Blind Tom—as Blind d'Arnault. In Lincoln, Herbert Bates, Cather's teacher at the University of Nebraska, appears as Gaston Cleric, Jim's teacher at the same school. Most important, Annie Sadilek Pavelka, the Bohemian girl whom Cather knew while growing up and whose friendship she renewed in middle age, appears as Ántonia Shimerda Cuzak.[9]

In *My Ántonia* particulars anchor the story, keeping it from floating away from this world. On their way to meet their new Bohemian neighbors, the Burdens pass through a natural paradise, with sunflowers making a gold ribbon across the prairie and one of the horses munching blossoms as he walked, "the flowers nodding in time to his bites" (20). The scene could easily seem a fantasy, yet the Burdens carry with them "some loaves of Saturday's bread, a jar of butter, and several pumpkin pies," and the everyday reality of the supplies, listed and identified by historical reality (the bread was baked on Saturday), keeps the scene within the here and now (19). The Shimerda's dough has the fairy-tale mystery of a witch's brew, yet it is mixed "in an old tin peck-measure that Krajiek had used about the barn" (31), and a storybook storm, when snow "simply spilled out of heaven, like thousands of feather-beds being emptied," takes place on January twentieth, Jim Burden's eleventh birthday (92).

Thus the ideal and the real, the general and the particular, are fused by the synthetic power of the imagination, especially strong in childhood. The ten-year-old Jim Burden sees his grandparents' hired men as Arctic explorers, his grandfather as a biblical prophet or an Arabian sheik, and their lives in Nebraska as more adventurous than those of characters in *The Swiss Family Robinson* and *Robinson Crusoe*. When transformed by the imagination, nature, like the Burdens' Christmas tree, is "the talking tree of the fairy tale; legends and stories nestled like birds in its branches" (83).

From the beginning Ántonia embodies these connections; she is a coming together of man and nature, a mediator between them. Her wild-looking hair, her eyes like the sun shining on brown pools, her spontaneity, make her seem nature's child, able to direct Jim's awakening to beauty. Her first act with him is to take his hand and lead him into the prairie, not stopping "until the ground itself stopped—fell away before us so abruptly that the next step would have been out into the tree-tops"; then from a nest in the long prairie grass, she points to the sky (25–26). As she will later stand in an orchard and reach out to a fruit tree or look up at the apples, so she here draws Jim toward the horizon, where this world stops and another begins—the bourne of heaven. She brings the Old World into the New (when an insect's song reminds her of Old Hata, the beggar woman in her childhood Bohemian village comes close to the Nebraska prairie), and she changes hardship into joy (when she tells of it, a hole dug into the wall of a primitive cave becomes a warm burrow, and a frightening encounter with a rattlesnake becomes a heroic adventure).

Nature fosters "alike by beauty and fear"—Wordsworth's words might have been Cather's description of the childhood section of *My Ántonia*, in which she included as an undercurrent to joy reverberations of loss and death. [10] Two black shadows flit before or follow after the children, Mrs. Burden's garden conceals a snake, Mr. Shimerda's smile suggests profound sadness, and the fullness of autumn's beauty contains "a shiver of coming winter in the air"

(38). This darker reality is conveyed especially by the story of Peter and Pavel, so powerful it is often the single episode people remember years after first reading *My Ántonia*. The story is simple. Returning home over snow, a wedding party is overtaken by wolves, and to lighten their load Pavel throws the groom and bride from his sledge. Even in the barest ouline it is a powerful incident, for as the snake in Mrs. Shimerda's garden represents the oldest Evil, so the story does our most basic fears. Cather intensifies its effect in the telling.

As the context for Pavel's story Cather establishes the vastness of a wilderness, the darkness of night, and, especially, the emptiness of silence. No one talks during the ride to Peter and Pavel's house; there, Pavel is asleep, awakening only to tell his story, then returning to sleep; following the tale Ántonia and Jim scarcely breathe. As is life within a wilderness or light within darkness, sound which breaks silence is dramatic; it is a principle Cather uses throughout this episode. Pavel begins his story in a whisper which grows to a raging cry, cut short by convulsive coughing, then by sleep. Ántonia's translation to Jim similarly builds from the merriment of the wedding guests to the shrieks of people and screams of horses attacked by wolves, then stops short, for Pavel could remember nothing of throwing over the bride and groom. When this silence too is broken by another sound, the reader expects still other wolves to be pursuing the last members of the wedding party, then realizes these are monastery bells in Peter and Pavel's village calling people to early prayer. Like the knocking on the gate in *Macbeth,* the bells signal a more profound horror than any thus far realized—a reentry of the ordinary world from which Peter and Pavel will henceforth be outcasts.

Repetition evokes the sense of ongoing truth. Three times friends journey home together, and three times the tale is told. Peter, Mr. Shimerda, Ántonia, and Jim travel by wagon to Peter and Pavel's house, where they hear of other friends traveling by sledge to their village; afterwards, they return by wagon to the Shimerda farm. Similarly, Pavel first tells his story in Russian; Ántonia repeats it in English; then Jim and Ántonia tell it to one another. Russian merges with English; cries of coyotes are answered by a man, and both echo those of wolves; screams of horses and of people combine; the moans of the wind seem spirits to be admitted, answered by a dying man soon to be among them.

Different voices combine to tell a truth so profound all of nature speaks of it, the tragedy of life in a wilderness.

The idea appears in various forms throughout this first section: during that first hard winter the Shimerdas faced starvation, Pavel died of consumption, Peter lost his land, and Ántonia's father committed suicide. Indeed, the childhood scenes contain such hardships that one wonders how a mood of joy survives. Again, Pavel's story suggests an explanation. Jim recalled that "for Ántonia and me, the story of the wedding party was never at an end. We did not tell Pavel's secret to anyone, but guarded it jealously—as if the wolves of the Ukraine had gathered that night long ago, and the wedding party been sacrificed, to give us a painful and peculiar pleasure" (61). This is the egocentricity of childhood, and it proves a saving protection.

Like Wordsworth, Cather recognized that nature ministers to the child, not literally, of course, but psychologically. Rowing late at night in a stolen boat and suddenly seeing the mountain uprear its head, the boy Wordsworth felt as if it were rising in response to him; in his recollection of the episode he is truthful to the childhood perception rather than to his adult understanding of the facts. Similarly, Cather presents a child's view of the outside world as if it existed for him. The wind hummed to Jim, a small frail insect sang for Ántonia, and people, like characters from a fairy tale, appear to tell their tales, then disappear. Not surprisingly, to Jim Russia seems as remote as the North Pole, and the personal lives of Peter and Pavel, strange men with unpronounceable names, are obscured in the distant realm of adulthood.

Through it all there is a child's belief that things will always be this way, made poignant by adult awareness of change. This is, after all, the middle-aged Jim Burden's recollection of his childhood, a retrospective Cather recalls by phrases repeated so often they become motifs—"I still remember," "they are with me still," and "I can see them now." Tension between innocence and experience increases with changes in Ántonia. By the end of their first year in Nebraska, Ántonia has left the security of childhood to work the land; she aches with exhaustion and, realizing other hardships lie ahead, wishes winter would not return. Meanwhile Jim, only eleven, is still reassured by the notion that it "will be summer a long while yet" (140).

"When boys and girls are growing up, life can't stand

still. . . . they have to grow up, whether they will or no" (193). In recognition that Jim was getting older and needed to attend school in town, the Burdens moved from their homestead to Black Hawk, a small prairie town halfway between the country and the city, wilderness and civilization. Ántonia followed them, to work as a hired girl for the Burdens' neighbors, the Harlings. The move signals the transition from childhood to adolescence, from receptivity to irrepressible energy. In Black Hawk the beauty of the immigrant girls suddenly shines forth, stunning within the narrow confines of a small community, and the energy of boys and girls alike spills over.

Music announces the change in mood. In the childhood scenes music provided an elegiac background: an insect singing before winter, Mr. Shimerda removing his violin from its box but never playing it, Fuchs singing a hymn while making a coffin and the community singing another by Mr. Shimerda's grave. In Part II, "The Hired Girls," the people are eased from the harsh struggle of those first years, and they burst into song. Jim Burden is drawn to his neighbors' home by the notes which filter from it: there everyone plays the piano, Ántonia hums as she works, children sing, and Mrs. Harling conducts them all. As Jim recalled, "Every Saturday night was like a party" (175). With Mrs. Harling at the piano it seems inevitable that they begin to dance, Frances teaching the younger children.

From the Harlings the dancers begin a procession which wends its way through Black Hawk. They go next to Mrs. Gardner's hotel, where the tempo changes dramatically. When Mrs. Gardner is out of town one Saturday, her carefully ordered establishment erupts into revelry, inspired again by a piano player—no longer the motherly Mrs. Harling but Blind d'Arnault. Looking "like some glistening African god of pleasure, full of strong, savage blood," d'Arnault played barbarously, wonderfully, awakening in his listeners their own savage blood, which erupts in a wild, frenzied dancing that he will not allow them to stop (191). Like him, they are blind to the consequences.

When the setting again changes, so does the mood. Three Italians come to Black Hawk and look over the children, then set up a dancing pavillion that is "very much like a merry-go-round tent, with open sides and gay flags flying from the poles" (194). From it come siren sounds to which the youth are irresistably drawn: "First the deep purring of Mr. Vanni's harp came in silvery ripples through the blackness of the dusty-smelling night; then the violins fell in—one of them was almost like a flute. They called so archly, so seductively, that our feet hurried toward the tent of themselves" (196). Upon hearing the music, Ántonia would hurry with her work at the Harlings, dropping and breaking dishes in her excitement, and "if she hadn't time to dress, she merely flung off her apron and shot out of the kitchen door. . . . the moment the lighted tent came into view she would break into a run, like a boy" (205). Energy until now barely contained spills over in animal heat. The iceman, delivery boys, young farmers, all come tramping through the Harlings' yard, and "a crisis was inevitable" (206). Told to cease attending the dances or to leave the Harlings' employ, Ántonia moves into the household of the notoriously dissolute Wick Cutter.

Still, the dancers do not stop. When the Vannises dismantle their tent and move away, the same people who attended it go to the Fireman's Hall Saturday dances. And as Ántonia earlier had broken from the Harlings, so now Jim breaks out, crawling from his grandparents' window on Saturday nights, kissing Ántonia as he has no right to do, and dreaming Lena Lingard turns to him saying, "Now they are all gone, and I can kiss you as much as I like" (226).

Two concluding episodes present two aspects of this energy, one pointing back, the other forward. In the first Jim and the hired girls return to the prairie for a picnic, feeling the idyllic contentment of childhood one last time. They play a game, then sit talking; it is one of the few scenes in this section in which they are physically still. The scene ends with one of the most famous images in Cather's writing, that of the plow momentarily transformed into heroic size by the blood-red energy of the sun, then fading into littleness. This is the passion of imaginative perception. The second episode points ahead ominously, to the dark side of passion that degenerates into debauchery. At Wick Cutter's, Ántonia is in danger of rape; and sleeping in her place, Jim is attacked. He emerges bruised and bitter, as if he had fallen and been trampled upon by the bacchanalian parade in which he had been dancing.

Having followed physicality to its darkest extreme, Jim turns away from it altogether. He moves from Black Hawk to Lincoln, where, at the university, he awakens to a world of ideas. Part III, "Lena Lingard," is complementary to Part I, "The Shimerdas": the two sections present two awakenings to two worlds, one of nature, the other of ideas. In this second awakening Jim again feels happiness so complete that it momentarily erases his past, for "when one first enters that world [of ideas] everything else fades for a time, and all that went before is as if it had not been" (258). Indeed, Jim jealously protects his new life from his former one, shutting his window when the prairie wind blows through it and begrudging "the room that Jake and Otto and Russian Peter took up in my memory, which I wanted to crowd with other things" (262). Not only Ántonia but nature itself seems remote; this is a time of interiors, and appropriately, it is set within Jim's rooms, Lena Lingard's workrooms, the theater.

Yet memories are there. As when he opened his window the earthy smell of the prairie outside wafted through, so "whenever my consciousness was quickened, all those early friends were quickened with it, and in some strange way they accompanied me through all my new experiences" (262). When Lena Lingard quietly but inevitably reenters Jim's life, she seems the physical form of the early memories accompanying him. And drawing upon those memories, Jim grasps the idea that great art arises from particulars: "If there were no girls like them in the world, there would be no poetry" (270).

During this period, however, Jim is far detached from those particulars in his own life. His first year at the university is as idyllic as was his first year in Nebraska—and as suspended from reality. Because Jim is totally absorbed in the mental world opening to him, his early friends are real only as ideas he holds within himself, "so much alive" *in* him that he "scarcely stopped to wonder whether they were alive anywhere else" (262). As Ántonia and Jim had once played in nature, so now Lena and Jim play with ideas; as innocence once protected Ántonia and Jim from suffering pains, so it now protects Lena and Jim from seeing reality. When they attend *Camille,* they are as innocent as "a couple of jack-rabbits, run in off the prairie," of what awaits them (272). And they are open to experience as only children can be. The curtain rises upon a brilliant world they have never before imagined, and they enter it so completely that they leave the real world behind. Dumas's lines alone are enough to convey the idea of tragic love, an "idea . . . that no circumstances can frustrate" (278), not an old, lame, stiff actress playing Marguerite or a disproportionately young, perplexed fellow playing her Armand, not faults in staging or weaknesses of the orchestra.

For a while Jim and Lena, luxuriating in newly discovered roles, are as oblivious to circumstances in their own lives as they had been to those in *Camille.* But when the school year comes to an end, so does their pastoral interlude. Gaston Cleric is offered a position at Harvard, and he proposes that Jim follow him in the fall. The return is comically abrupt. Jim goes to Lena with the rather self-serving but noble resolution that he has been standing in her way, "that if she had not me to play with, she would probably marry and secure her future," only to learn that she has no intention of marrying him or anyone else (289).

Thus closes Jim's chapter with Lena, and one of Cather's most interesting characters recedes from view. By temporarily moving Ántonia to the background of the narrative and the recesses of Jim's memory, Cather releases Jim to revel in ideas. Appropriately, he does so with Lena, the idea of sexuality without its threatening reality. She is sensuously beautiful, and not surprisingly, men cluster about her: in Black Hawk Ole Bensen, Sylvester Lovett, and Jim Burden; in Lincoln the Polish violin-teacher Ordensky, old Colonel Raleigh, and (again) Jim Burden. What is striking is the contrast between these men paying court to Lena and those clustering about Ántonia in Black Hawk. The courtship of Lena is conducted languidly, devoid of animal vitality, by old men and boys to whom she appeals because she knows they are only playing at love. Nobody needed to have worried about Ole Bensen, she recognized, because he simply liked to sit and look at her; similarly, she allows the old men of Lincoln to court her, for "it makes them feel important to think they're in love with somebody" (290). Implicitly she has a similar bemused affection for the schoolboy Jim Burden.

Even while Jim is most detached from Ántonia, however, the memory of her remains, awaiting a return. Part IV, "The Pioneer Woman's Story," tells of beginning that return. Ántonia has continued to live her own life, following Larry Donovan to Denver, becoming pregnant, and returning alone and unmarried to give birth to a daughter. Bitterly disappointed in her, Jim has tried to shut her out of his mind until, seeing a crayon enlargement of her daughter displayed prominently in a Black Hawk photographer's window, he feels he must see her again. He goes first to the Widow Steavens, the Shimerdas' neighbor who assisted Ántonia in the preparations for her marriage and in the delivery of her baby; from her, Jim learns Ántonia's story. Only then does he go to the Shimerdas' homestead, where he sees Ántonia. Their brief meeting builds to Jim's declaration of faith: ["Do you know, Ántonia, since I've been away, I think of you more often than of anyone else in this part of the world. I'd have liked to have you for a sweetheart, or a wife, or my mother or my sister—anything that a woman can be to a man. The idea of you is a part of my mind; you influence my likes and dislikes, all my tastes, hundreds of times when I don't realize it. You really are a part of me" (321).]

The moment is important in Jim's imaginative return, as interesting for what it does not include as for what it does. Jim here affirms his idea of Ántonia as archetypal woman—that much is clear: he sees her face "under all the shadows of women's faces, at the very bottom of my memory" (322). But this is *his* idea only, and when he imagines linking that idea to the real world, he rather indiscriminately wishes she could be whatever a woman can be to a man—sweetheart, wife, mother, sister—apparently it doesn't matter. There is strikingly little of Ántonia in this meeting; the scene is almost wholly centered upon Jim, with only perfunctory references to Ántonia's life or child. Because he has not yet grasped her particularity, he is as yet unable to conceive of Ántonia as apart from him; and without the yoking of the idea with the particular that enables the romantic to unite subject and object in symbolic perception, Jim's return is incomplete.

Part V, "Cuzak's Boys," is the closing of the circle. Allegiance to his idea has kept Jim away from Ántonia for twenty years, for he has heard that she had married an unsuccessful man and lived a hard life. Perhaps it was cowardice, he recalled, but "I did not want to find her aged and broken; I really dreaded it. In the course of twenty crowded years one parts with many illusions. I did not wish to lose the early ones. Some memories are realities, and are better than anything that can ever happen to one again" (328). Again, Lena Lingard acts as an intermediary. As she had appeared in Jim's student rooms and brought with her memories of his past, so years later she gives Jim a cheerful account of Ántonia and urges him to see her.

When the middle-aged Jim returns to the scenes of his childhood, it is to fuse the idea and the particular by seeing what Coleridge called "the universality in the individual, or the individuality itself."[11] First Jim sees Ántonia in all her physical reality, an aging woman with grizzled hair, missing teeth, and hands hardened from work; then he realizes the timeless truth that resides within that reality. For the first time it is her identity rather than his idea of her that he affirms.

As if "experience . . . repeated in a finer tone," scenes from childhood recur, metamorphosed.[12] Jim enters by wagon (then as a boy, now as an adult) and looks about a kitchen (then Jim's grandmother's sunny one, now Ántonia's); Jim at first sees Ántonia and especially her eyes (then of a girl, now a woman), and they talk alone on the prairie (then a wild spot, now planted with an orchard); Jim witnesses an unexpected explosion of life from the earth (then the Shimerda's cave, now Ántonia's fruit cellar), and he lies down in nature, feeling great contentment (then in the garden, now a hayloft). Even the most apparently ordinary detail resonates with childhood memories: Ántonia's white cats sunning among yellow pumpkins echo Jim's first morning in his grandmother's garden, sunning himself among other pumpkins.

With each scene there is the familiarity of recognition coupled with an explosion of meaning, as the particular is fused with an idea and experienced as a symbol. This is the return of the romantic sensibility, now refined and able to understand the emotional pattern that emerges from the experience:

Ántonia had always been one to leave images in the mind that did not fade—that grew stronger with time. In my memory there was a succession of such pictures, fixed there like the old wood cuts of one's first primer: Ántonia kicking her bare legs against the sides of my pony when we came home in triumph with our snake; Ántonia in her black shawl and fur cap, as she stood by her father's grave in the snowstorm; Ántonia coming in with her work-team along the evening skyline. She lent herself to immemorial human attitudes which we recognize by instinct as universal and true. I had not been mistaken. She was a battered woman now, not a lovely girl; but she still had that something which fires the imagination, could still stop one's breath for a moment by a look or gesture that somehow revealed the meaning in common things. She had only to stand in the orchard, to put her hand on a little crab tree and look up at the apples, to make you feel the goodness of planting and tending and harvesting at last. All the strong things of her heart came out in her body, that had been so tireless in serving generous emotions.

It was no wonder that her sons stood tall and straight. She was a rich mine of life, like the founders of early races. (352–53)

Here is the peace of resolution. When Jim leaves the Cuzak farm, he feels a sense of loss, yet reassures himself with the possibility of return. Ántonia—and her children after her—will endure, and the memories of her are "spots of time" by which he can renew himself.

The overall pattern of *My Ántonia,* with its separation, resolution, and return to separation, is familiar to readers of romantic literature: one need think only of Wordsworth's "Tintern Abbey," Coleridge's conversation poems, and Keats's odes. Like her predecessors in romanticism, Cather uses that pattern to write of the individual imagination perceiving the world symbolically. Unlike them, however, she uses gender assumptions to heighten tension between her subject and object. As her early essays make clear, Cather was acutely aware that our culture assigns to men the position of subject and to women that of object, and she incorporates those assumptions into her novel. Jim Burden expresses conventionally male attitudes: he assumes the subject position, moves outward, engages in change and progress, and writes possessively about *his* Ántonia as the archetypal woman who provides an anchorage for his travels and a muse for his imagination. Through Jim, Cather presents myths of male transcendence, of man as a liberating hero, romantic lover, and creative genius; of women to be rescued, loved, and transformed into art. In Ántonia, however, Cather contradicts these assumptions by creating a woman who works out her individual destiny in defiance of her narrator's expectations. [13]

My Ántonia is Jim's account of all that Ántonia means to him, or more precisely, of his youthful attempt to *make* her "anything that a woman can be to a man" (321). By his account Ántonia seeks primarily to nurture by giving—to give her ring to the ten-year-old Jim and to admire his exploits, to give her love to Larry Donovan, and to give to her children a better chance than she had. As important, she makes no demands upon the world or upon others in it. Even after becoming pregnant, Ántonia does not press Larry Donovan to marry her, for "I thought if he saw how well I could do for him, he'd want to stay with me" (313). Her husband, Cuzak, affirms "she is a good wife for a poor man" because "she don't ask me no questions" (365–66). Ántonia offers unconditional love; both her strength and her weakness are that she could never believe harm of anyone she loved (344; see also 268, 343). Through her love, Ántonia, like the orchard she tends, offers "the deepest peace" of escape from worldly demands (341). To Jim, Ántonia is a wellspring for male activity in the larger world. On a physical level she bears sons. Jim titles his final chapter "Cuzak's Boys," and he concludes, "It was no wonder that her sons stood tall and straight." On a spiritual level she is a muse to Jim, for she "had that something which fires the imagination" (353).

At the same time that Cather uses Jim to present "the collective myths" about women,[14] she builds tension against his account. There emerges a certain ruthlessness about Jim's affection for Ántonia that belies his stated affection for her. His love, unlike hers, is conditional. He is proud of Ántonia when he believes her to be "like Snow-white, in the fairy tale" (215); he turns from her when she asserts her individuality. He resents her protecting manner toward him, is angered over her masculine ways when she works the farm, is bitter when she "throws herself away on . . . a cheap sort of fellow" and, once pregnant, falls from social favor. Jim's allegiance is consistently to his ideas; when they conflict with reality, he denies the reality.

The world and the people in it just as consistently belie the myths Jim attempts to impose upon them. Otto Fuchs is not a Jesse James desperado but a warmhearted ranchhand; Lena Lingard is not a wild seductress but a strong-minded girl who becomes an independent businesswoman; Jim himself is not the adventurer, the lover, or the poet he pretends to be. By contrasting the boast and the deed, Cather suggests comic, self-serving, and ineffectual dimensions of male gallantry. Picturing himself as a dragon slayer, Jim kills an old, lazy rattlesnake. Drafted by his grandmother into service as Ántonia's rescuer, Jim sleeps at the Cutters, saving Ántonia from rape but feeling something close to hatred of her for embarrassing him. Resolving to "go home and look after Ántonia" (268), Jim returns to her only twenty years later, after being assured that he will not have to part with his illusions. Finally, Ántonia and Lena, the objects of Jim's benevolence, react to his promise with smiles (322–23) and "frank amusement" (268). They get on with their lives basically independently from men, whether by design, as when Lena resolves that she will never marry, or by necessity, as when Ántonia proceeds to rear her daughter alone.

Tension against Jim's account increases as his narrative role changes. In the initial sections Cather presented Ántonia through Jim's point of view. Jim measured Ántonia against his idea of women, approving of her when she assumed a role he expected of her. But in Book IV, "The Pioneer Woman's Story," Cather moved Jim aside, to the position of tale recorder, and made the midwife who attended Ántonia the tale teller. The Widow Steavens provides a woman's account of a woman's experience, and with it a significant change in tone toward Ántonia. She relates her story with understanding and sympathy rather than with Jim's shocked and bitter insistence that Ántonia play her part in his myth.

By Part V, Jim and Ántonia have reversed roles. Jim began the novel as the story teller in several senses, telling the account he titles *my* Ántonia, and also telling it in terms of stories he has read or heard—*The Life of Jesse James, Robinson Crusoe, Camille,* the *Georgics.* But the child Jim grew into a man who followed the most conventional pattern for success: he left the farm to move to town, then attended the university, studied law at Harvard, married well, and joined a large corporation. In the process, his personal identity seems to have faded. Ántonia, who began the novel as a character rendered by Jim, in the fifth section breaks through myths Jim had imposed upon her and emerges powerfully as herself. With her children around her, she is the center of "the family legend" (350), to whom her children look "for stories and entertainment" (351). Ántonia's stories, unlike Jim's, are not from literature. They are instead domestic ones drawn from life, "about the calf that broke its leg, or how Yulka saved her little turkeys from drowning . . . or about old Christmases and weddings in Bohemia" (176).

As Jim leaves the Cuzak farm in the last paragraphs, Ántonia recedes into the background. One of a group standing by the windmill, she is waving her apron, as countless women have said goodbye to countless men. Returning to the larger male world, Jim spends a disappointing day in Black Hawk, talking idly with an old lawyer there. Finally, he walks outside of town to the unploughed prairie that remains from early times. There Jim's mind "was full of pleasant things," for he intended "to play" with Cuzak's boys and, after the boys are grown, "to tramp along a few miles of lighted streets with Cuzak" (370). But these plans seem curiously empty, irrelevant to the center of life represented by the female world of Ántonia. The early male myths of adventure have led to pointless wandering and lonely exile, and the women, originally assigned roles of passivity, have become the vital sources of meaning.

Part III. The World Split in Two

At Bread Loaf School in Middlebury, Vermont, 1922

7 *One of Ours:* An American Arthurian Legend

> They lingered awhile, however, listening to the soft, amiable bubbling of the spring; a wise, unobtrusive voice, murmuring night and day, continually telling the truth to people who could not understand it. [1]

Willa Cather's early Nebraska novels — *O Pioneers!*, *The Song of the Lark*, and *My Ántonia* — are celebrations of certain qualities of feeling and imagination" that were, along with "sturdy traits of character," the legacy of European pioneers and their descendents to the New World. [2] Theirs was a "gift of sight" that affirmed continuities, for with it one could recognize connections among apparently disparate things and infuse the present with meaning from an apparently distant past.

In *One of Ours,* Cather further explored the relation of American consciousness to its Old World heritage, this time in terms of discontinuities threatened by World War I. As she saw other matters, so Cather saw the war in terms of the imagination: "She was the last person to have set out deliberately to write a 'war novel.' " Edith Lewis wrote, "She felt strongly about the war from its beginning, for it threatened everything in the world of the mind's endeavour that was most precious to her; she saw it beforehand, I think, as many people saw it afterward. But she talked very little about it, and it would not, I am sure, have occurred to her to write about it except for an accident." [3]

The accident was the death of G. P. Cather, Willa Cather's young cousin, who died at Cantigny, leading his men in the first American offensive. Cather had never intended to write a war story, but then found she was unable to go on to anything else before telling the story of the young Nebraska boy who believed he had met his destiny in France. To prepare for doing so, she read her cousin's letters to his mother, Cather's Aunt Franc; she saw and talked with soldiers brought to her by one of her former students, who was stationed on a New York army post; she visited wounded soldiers in a New York hospital and read the diary of a doctor who had served on a troop ship during a severe outbreak of influenza;

later she traveled to France, where she lived for six or seven weeks in Paris, then went with Isabelle and Jan Hambourg on a tour of the battlefields and devastated parts of France, then through southern France.[4] Mostly, though, she recalled her cousin. Edith Lewis specifies: "In *One of Ours* [Willa Cather] did not choose the war as a theme, and then set out to interpret it through the experience of an individual. The whole story was born from a personal experience (as I think was the case with all her novels); from the way in which the news of her cousin's death at Cantigny brought suddenly before her an intense realization of his nature and his life, and their significance."[5]

Cather pointed her readers to that significance when, shortly after completing *One of Ours,* she spoke of the novel, saying "I have cut out all descriptive work in this book—the thing I do best. I have cut out all picture making because that boy does not see pictures."[6] For Cather "picture making" involved an imaginative movement toward a revelatory experience in which one recognizes similarities among apparently disparate parts and participates in the relationship between the finite and the infinite: Alexandra Bergson's vision on the Divide, Thea Kronborg's in Panther Canyon, Jim Burden's of Ántonia. Cather organized previous novels about such experiences. In *My Ántonia,* for example, Jim recalls Ántonia by a succession of pictures: Ántonia driving cattle home; Ántonia telling stories to her children; Ántonia standing in the orchard; Ántonia emerging from the fruit cellar, followed by her children. With each Jim responds to "a look or gesture" that "somehow revealed the meaning in common things." When Jim sees Ántonia emerge from the fruit cellar, he connects the specific experience to "immemorial human attitudes which we recognize by instinct as universal and true," and feels the happiness of being "dissolved into something complete and great."[7] Creating such experiences is a measure of a writer's achievement:

The "scene" in fiction is not a mere matter of construction, any more than it is in life. When we have a vivid experience in social intercourse, pleasant or unpleasant, it records itself in our memory in the form of a scene; and when it flashes back to us, all sorts of apparently unimportant details are flashed back with it. When a writer has a strong or revelatory experience with his characters, he unconsciously creates a scene; gets a depth of picture, and writes, as it were, in three dimensions instead of two.[8]

When Cather said that she "cut out all picture making because that boy does not see pictures," then, she made a profound statement about her character, her book, and her concerns for American consciousness. For *One of Ours* is, as the title indicates, a novel about youth that springs from *American* sensibilities. Unlike Alexandra Bergson, Thea Kronborg, and Ántonia Shimerda, Claude was not exceptional, "except in the way that every individual is exceptional"; he was like many American boys she had known.[9] With him, Cather shifted her vantage point toward the relationship of America to its European heritage. In her earlier novels Cather showed the Old World infusing the New through characters who brought that tradition with them (Alexandra Bergson and Ántonia Shimerda immigrate) or had close relationships with Old World representatives (Thea Kronborg learns from the Kohlers and Herr Wunsch). In *One of Ours* Cather reverses this movement by creating a character who is reared in America, then goes to Europe, taking with him his New World consciousness. As if extending Frederick Jackson Turner's frontier thesis, Cather explores the results of discarding the past and forming a national character in the crucible of a frontier. What would that American consciousness be?

For her answer, Cather wrote an American version of Arthurian legend that sets a would-be knight in search of a hero he could admire, an order he could join, and a chivalric ideal he could follow. Claude Wheeler is a farm boy who, in search of "something splendid," wends his way through a modern wasteland and battles the foe of materialism. Again, Cather described her book by the duality basic to her romanticism. In 1921 she spoke of placing two objects — an orange and a vase — on a table, and said she was interested in the reaction between the two. On the one hand there was Claude, a sensitive youth burning with desire to find meaning; on the other, there was his world — intractable, immediate, alien. The tension was familiar in Cather's writing, but her emphasis here was different. It was as if she turned around the old question, How can subject and object meet? to ask, What would a life be if subject and object were forever separate?[10]

She answers by telling the story of a romantic caught in a nightmarish world of realism.[11] Claude Wheeler perceives a material world that asserts its own alien reality, as if refusing to be absorbed into human experience. Dark sediments ring his wash bowl, undissolved by the water; Mr. Wheeler's rumpled shirt bulges, escaping the restraint of his belt; and the food within Claude's mouth "grew stiff and heavy." Ordinary objects seem to have a life of their own, disrupting rituals and overturning expectations. The Ford car is surprisingly little, the "two-pint sugar bowl" grotesquely large, and Mr. Wheeler's silky alpaca coat inexplicably fine; all are part of an intractable material world that thwarts Claude's romantic aspirations, as mud encrusts the car wheels designed for movement and the windshield designed for sight.

The irony is that another material world—that of nature—offers him great possibility. When Claude leaves his house to go to the barn, "the sun popped up over the edges of the prairie like a broad, smiling face; the light poured across the close-cropped August pastures and the hilly, timbered windings of Lovely Creek—a clear little stream with a sand bottom, that curled and twisted playfully about through the south section of the big Wheeler ranch" (2). Here, as elsewhere, Cather shows nature as an alternative to Claude's limited sight. Nature suggests the personal self Claude is unable to express: playful in the early scenes when a young Claude is on his way to the circus and, later, sensuous when he is courting Enid; idyllic when an older Claude is in the French countryside, and horrific when he is in the trenches. "A wise, unobtrusive voice, murmuring night and day, continually telling the truth to people who could not understand it" (153), nature expresses universal truths Claude seeks but cannot find. Like Jo in *Bleak House,* the novel his mother reads to him, Claude is imprisoned in his ignorance, "in utter darkness as to the meaning, of those mysterious symbols, so abundant" about him.[12]

Claude is, above all, ignorant of himself. He is unsure and distrustful of his own feelings, the means by which he might convert objects into human experience; as a result, he subjects himself to the materialism he is so desperately attempting to escape. In school Claude does move beyond the narrowly denominational Temple College and enroll in the university, where in a history class he glimpses the freedom offered by ideas. But when he writes his paper on Joan of Arc, he flatters himself "he had kept all personal feeling out of the paper; that it was a cold estimate of the girl's motives and character" (61). Betraying the living figure of his mind and affirming dry, lifeless fact, Claude reveals the inability to extend himself imaginatively that limits him in all he does. For Claude farming too is a purely physical endeavor. Like Alexandra's brothers, he treats the land as an adversary to be overpowered: "day after day he flung himself upon the land and planted it with what was fermenting in him" (78), wearing himself out in such a fury of discontent that he "went to bed defeated every night, and dreaded to wake in the morning" (102).

Claude's failure of imagination is most evident in the central action of the American sections, his courtship and marriage. In her title for Book II, "Enid," as well as in plot, theme, and characterization, Cather echoes the Enid and Geraint idylls of Tennyson's *Idylls of the King;* indeed, Tennyson originally used the single title "Enid" for the material he subsequently divided under the headings "The Marriage of Geraint" and "Geraint and Enid."[13] Like Claude, Geraint has the manly physique, muscular arms, agility, and strength of a hero, but he is limited by his pride and his subsequent capacity for being deluded. Enid the Fair, Enid the Good, is courted and married by Geraint after he finds her in her father's ruined castle, a dark, mysterious, fern-and-ivy-covered setting similar to the Royce Mill House, within which her delicate beauty shines. The archetype of comely womanhood, Enid represents salvation. Geraint loves Enid "as he loved the light of Heaven" (1, 5); similarly, Claude believes Enid Royce will "put him right with the world" (145) and that marriage will "restore his soul." In both stories Enid's redeeming power is demonstrated when she nurses her injured lover to health. Other than the fact Tennyson wrote in poetry, Cather in prose, the description of one could replace the other:

> And Enid tended on him there; and there
> Her constant motion round him, and the breath
> Of her sweet tendance hovering over him,
> Filled all the genial courses of his blood
> With deeper and with ever deeper love.
> (923–27)

Complications in both stories result from the lover's confusion of appearance and reality. Both men, unable to conceive of the world objectively, interpret life through their hopes and desires. Despite overwhelming evidence of her love, Geraint believes Enid is unfaithful when he overhears her words, "O me, I fear that I am no true wife." Trusting to appearance and ignoring his own experience of his wife's goodness, Geraint illustrates the theme of the idylls, the pain of persons who grope their way through "the feeble twilight" of a modern world.

> O purblind race of miserable men,
> How many among us at this very hour
> Do forge a life-long trouble for ourselves,
> By taking true for false, or false for true;
> Here, through the feeble twilight of this world
> Groping, how many, until we pass and reach
> That other, where we see as we are seen!
>
> (1–7)

Like Geraint, Claude is the dupe of appearance, but his is a more basic error. Geraint believes circumstances surrounding Enid, thinking her unfaithful to him. Claude believes the *appearance* of Enid, believing that she will be faithful to him. He assumes that because Enid appears graceful, she will be generous, and he persists in his illusion despite warnings to the contrary. Enid tells him she is unsuited for marriage, as does her father, though indirectly. More importantly, Claude's own feelings warn him. Throughout their engagement he "was not altogether happy" about her, recognizing, for example, that "she seemed more interested in the house than in him." Yet he continued to deny his experience and to believe "in the transforming power of marriage" (176). Not surprisingly, Claude is happiest when Enid is remote, sitting gracefully on the porch of the house they are building, or "still and unconscious like a statue" (145) in his dreams. Less surprisingly, despite her graceful appearance Enid remains as inflexible as the "black cubical object" in which she travels about the countryside, advocating Prohibition. At the end of the courtship-marriage action, Enid leaves for China and Claude closes his house, once again painfully aware of his loneliness in an alien world.

Supporting characters fall into groups according to their attitudes toward the material world. Those in the larger of these groups dramatize the evasions and substitutions Cather attacked in the American scene. At one extreme, Bayliss indiscriminately de-votes himself to making money as currency that is detached from, even hostile to, human comfort. He is a thin, dyspeptic, vegetar-ian who warns against food, "a virulent Prohibitionist" who cam-paigns against drink (8). A wealthy homeowner, he plans to tear down the historic mansion he has purchased. Ralph is similarly indiscriminate in buying mechanical toys that cause more work for his mother and Mahailey or, unused, clutter the basement. And Mr. Wheeler has land he doesn't need, his surplus a form of deca-dence.

Women in this group represent another extreme — a denial of physical reality and an indiscriminate adherence to abstraction. Mrs. Wheeler, lost in religious meditation or in recollections of old books, has so left the physical world that "her flesh had almost ceased to be concerned with pain or pleasure, like the wasted wax images in old churches" (69). And Enid Royce, the Prohibitionist driving her coffinlike black car about the countryside, coldly de-nies physical existence with a distorted spirituality remarkably similar to Bayliss's distorted business acumen.

A second group of characters offers an alternative. Mahailey, the Wheelers' servant, lives instinctively, her simplicity protect-ing her from the corrupting society about her. Unlike Ralph, who strives "to keep up with the bristling march of invention" by indis-criminately buying whatever is new, Mahailey values things that have their own personal history. The kitchen table, her rolling pin, her butcher knife, were "objects [that], after they had been mended, acquired a new value in her eyes, and she liked to work with them" (22). Unlike Enid, Gladys Farmer has "a passionate heart" (156) and "a warm imagination" that enabled her "to see a great deal within a few miles of Frankfort" (152); and unlike the apparently wealthy but emotionally impoverished Wheelers, the Erlichs enjoy what they have to the fullest.

Whether or not they are from Europe, these are characters with Old World imaginations. Each has learned to see beauty in the ordinary. Cather uses Ernest Havel, Claude's foil in the Nebraska scenes as David Gerhardt is in the France scenes, to articulate the difference between European and American sensibilities: "You Americans are always looking for something outside yourselves to warm you up, and it is no way to do. In the old countries, where not very much can happen to us, we know that, —and we learn to make the most of little things" (53).

Ernest illustrates that difference. Cultivating his bright, glistening young cornfield, Ernest whistles

an old German song which was somehow connected with a picture that rose in his memory. It was a picture of the earliest ploughing he could remember.

He saw a half-circle of green hills, with snow still lingering in the clefts of the higher ridges; behind the hills rose a wall of sharp mountains, covered with dark pine forests. In the meadows at the foot of that sweep of hills there was a winding creek, with polled willows in their first yellow-green, and brown fields. He himself was a little boy, playing by the creek and watching his father and mother plough with two great oxen, that had rope traces fastened to their heads and their long horns. His mother walked barefoot beside the oxen and led them; his father walked behind, guiding the plough. His father always looked down. His mother's face was almost as brown and furrowed as the fields, and her eyes were pale blue, like the skies of early spring. The two would go up and down thus all morning without speaking, except to the oxen. Ernest was the last of a long family, and as he played by the creek he used to wonder why his parents looked so old. (137)

This is Cather doing what she did best, writing scenes in which ordinary things become universal symbols. Ernest's mother and father stand for all the cultivators of the land from time immemorial, and from his picture of them, we understand feelings Ernest could never put into words, about his sense of himself in continuing time. Were this Ernest Havel's story instead of Claude Wheeler's, Cather could subsequently evoke his Old World values by an unobtrusive particular: a later Ernest, for example, plowing with downcast eyes would connect with the former picture that rose in his memory.

But *One of Ours* is Claude Wheeler's story, and Claude does not see pictures. He is capable of intense emotion but incapable of the erasure of personality essential to learn the truth of a thing. The few scenes in which he lets himself go are exceptional: his accepting from Julius Erlich a dinner invitation that was so unexpected he didn't have time to become nervous; his similarly unexpected sickroom visit from Enid, who put him at his ease with her calm, impersonal manner; his drive about Denver with a girl who talked so pleasantly he forgot to be embarrassed. The pattern, however, is of Claude's intense self-absorption, and when one thinks of him, one thinks of a character who wishes for something great, then blushes, stammers, and retreats. In the terms of Robert Langbaum, Claude is capable of affirmation and denial, but incapable of reaffirmation.[14] He affirms an ideal (of friendship, for example, or marriage), then expects the abstract ideal to perform a miracle, and he turns away bitterly when circumstances disprove his illusions. He feels personally betrayed when Gladys, his "aesthetic proxy," accepts favors from Bayliss; he is humiliated when Enid remains herself—a distant, cool, self-satisfied woman, capable of abstract discipline but incapable of a personal relationship.

As a result, the pattern in *One of Ours* is of discontinuity, by which innumerable instances of throwing away present the waste of human resources. Objects that might become "three dimensional" (Cather's term for the revelatory experience that creates a scene with "a depth of picture") appear, then disappear.[15] Mahailey's quilts, for example, appear in several scenes, gradually acquiring their own history, infused with human feeling. They are three quilts of different designs—the log cabin, the laurel leaf, the blazing star—lined with wool from Virginia sheep, made by Mahailey's old mother, then given to Mahailey for a marriage portion. Mahailey brought the quilts with her to Nebraska, cared for them, and saved her favorite, the blazing star, to give Claude when he married. On the night before Claude's wedding, Mahailey goes to the attic to get the quilt, "took it out of the chest, unfolded it, and counted the stars in the pattern—counting was an accomplishment she was proud of" (186). Mahailey's quilt has become a symbol of domestic pride and fidelity and devotion and love. In *O Pioneers!* and *My Ántonia* such a quilt might reappear unobtrusively, perhaps as a detail in a scene between husband and wife or as an object whose story would be told: a parent might tell his children its history as Alexandra told Emil about the desk she used for writing, brought by her father from the old country. But in *One of Ours* after Mahailey prepares the quilt "to go down to the mill house with the other presents" (186), it disappears, becoming forceful by its absence, as if the mill house grinds objects into insignificance as it once ground grain, and Claude's marriage with

Enid is a vacuum in which meaning is lost. The book abounds with such objects cluttering the landscape as reminders of waste: the discarded machines looming in the basement; the cherry tree that is cut, its trunk bleeding; the house Claude built for Enid, then closed up and left; Enid herself, who, leaving for China, vanishes from Claude's thoughts.

Eventually, Claude discards his own past. He enlists, abrogating his responsibility for his own identity by becoming one of the "boys" heading "over there." In a scene reminiscent of Stephen Crane, Cather describes the troops departing, caught within forces they can neither control nor understand. While the men waited on dock, "there was little to be seen" (270): even the water upon which they would sail was not visible, and the city they would leave "looked unsubstantial and illusionary" (272). As Crane described men like "lice which were caused to cling to a whirling, fire-smote, ice-locked, disease-stricken, space-lost bulb,"[16] so Cather describes troops clinging to a ship lost in space, coating it like bees in a swarm, making vows to a Statue of Liberty they at first cannot see at all, then make out only as "a bronze image in the sea" (274).

This quest is, as Cather writes, "quixotic," for like Cervantes' character, Claude pushes ahead with a willed blindness. Incongruities are, if anything, more jarring than ever. Claude is going to fight an enemy he had always believed "pre-eminent in the virtues Americans most admire" (166), a contradiction he dismisses by assuming "the world simply made a mistake about the Germans all along" (170). On the *Anchises,* during a voyage that serves as a transition between the novel's two major parts, Claude avoids troubling incongruities by leading a double life. He mechanically carries out his duties, all the while reveling in a released inner life, which he protects by ignoring any reality that would disprove it. His belief that the troops had "come to be worth the watchfulness and devotion of so many men and machines, this extravagant consumption of fuel and energy" (283–84), is unchanged by the decrepit state of the ship. Rusty pipes and unpainted joinings directly over his bed reveal the truth this was "the 'Old Anchises'; even the carpenters who made her over for the service had not thought her worth the trouble and had done their worst by her" (300). His feeling that "they were Fate, they were tomorrow" (269) is unchanged by the reality that they are caught on a death ship, infected with influenza of a peculiarly bloody, malignant type. And Claude's sense of purposeful well-being is unaffected when the ocean itself mocks them: the ship sails against "a sinister sunset" under clouds that "came up out of the sea, —wild, witchlike shapes that travelled fast and met in the west as if summoned for an evil conclave" (293). The murmur of nature has become a scream, still speaking truths that Claude cannot understand.

As in Nebraska, when he was happiest apart from Enid, Claude continues to embrace isolation from threatening reality. He welcomes the fog that surrounds the ship as "a shelter . . . hiding one from all that had been before. . . . The past was physically shut off; that was his illusion" (304). Entering France, Claude remains oblivious to increasingly ominous warnings that it is madness to discard history. In Paris Claude sees a one-armed psychopathic patient who "has forgotten almost everything about his life before he came to France" (337), yet he cannot recognize the similarity between the patient's amnesia (especially about women) and his own belief he had left his past (and especially Enid) behind him. Moving deeper into France, Claude exclaims over the poppies spilling about them, ignorant that in literature poppies threaten forgetfulness and unable to know that these are the flowers that will one day be worn on Armistice Day, "lest we forget" the devastating fields of Flanders. Claude observes but does not apply to himself Captain Owens' folly in believing "everything was in the foreground" (370), and he hears but does not understand David Gerhardt's moving recognition that his life as a concert violinist is as irretrievably lost as his smashed Stradivarius. Indeed, Claude welcomes this landscape of devastation. The pitiful groups of humanity, the psychopathic victims, the earth itself, "long lines of gaunt, dead trees, charred and torn; big holes gashed out in fields and hillsides . . . winding depressions in the earth" are to Claude "reassuring signs" (358).

Yet even as Claude seeks to escape his American past, he is limited to a sensibility shaped by it. He proceeds by the most simplistic and dangerous of New World myths. The American belief in new beginnings seems touchingly naive when Claude assumes he may physically cut off the past (304); the American myth of moving west seems comic when Claude vaguely hopes that, though there is no longer an American West, "perhaps he could find something below the Isthmus" (118); and a frontier society's lust for adventure seems tragic when American youth mindlessly flock together under the cry, "Bidding the Eagles of the West Fly On."[17] In France, then, Claude is fighting a war he understands only by blatantly distorted propaganda; he believes he is fulfilled in a country he knows under tragically artificial circumstances, among a people with whom he can communicate in only the simplest schoolboy phrases.

Here as in the Nebraska sections, Cather sets her story against a background of the grail quest. Resemblances to *Parsifal*, Wagner's opera of salvation through compassion, renunciation, and suffering, recall an ideal of heroic achievement. Cather had originally titled her final section, "The blameless Fool, by Pity Enlightened," and at first glance Claude Wheeler does resemble Parsifal, the "guileless one" who is "by pity 'lightened." [18] Like Parsifal, Claude embarks upon a quest for vision, proves his purity by resisting temptation, especially from women, and loses himself in divine mission. But Cather's hero is not Wagner's "guileless one" but a "fool," easily duped, at times almost a buffoon. Nowhere is the difference more striking than in the salvation each reaches. Proven worthy, Parsifal heals the wounded, sees and bows before the Grail as a holy light annoints him, then, as others bow before him, raises the Holy Grail in a renewal of consecration. This is very like the destiny Claude *feels* as he leads his men in battle; but Claude's salvation is only in his mind. The holy light he sees is enemy fire, the god he prays to remains silent, and the friend he dies for had been blown to pieces long before, while running blindly across a smoke-filled battlefield.

Actually, Cather's Holy Grail story resembles not Wagner's so much as Tennyson's, whose *Idylls of the King* tells of heroism debased in a modern wasteland. In "The Holy Grail" Tennyson wrote of would-be knights who, like Claude, "wish to leap instantly to grace."[19] Unlike Galahad, who sees the vision, the other knights perversely swear allegiance because they do *not* do so, then set out blindly, defying Arthur's warning that they "follow wandering fires / Lost in a quagmire. Many of you, yea most, / Return no more." When truth is so uncertain, the quest itself may seem valuable, for it provides at least the illusion of purpose. On it Percivale joyously believed the heaven appeared bluer and

the earth greener than ever, yet these were only his desires projected upon a world that turned to dust as he approached it. A
woman spinning by a house rose as if to greet him, but when Percivale touched her, she "fell into dust and nothing," her house became a broken shed in which he found a dead baby, "and also this /
Fell into dust, and I was left alone." A warrior in golden armor,
bedecked in jewels, opened his arms as if to embrace Percivale, but
then "he too, fell into dust, and I was left alone." A city that
seemed glorious, "the spires / Prick'd with incredible pinnacles
into heaven," became foreign when Percivale entered it and found
no one who spoke to him.

Cather too places a befuddled hero in a landscape of projected
desires that turn to dust as he approaches. Claude pities a woman
with children, only to learn the baby he carries for her is German.
He idealizes Victor Morse, a flyer as bedecked with medals as Percivale's warrior was with jewels, then learns his hero is from Iowa.
And as Percivale approached a heavenly city, so Claude and the
other troops imagine Paris a city of "spires and golden domes past
counting, all the buildings . . . brilliant—dazzling brilliant"
(341), then upon entering it find it a foreign labyrinth whose inhabitants cannot speak to them.

Percivale follows Galahad through a landscape of devastation,
"a great black swamp of an evil smell, / Part black, part whiten'd
with the bones of men," and glimpses the Grail not independently
but over Galahad's head. In the end Percivale returns to Arthur,
who again questions would-be knights who seek an ideal by leaving the world. Arthur, the ideal man, tells them one must live by
an ideal, yet practically and in this world. But Percivale remains
blind. His final words, "So spake the King: I knew not all he
meant," underscore both his limitations and the inadequacy of his
solution.

Like Percivale, Claude is dependent upon an intermediary: the
closest he comes to divine truth is through David Gerhardt. And
like Percivale, Claude has visions, but private, distorted ones,
undercut first by comic, then tragic irony. Sitting solemnly in
what he believes to be the Cathedral at Rouen, Claude looks at the
stained glass windows: he attempts to remember textbook lessons
about Gothic architecture, then, giving up the effort, "felt distinctly" the light that "went through him and farther still . . . as

if his mother were looking over his shoulder" (343). The experience is genuine but out of joint; the scene ends as a huge practical joke. When Claude rejoins the others, "they had the laugh on him," for he had not been in the Cathedral at all, but in the Church of St. Ouen (343).

The idea of blindness continues as the troops move more deeply into France and incidents contain an increasingly dark humor. The trench Claude believes "quite a comfortable little hole" (365) is actually a grave containing badly buried bodies, and the shell hole that seems a picturesquely situated bathing pond (365) emits "big sleepy bubbles" (366) from a body within its depths. As time passes, the disparity between Claude's perception and reality widens, for the external world comes to seem malevolent, transforming itself into a grotesque mockery of nature. This is a landscape in which instead of a hill there is "a pile of corpses . . . faintly discernible in the darkness" that seems to come alive, as "rumbling, squirting sounds began to come from this heap, first from one body, then from another" (445). The presumably stable earth beneath the troops' feet "worked and moved as if boa constrictors were wriggling down there—soft bodies, lightly covered," and from the presumably protecting earth walls of their trenches "a dark hand reached out" (445, 447).

In the end Cather's story is darker than Tennyson's. Percivale *does* return to Arthur, who *does* represent hope, despite men's blindness to it. And Tennyson concludes with a call to right action: if one is not a Galahad, he would do best to live in this world, do his duty by it, comprehend it by loving it, and reach beyond it to the spiritual. Claude, however, dies in battle, and Cather's truth-sayer is not Arthur but the dead boy's mother, who feels relief that her beloved son did not return to inevitable disillusionment. By concluding *One of Ours* with the idea that Claude is best out of a world so shattered, Cather continued the pattern of the novel: affirmation, then denial.

Completing her book did not bring relief to Cather. She had become more personally involved with Claude than with any of her other characters, feeling she had come to know him better than she knew herself; and she felt bereft when she no longer had his company each day.[20] Because she cared so deeply, and undoubtedly because she wanted this, her first novel with Alfred Knopf, to do well for her new publisher, she took extraordinary pains to smooth the way for it. She arranged, for example, with Dorothy Canfield Fisher to write the major review of it, which appeared in the *New York Times*. [21] In some ways Cather's hopes for her novel were met: *One of Ours* was Cather's first popular success and the book for which she received the Pulitzer Prize. Appreciative letters from servicemen poured in.

But critical reception was harsh. By this time Cather had attracted considerable attention, much of it favorable; by 1919–20, H. L. Mencken was acclaiming her a major writer. [22] But following *One of Ours* Edmund Wilson asked, "Can H. L. Mencken have been mistaken when he decided that Willa Cather was a great novelist?" then judged her new novel "a pretty flat failure" with cardboard characters rather mechanically "put through the paces of puppets." Wilson faulted in particular the latter part of the book, "where Miss Cather has imposed on herself the special handicap of having to imagine her hero in relation to the ordeal of the war." [23] The war scenes have always been considered the most disappointing part of the novel, and Hemingway's remarks upon them have become famous in their own right: "Look at *One of Ours.* . . . Prize, big sale, people taking it seriously. You were in the war weren't you? Wasn't that last scene in the lines wonderful? Do you know where it came from? The battle scene in *Birth of a Nation.* I identified episode after episode, Catherized. Poor woman she has to get her war experience somewhere." [24]

To some extent Cather had anticipated the criticism. She recognized that, unfortunately, *One of Ours* would be read as a war novel, even though in it she told the story of Claude, not of war. Nevertheless, a recurrent question has been whether Cather presented an accurate account of war, and that question too reveals misunderstanding. According to Cather's views of art, to follow a criterion of "accuracy" would be to write fiction as meaningless as Claude's objective and lifeless report on Joan of Arc. The truth of the war lay in a boy's experience of it, and this boy was young, naive, and romantic. When Claude embraces the war, he is as willfully uncritical as he was earlier of Enid. Most certainly his views were shaped by convention; that is the point.

I am not arguing that the book is without problems, and I would not place it among Cather's best writing. Certain scenes fall flat, sometimes embarrassingly so. One example will suffice. In describing the sounds that come from a pile of corpses, "gasses, swelling in the liquefying entrails of the dead men," Cather wrote, "they seemed to be complaining to one another; *glup, glup, glup*" (445–46). I am arguing, however, that *One of Ours* is better than has been recognized and that critics' difficulties may come partially because Cather attacks precisely those expectations by which it is being evaluated. These concern male characters and, especially, war novels, and they are represented most memorably by Hemingway.

According to Hemingway war presents reality so immediately, intensely, and unavoidably that it serves as a crucible for a character's formation of manhood. In battle the present moment is everything; past and future cease to exist. The Hemingway character is admirable not because he affirms continuities, as Cather's heroes do, but because he confronts unalterable loneliness with dignity. He is not "messy"; that is, he holds his liquor well, knows and abides by certain rituals, is self-contained and, above all, in control. These are precisely the qualities of American culture Cather exposed in *One of Ours,* where to be a man is to seldom voice an opinion and never to explain it, to dominate others, to be in control. As Claude put it, to be a man was to be "prosaic and commonplace" (127).

Claude's agonized question, "What is wrong with me?" runs like a motif through the first part of the book. He is painfully sensitive, socially awkward, unable to enter a saloon and purchase a beer. He yearns for culture and good talk, fine clothes and elegant manners, but because he lives in a world governed by gender rules almost as rigid as those Hemingway wrote of, he is able to express his feelings only through a woman serving as his "aesthetic proxy" (112). For what Claude wants, finally, is to live as convention would allow only a woman to live: not to possess or master, but to give himself up to something more powerful than himself.

In a provocative essay Stanley Cooperman argues that Cather, in writing of Claude's search for manhood, created "a story of erotic war motivation unequalled until John Hersey's *The War Lover.*" Recognizing how closely Cather associates Claude with violence, Cooperman interprets him as a "war lover" because of his "stimulation by violence; dutiful application of 'ideals' to sanction violence;

and—when the rational edifice of consciousness is most relaxed—
the translation of violence into erotic fulfillment."[25] Yet one could
argue Claude is most himself when he is most domestic. In the
Nebraska scenes he is happiest when he is reading with his mother,
hearing Mrs. Erlich talk about cookery, lavishing tender care upon
his little house, lying quietly in the grove. Furthermore, his best
moments are those in which he assumes conventionally female
roles. While he is sick and, therefore, given permission to be passive, he is visited by Enid in a kind of courtship, complete with
flowers. When they are engaged, Claude again is most content
when lost in the conventionally female and passive dream that
marriage will bring happiness. Conversely, he is most miserable—and violent—when doing what is expected of him as a
man.

When he enlists, Claude at last is able to live without complications of gender, for in war—the unquestioned realm of men
—he is released from having to prove himself manly. Because
there are no women, men can assume conventionally female duties:
nursing, cooking, cleaning, nurturing. The result for Claude is
the unexpected sense of domesticity which builds during the
French section and culminates in the war scenes. Seeing columns of
smoke rise from German lines across "No Man's Land," Claude
reflects, "Everything was comfortable and natural" (363), and
when the sky flames with color, he decides to "enjoy the scenery a
bit" (364), rather as if he were on a Sunday stroll. When he reaches
the dugout he will share with Gerhardt, he begins to set up housekeeping:

The former occupants had left it clean. There were two bunks nailed
against the side walls, — wooden frames with wire netting over them,
covered with dry sandbags. Between the two bunks was a soap-box table,
with a candle stuck in a green bottle, an alcohol stove, a bain-marie, and
two tin cups. On the wall were coloured pictures from *Jungend,* taken out
of some Hun trench.

He found Gerhardt still asleep on his bed, and shook him until he
sat up.

"How long have you been out, Claude? Didn't you sleep?"

"A little. I wasn't very tired. I suppose we could heat shaving water
on this stove; they've left us half a bottle of alcohol. It's quite a comfortable little hole, isn't it?"

"It will doubtless serve its purpose," David remarked dryly. "So sensitive to any criticism of this war! Why, it's not your affair; you've only just arrived."

"I know," Claude replied meekly, as he began to fold his blankets. "But it's likely the only one I'll ever be in, so I may as well take an interest." (364–65)

This is the only war Claude will ever be in; ironically, in it he finds the only family he is actually a part of, and with David, he enjoys the life he had hoped to have with Enid: the snug home made comfortable by the thoughtful consideration of its inhabitants.

With such scenes, Cather suggested something she had felt upon talking with even the most unlikely of soldiers. She recalled meeting the violinist David Hochstein, upon whom she based David Gerhardt. Shortly after enlisting Hochstein was disspirited over the deadly routine of camp life, Cather recalled; but when she saw him some months later, she was struck by changes in him. He was again confident and enthusiastic, saying he wouldn't have missed the life at camp, for "he had found something there that he had vaguely felt the lack of all his life. . . . his relation to other young men. He didn't mention the war, didn't seem to be dwelling on the larger issues of it. His whole attention now seemed fixed upon his company and what was going on at Camp Upton. We asked him if he wasn't bored. No, not at all now; the men were splendid."[26]

It was this sense of camaraderie that Cather infused into Gerhardt and, especially, into Claude. With the boys in his company he finds companionship akin to that he so admired in the Erlichs' family: lively talk, good humor, constant variety. Such comradeship is the reality, the war strangely unreal. Even in battle, when his company is defending the Boar's Snout and Claude leaps to the parapet to encourage his men, he is oblivious to the violence about him, thinking only that he commanded wonderful men and that David would find them all there when he returned: these are ideals of devotion, fidelity, trust, and, most importantly, love.

We have become sensitive to ways in which Cather broke through hidebound conventions regarding women, yet generalizations about Cather's male characters remain largely unexamined. Cather created weak men, we are told, because they are often supportive, reflective, sensitive, poetic, emotional, onlookers rather than at the center of the action. Most damning, they are often eclipsed by powerful women. Nowhere does Cather evoke questions about those assumptions more powerfully than in *One of Ours,* but her exploration of effects of gender conventions upon men extends through her writing. Carl Linstrum is the first of a long line of male characters that includes Claude Wheeler and culminates in Anton Rosicky, men who are admirable because they have the sensitivity to feel deeply and the strength to love well.

Critics were greatly relieved when Cather's next book appeared, and it was again in the symbolic mode at which she excelled. They hailed *A Lost Lady* as a nearly perfect novel. But Cather was never to renounce the book she had so long called simply "Claude."

"I like best of my books the one that all the high-brow critics knock," Miss Cather confessed. "In my opinion, 'One of Ours' has more of value in it than any one of the others. I don't think it has as few faults perhaps as 'My Antonia' or 'A Lost Lady,' but any story of youth, struggle and defeat can't be as smooth in outline and perfect in form as just a portrait. When you have an inarticulate young man butting his way thru the world you can't pay that much attention to form."[27]

8 *A Lost Lady:* A Prose-Poem
of Symbolic Experience

From that disparity, he believed, came the subtlest thrill of her fascination. She mocked outrageously at the proprieties she observed, and inherited the magic of contradictions.[1]

By 1923 Willa Cather's career had taken on a rhythm, with a labored book followed by a spontaneous one, a full-bodied narrative followed by one with the quality of poetry. It was as if Cather assembled thematic materials in one book, then in the next threw "all the furniture out of the window and along with it, all the meaningless reiterations concerning physical sensations, all the tiresome old patterns, [leaving] the room as bare as the stage of a Greek theatre, or as that house into which the story of the Pentecost descended; [leaving] the scene bare for the play of emotions, great and little."[2] She first wrote *Alexander's Bridge,* a mechanical book about the imagination; she then wrote *O Pioneers!,* a spontaneous creation of the imagination. In *The Song of the Lark* she gathered materials about growing up; in *My Ántonia* she created the experience itself. *One of Ours* was a detailed narrative about a young romantic's search for something splendid amidst dissolution of tradition. Cather's next book, *A Lost Lady, is* this search, so poetic that reading it is akin to reading a Keatsian ode.

Cather's well-known description of the *novel démeublé* (or unfurnished novel) is especially apt for *A Lost Lady,* her best example of the type. Its theme was one Cather accepted rather than chose; she recalled that the story descended upon her, as a revelation. While visiting in Toronto, Cather learned that Mrs. Lyra Garber had died, a woman she had "loved very much in my childhood," whose "lovely hair and laugh . . . made me happy clear down to my toes."[3] Cather went to her room, lay down to rest, and though she had never before thought about writing of Mrs. Garber, found that the story came to her within an hour, as if she had read it elsewhere. Suddenly there was the right form for an emotion she had been carrying with her: "'A Lost Lady' was a beautiful ghost in my mind for twenty years before it came together as a possible subject for presentation. All the lovely emotions that one has had some day appear with bodies."[4]

Though the story came to Cather effortlessly, the writing of it initially presented more difficulty than had her other books.[5] Perhaps part of that difficulty resulted because Cather knew so clearly what she wanted—and what she didn't want. She did not want to make a conventional story of love and intrigue, nor did she want to make a character study (when she was little she wasn't interested in Mrs. Garber's character). Instead she wanted "to get her just as I remembered her and produce the effect she had on me and the many others who knew her." She wanted to create an emotion—the happiness of hearing Mrs. Garber laugh, the joy of seeing her beauty. And she was determined "not to care about anything else in the story. . . . Everything else is subordinate."[6]

To present the effect of her character, Cather "had to have something for Marian Forrester's charm to work on," and so she created Niel Herbert. The problem lay in getting the right balance. In *My Ántonia,* where she had last used a male figure to recall a woman, Cather had told Jim Burden's story of remembering his childhood. Now she wanted to tell, not a young boy's story, but Marian Forrester's effect upon him. She tried writing in the first person, but eventually realized that as a character in his own right Niel "would get too fused up over the story. He would have to have a certain love theme, and in his telling the bank failure would be made a great deal of, and so it would end in being a conventional novel." So Cather began again, this time with Niel not a character but "just a peephole into that world. . . . only a point of view."[7]

Perhaps, too, as Edith Lewis conjectured, Cather's difficulty with balance arose "from the fact that Mrs. Forrester was a more direct portrait than any of her other characters except Ántonia."[8] Marian Forrester's life closely follows that of Lyra Garber, wife of an early builder of Nebraska. While he was a captain in the Union Army, Silas Garber heard stories of the beautiful Republican Valley. After the war he visited the area, filed a claim, helped build a stockade, organize schools, and plan for the town he wished to name Red Cloud. Garber's fortunes rose with those of the country he was helping to settle. He became governor of Nebraska in 1873, then, while visiting in California, met the beautiful younger sister of his brother's wife. The widower Garber married Lyra

Wheeler and brought her to Nebraska, where she was a brilliant hostess, first of the governor's mansion in Lincoln, and after that of the Garber home in Red Cloud. When the bank he founded failed, however, Mr. Garber lost his fortune; and after he was thrown from a carriage in Lincoln, he lost his health. Lyra Garber tended him faithfully and, though the townspeople gossiped, continued to entertain frequently. Following her husband's death, Mrs. Garber lost what money remained, "and with it her perspective," eventually moving away from Red Cloud.[9]

After Mrs. Garber left Red Cloud and until her death in 1921, Cather apparently heard only the most general news of her: she had returned to California, where she had remarried. But Cather's memories remained vivid: of going up the tree-lined road and crossing Crooked Creek to visit the Garber home or to play in the cottonwood grove growing behind it. "Wasn't she a flash of brightness in a grey background, that lady? Can't you hear her laugh?" Cather recalled.[10] And in later years Cather said that to write well, she had to get up in the morning feeling thirteen and going for a picnic in that grove.[11]

When critics have moved beyond recounting the genesis of A Lost Lady to interpreting it, they have stressed its themes: the frontier's downfall, the noble pioneer's passing, materialism's onslaught, woman's plight in a patriarchal society. Certainly those themes are there. One can argue, for example, that characters and settings symbolize ideas in a social allegory of the decline of the West: the old pioneer order and virtues in Captain Forrester, the vulnerable beauty of the pioneer dream in the fragile march and the young wife; corrupting materialism by Ivy Peter.[12]

While all this is accurate enough, it is not true to my reading of A Lost Lady. It is only after I put the book down and begin to classify, categorize, and interpret that I equate characters and settings with ideas. While I am reading I am engaged on quite another level. I experience Marian Forrester; I help to create her. And realizing this, I have come to believe that Cather's achievement in A Lost Lady was that she did precisely what she set out to do. She wrote about the experience of the thing and not the thing itself, the effect of Mrs. Forrester and not the character. In doing so, she was classically romantic. When traditional orders collapse, the romantic turns to subjective experience; confronted with historical loss, the romantic affirms the soul's need for primitive or sacred understanding, for spiritual attitudes and intuitive, symbolic experience. Largely through Niel Herbert, the "peephole character" she revised so extensively to get right, Cather presented this experience. [13]

Unlike Jim Burden, Niel Herbert is not highly individualized. Cather provides enough background to give him a place within Sweet Water (he is Judge Pommeroy's nephew; he lives with his father and Cousin Sadie on the edge of town) and to establish in him a certain temperament. Niel is painfully aware that a noble past is closed to him (he realizes he lives at "the very end of the road-making West. . . . It was already gone, that age; nothing could ever bring it back" [168–69]), and he yearns for a noble life lived by high ideals. Other details further establish that temperament: like his mother, he is proud and somewhat aloof; he is disappointed, even ashamed of his father, a widower who passes all his time at his office, investing other people's money after having lost his own; and he is curious about the great world of the past, which he enters by reading *Don Juan*, *Tom Jones*, *Wilhelm Meister*, Montaigne, Ovid. He is a romantic, condemned, as it were, to seek spiritual values in a world giving way to materialism.

Not unexpectedly Niel's experience takes the form of tension between ideal and reality, dream and disappointment. As such it resembles that of a Keatsian ode, in which the drama is of a mind engaged with an object. On the one hand, there is Niel, trying to possess Mrs. Forrester imaginatively, to see his ideal in her and to discover her secret; on the other hand, there is Mrs. Forrester, elusively separate, teasingly contradictory. Movement is between expectation and experience, ideal and reality. The mind, frustrated so long as it projects itself upon an object, is satisfied only when it ceases to be self-conscious and feels what it is to *be* it (by what Keats called negative capability and Cather the gift of sympathy). Satisfaction is short-lived, however, for inevitably the mind again becomes self-conscious, and the object reasserts its own identity. In the end it is not any settled truth but the experience itself that has been real and valuable.

A Lost Lady contains a bustle of activity that forms an overall pattern of rising and falling motion, of expectation and disappointment. The pioneers live and die, people come and go, the economy rises and declines, light dawns and fades, flowers open and close, even Mrs. Forrester's laugh rises and descends. The plot reflects this pattern: Marian Forrester comes to Sweet Water as the young bride of Captain Forrester, and she leaves after his death; at the beginning of the action, the boy Niel Herbert first enters the Forrester place, and at its conclusion an older Niel departs "for the last time." Scenes suggest this pattern in miniature, characteristically beginning with Niel's coming up the hill approaching the Forrester house and ending with his going down the hill after leaving it.

Yet although movement surrounds episodes of *A Lost Lady,* there is a profound stillness at its center. Episodes contain moments of recognition that seem frozen in time, and these moments make up the essential experience of the novel. Like Ántonia, who could "leave images in the mind that did not fade, that grew stronger with time,"[14] so does *A Lost Lady* leave such images: Mrs. Forrester bringing cookies to the boys in the marsh; Mrs. Forrester listening to Captain Forrester tell their dinner guests of first coming to Sweet Water and, later, presiding over her own dinner party, telling quite different guests of her meeting Captain Forrester; Niel stooping to place a bouquet of flowers outside her bedroom window, then hearing from within the sound of her laughter mingled with that of her lover.

These two effects of movement and stillness, change and timelessness, derive from two impulses that run through the novel: one is a historical account of Mrs. Forrester, the other an emotional experience of her. The first works in the manner of conventional fiction, the second in the manner of a poetic symbol. In the historical narrative, Mrs. Forrester is a woman who lives in time. She comes to Sweet Water and presides over her husband's home as a brilliant hostess, takes a lover, cares for her husband during his prolonged illness, abandons the principles of his generation after his death, has an affair with a shyster lawyer, and moves from Sweet Water to seek her fortune elsewhere. Throughout this progression, she participates in cause-and-effect relationships in time: she flourishes as a result of her husband's prosperity and suffers by his loss of fortune; she enjoys youthful beauty, then gradually grows old. Were this the substance of the book, *A Lost Lady* would follow "the usual fictional pattern," and Marian Forrester would be "a standardized heroine."[15]

But Cather tells of a second effect associated with Marian Forrester—the experience of her. While the events of her life occur
within time and in terms of cause-and-effect relationships, the experience of her exists out of time and comes from the integration of
apparently disparate elements: her suspicious past and her respectability as Captain Forrester's wife; her aesthetic otherworldliness
and her sensuality; her fragility and her strength; her exquisiteness
and her coarseness; her artlessness and her artifice; her mocking,
guarded veneer and the living reality beneath it.

The novel's intensity builds on both levels. First, there are the
increasingly desperate circumstances of Mrs. Forrester's life—of
her struggle to avoid entrapment by the restricting effects of her
husband's loss of fortune and death, of living in Sweet Water, of
growing old. Second, and far more important, intensity builds as
she reveals ever greater discrepancies. Initially, the contrasts she
presents are relatively easy to resolve: she seems a lady far above and
detached from other people, yet she enters the ordinary world of
childhood when she brings cookies to young boys playing in the
marsh. Gradually, she reveals wider contrasts—between the spiritual and the physical, the common and the uncommon, fidelity
and betrayal—and resolution becomes correspondingly more difficult.

Niel Herbert, the sensitive observer of Marian Forrester, is the
major vehicle for this expanding experience. It is Niel who feels
most intensely her "magic of contradictions," and it is he who
attempts most arduously to deny those contradictions. The overall
movement of the novel follows Niel's responses and consists of two
major imaginative expansions and contractions, followed by a
resolution.[16] In the first part, scenes expand the experience of Mrs.
Forrester through a dialectic between her otherworldly grace and
her physical reality. Early expansive movement occurs when the
young Niel thinks of her as a spiritual goddess, then perceives her
playful, teasing, human qualities. Expansion continues as the
adolescent Niel becomes aware of other incongruities in her: a
scandalous past and a present respectability, a mocking manner
and a deep interest in people, fragility and vitality: "From that
disparity, he believed, came the subtlest thrill of her fascination.
She . . . inherited the magic of contradictions" (79).

Niel's imaginative, emotional response is far deeper than he is conscious of and greatly exceeds his capacity to understand her. Cather prepares for this disparity by a sequence of episodes: the dinner party, culminating Niel's initial response to Mrs. Forrester, is followed by the cedar-bough-cutting episode, which occurs outside Niel's knowledge and in which the nonjudgmental Adolph Blum provides the lens for presenting profoundly sexual qualities in Mrs. Forrester. Thus in the following chapter, when Niel attempts to explain his interest in Mrs. Forrester, there is an enormous ironic difference between his explanation that "it was as Captain Forrester's wife that she most interested Niel, and it was in her relation to her husband that he most admired her" (78) and the reader's knowledge of qualities in her that lie far outside this explanation.

Through this expansion, tension builds with intrusions by Frank Ellinger and culminates when Niel overhears Mrs. Forrester with Ellinger in her bedroom. Unable to accommodate sexuality in his imaginative conception of her, Niel draws back in bitter disillusionment, breaking the imaginative expansion with logic: "He burned to ask her one question, to get the truth out of her and to set his mind at rest: What did she do with all her exquisiteness when she was with a man like Ellinger? Where did she put it away? And having put it away, how could she recover herself, and give one—give even him—the sense of tempered steel, a blade that could fence with anyone and never break" (100). Niel's question reveals an analytic impulse and an underlying denial of paradoxes. He assumes that Mrs. Forrester puts away her exquisiteness when she is with her lover and that, after having given herself up to sexuality, she "recovers herself," putting aside sexuality and resuming her former nature. Intensifying the question is Niel's almost violent impulse to force a response from her, a yielding to him, as he "burned . . . to get the truth out of her."

In the novel's second part, Niel's response is again expansive as scenes further present Mrs. Forester's complexity. Seldom leaving Sweet Water during her husband's last years, Mrs. Forrester reveals gentleness in her ministrations to her dying husband and fierceness in her own desire to live, exhaustion and strength, generosity and greed. This expansion culminates when Mrs. Forrester presides at her own dinner party after her husband's death and, despite her great fatigue and her guests' insensitivity, trans-

forms those present with the story of her first meeting Captain Forrester.

Throughout this expansion, tension builds as Ivy Peters assumes the role previously held by Frank Ellinger—the lover who
elicits contradictory features in Mrs. Forrester. Contraction occurs
when Niel, seeing Ivy Peters "unconcernedly put both arms
around her, his hands meeting over her breast" (169), turns from
her in bitter disillusionment, resolving never to return to the Forrester place. Again Niel attempts to deny contradictions in her:
she is either common or uncommon, worthy or unworthy. Recalling her, Niel wishes to "challenge [her], demand the secret of that
ardour," just as he had earlier wished "to get the truth out of her."
Yet the futility of this last wish is apparent. Mrs. Forrester "had
drifted out of his ken"—she had moved to South America, remarried, and died—and the image of her drifting away combines with
Niel's wish "to call up the shade of the young Mrs. Forrester, as the
witch of Endor called up Samuel's" (171), to convey a dreamlike,
imaginative quality in his response.

Resolution comes when Niel, ceasing his attempts to explain
Mrs. Forrester or to force her to explain herself, pays tribute to her
on another level. Removed in time and place from the cause-and-
effect relationships of the narrative, Niel hears again of his "long-
lost lady," an account relayed by a childhood friend, Ed Elliott. In
this final description, Mrs. Forrester remains enigmatic: she had
aged, yet hadn't changed in essentials; she had married a man
reputed to be "quarrelsome and rather stingy," yet "she seemed to
have everything"; most remarkably, she had "come up again" after
having "pretty well gone to pieces before she left Sweet Water."
But Niel responds, "So we may feel sure that she was well cared for
to the very end. . . . Thank God for that!" The resolution here is
in Niel's attitude to Mrs. Forrester, an acknowledgement of the
truth of his subjective experience of her. His "Thank God!" reveals
the strength of his feeling; his friend interprets the reaction as feeling ("I knew you'd feel that way"); then the narrator affirms this
interpretation in the novel's final clause, "a warm wave of feeling
passed over his face" (172–74).

At the end, we too try to "get at" Mrs. Forrester's secret—to
explain and judge her as strong or weak, noble or fallen. But just as
there is a problem with the "real" meaning in "Ode on a Grecian

Urn," so there is a problem with the "real" meaning of Marian Forrester and, through her, of *A Lost Lady*. We finally return to our experiences of the woman and, as we do so, recognize as Niel does the expanding significance that radiates from her, infusing every part of the novel: "She had always the power of suggesting things much lovelier than herself, as the perfume of a single flower may call up the whole sweetness of spring" (172).

This experience of Mrs. Forrester, the single effect to which Cather subordinated everything else in the story, is symbolic experience. Its essential quality is its infusing power. As Coleridge wrote, a symbol "partakes of the Reality which it renders intelligible [and] . . . abides itself as a living part in that Unity, of which it is the representative."[17] It follows, then, that we would expect the parts of a symbolic prose narrative—as Karl Kroeber does those of a symbolic poem—"to be dynamically interrelated."[18] And so they are. To develop the expanding symbolic experience of Mrs. Forrester, Cather uses a form of incremental repetition, repeating descriptive phrases so that the significance of the reference changes in the progress of the novel. By repetition, things become familiar: they appear, then reappear, with each reappearance bringing forward the accumulated associations of their past. When the boy Niel is taken into Mrs. Forrester's bedroom after breaking his arm, for example, he sees light coming through closed green shutters; later, an older Niel, having gathered a bouquet for Mrs. Forrester in the early morning, goes "softly round the still house to the north side of Mrs. Forrester's own room, where the door-like green shutters were closed" (86). The familiar shutters subtly evoke the earlier scene in which Niel was inside the room and secure in his youthful idealization of Mrs. Forrester, and thus they contribute to the dramatic impact of the disillusionment scene.

As the effect of incremental repetition expands, objects take on qualities of their perceivers, further suggesting a world informed with symbolic significance. The poplars bordering the road to the Forrester place are initially simply objects in a rather flat nature: "The Captain's private lane [was] bordered by Lombardy poplars" (11). Gradually, however, the trees become sentinels of the coming and going of visitors to the Forrester place, familiar landmarks in a world we come to recognize. Eventually, they participate in the symbolic meaning that radiates from Mrs. Forrester, trans-

formed by Niel following his experiences with her. Leaving the
Forrester place, "Niel paused for a moment at the end of the lane to
look up at the last skeleton poplar in the long row; just above its
pointed tip hung the hollow, silver winter moon" (42). When
Niel leaves the Forrester place "'for the last time,'" the narrator
affirms, "it was even so; he never went up the poplar-bordered road
again" (170)—and the reference to the poplars, with their many
associations from the past, suggests the symbolic resonances Niel
is turning from.

Finally, by building to symbolic climaxes, the accumulative
meaning of details enables moments of recognition. References to
roses, for example, underlie the novel's first major expansive movement. When Mrs. Forrester sees Niel and the other boys on their
way to the marsh, she is arranging roses; when she comes to the
door to talk with them, she is holding a single rose. The rose,
tamed and domesticated inside Mrs. Forrester's parlor, reappears
in the marsh in profusion as "wild roses [that] were wide open and
brilliant" (17), the image subtly foreshadowing the sensual, even
wild potential in Mrs. Forrester's own nature and suggesting
Niel's response to that potential. On the one hand, the intimation
of sensuality is a major element in his fascination with her; on the
other hand, it is this quality in her that he is unable to face.

Roses appear again in the early morning scene in which Niel
gathers a bouquet for Mrs. Forrester. The extended image begins
with a relatively objective description of "thickets of wild roses,
with flaming buds, just beginning to open." Then, as the objects
by their own beauty and by their past association with Mrs. Forrester draw forth fuller perception, the description moves from the
roses themselves to Niel's mind as he perceives them: "Where they
had opened, their petals were stained with that burning rose-
colour which is always gone by noon, —a dye made of sunlight
and morning and moisture, so intense that it cannot possibly
last . . . must fade, like ecstasy." The rose unifies aesthetic and
sensual responses into a single intense moment. Finally, Niel begins to cut stems of the flowers, resolving, in highly metaphorical
terms, that "he would make a bouquet for a lovely lady; a bouquet
gathered off the cheeks of morning . . . these roses, only half
awake, in the defenselessness of utter beauty" (85). Far more than
the action, the roses here convey the transitoriness of such a mo-

ment and the vulnerability of one who experiences it, anticipating Niel's disillusionment at the end of that scene. As preceding references to roses foreshadow this scene, succeeding references echo it. Roses, again reduced to objects but now containing symbolic resonances, reappear after Captain Forrester's death, when the Blum brothers bring a box of yellow roses to Mrs. Forrester and, later, when she resolves to plant some of her husband's rosebushes over his grave (145–46).

Incremental repetition illustrates, then, the way in which symbolic experience works by accumulation, expansion, and infusion, its movement quite different from the cause-and-effect patterns in the historical account. Through this contrast, the symbolic and historic elements work off one another. Scenes customarily begin in time, move to a core episode that contains a moment of recognition and an escape from time, then return abruptly to the historical, real world. The Forrester place resides at the center of this movement, offering apparent security and constancy and containing Mrs. Forrester, with her magical power of transformation. But experiences there are surrounded by ominous images of incompletion, change, and death that suggest inevitable intrusions from the real world. When Niel is taken to Mrs. Forrester's room after breaking his arm, he becomes aware of a "different world from any he had ever known" (42). His involvement intensifies until, when "Mrs. Forrester ran her fingers through his black hair and lightly kissed him on the forehead," he loses himself in the fullness of the experience: "Oh, how sweet, how sweet she smelled!" With the next line, however, the world of change intrudes: "Wheels on the bridge; it's Doctor Dennison. Go and show him in, Mary." Niel's return to the real world is dramatized as Doctor Dennison takes him home, a home "set off on the edge of the prairie" and "usually full of washing in various stages of incompletion" (29). The wholeness Niel felt with Mrs. Forrester intensifies his later sense of incompletion; his happiness sharpens his dissatisfaction; his fleeting sense of belonging heightens the loneliness of his daily life.

Subsequent episodes follow a similar pattern. Niel feels exultation over an evening talk with Mrs. Forrester; then, leaving the Forrester place, he stops "at the end of the lane" to look at the last skeletal poplar pointing to a hollow winter moon (42). At Captain Forrester's dinner party, Niel again feels a deep sense of security, this time through loss of self in Captain Forrester's story of coming to Sweet Water; then "just before midnight" he returns to a world of separation and incompletion as the guests sing "Auld Lang Syne" and "hadn't got to the end of it" when they hear "a hollow rumbling down on the bridge" and then "see the Judge's funeral coach coming lurching up the hill, with only one of the side lanterns lit" (57). Other scenes come to mind: Niel's gathering flowers for Mrs. Forrester and reveling in the "almost religious purity about the fresh morning air," then abruptly returning to the real world at the sound of laughter from within the bedroom (84–87); Niel's losing himself in Mrs. Forrester's story of first meeting Captain Forrester and then, in the next scene, planning to leave Sweet Water and feeling he was "making the final break with everything that had been dear to him in his boyhood" (168).

What emerges is a buildup of tension between the encroaching real world of change and the experiences of unity—of symbolic meaning—that become increasingly difficult to reach in that world. The contrasting dinner parties illustrate the heightening of tension. In the first, a young Mrs. Forrester appears effortless as she assists her husband in transforming the evening; in the second, an older, widowed, impoverished Mrs. Forrester appears haggard, and it is only by a supreme act of will that she again electrifies her guests. The strong sense of incompletion throughout the narrative contributes to this tension: Sweet Water does not fulfill its early promise; Captain Forrester's career as a builder is cut short by an accident; the heirs apparent to the pioneer generation, Marian Forrester and Niel Herbert, leave without bringing renewal.

Finally, changes in point of view reinforce this tension. The overall progression of point of view is from the public meaning of a storyteller to the private meaning of subjective experience. The novel begins with a narrator who recalls, "thirty or forty years ago, in one of those grey towns along the Burlington railroad, which are so much greyer today than they were then, there was a house well known from Omaha to Denver for its hospitality and for a certain charm of atmosphere," then modifies this observation—"well known, that is to say, to the railroad aristocracy of that time." The effect is of ongoing reminiscence, of the actual presence of a storyteller who offers an observation as it occurs to her. Because she is casual about time (referring to "thirty or forty years ago" and to "long ago") as well as about place (referring to "one of those grey towns along the Burlington railroad"), the storyteller herself emerges strongly in the opening passage, seeming more immediate, real, and accessible than her subject.

Recounting comings and goings, sequences and changes, the storyteller provides a logical organization of these movements. She establishes a chronology of events ("for the next few years Niel saw very little of Mrs. Forrester" [31]; "during that winter . . . Niel came to know her very well" [103]; "Captain Forrester's death . . . occurred early in December" [144]), and she explains events through their sequence of cause and effect within that chronology ("For the Forresters that winter was a sort of isthmus between two estates; soon afterward came a change in their fortunes. And for Niel, it was a natural turning point" [69]). The narrative conveys a sense of movement; its meaning is objective, factual, settled.

But the stillness at *A Lost Lady*'s center derives from a quite different experience, one that is subjective, imaginative, and expanding. For it Cather moves from the storyteller's omniscience to the limited points of view of individual characters, such as Niel. This movement involves a gradual narrowing from the storyteller's long view to a specific episode, to one character within the episode, and finally, to the episode as it is being processed in that character's mind. Beginning with the long view, for example, the storyteller explains, "It was two years before Niel Herbert came home again," then presents Niel having come to the Forrester place, summarizes his meeting with Captain Forrester, and follows Niel "round the house to the gate that gave into the grove," where he saw first a hammock between two cottonwoods, then a still, slender, white figure in it. The account gains in immediacy as Niel, approaching, discerns more details: "As he hurried across the grass he saw that a white garden hat lay over her face" and was "just wondering if she were asleep, when he heard a soft, delighted laugh," stepped forward, and caught her suspended figure. Suddenly, the point of view presents Niel's mind encountering the object: "How light and alive she was! like a bird caught in a net. If only he could rescue her and carry her off like this" (103–10).

Within specific scenes, Cather interweaves omniscience with individual perceptions, keeping the point of view in motion and maintaining dialectical tension through which symbolic meaning emerges. The storyteller contrasts descriptions from the "long ago" (of the young Mrs. Forrester, "bareheaded, a basket on her arm, her blue-black hair shining in the sun") to later time ("it was not until years afterward that she began to wear veils and sun hats" [17–18]). Similar movement occurs as a result of changes in Niel. Niel's youthful idealization of Mrs. Forrester contrasts with his later disillusionment and his still later gratitude to her. And the storyteller contrasts individual points of view: Adolph Blum's seeing Mrs. Forrester come from an assignation with her lover contrasts with Niel's seeing her only as Captain Forrester's wife; Captain Forrester, watching her with Niel and thinking of her "as very, very young" (75), contrasts with Niel's general view of her as an older woman.

Within the novel as a whole, changes in point of view suggest the effects of a disintegration of traditional, communal values and a corresponding stress on personal, symbolic meaning. Initially, the storyteller identifies individuals in terms of her community: Marian Forrester, seeing a group of boys approach, "knew most of them" as members of the community. Niel is "Judge Pommeroy's nephew"; the others include the "son of a gentleman rancher," "the leading grocer's . . . twins," and "the two sons of the German tailor." Recognition is personal and intimate, based on gossip about the boys as well as on the professional standing of their fathers. Ed Elliot, for example, is the boy "whose flirtatious old father kept a shoe store and was the Don Juan of the lower world of Sweet Water" (14). Similarly, the boy Niel approaches the Forrester place in terms of alignment and congruity: it represents the values he upholds and the life to which he aspires.

By the end of part 2, however, Niel returns to a community from which he is alienated. Cather has replaced Marian Forrester with Ivy Peters to describe Niel's return, and Peters identifies Niel not by community relationships but by his clothes. A shift in power and in communal values is suggested by the shift from Mrs. Forrester, who greets guests as a representative of her husband and the best of Sweet Water, to Ivy Peters, who greets guests as the leader of materialistic, unscrupulous elements that have gained power in the same community. Tension heightens as Niel believes Mrs. Forrester is aligning herself with the new "generation of shrewd young men, trained to petty economies" (107), represented by Ivy Peters.

As Niel's alienation deepens, his subjective, imaginative response is increasingly at odds with his rational appraisal of the "lost lady." Logically and objectively, Niel comes to believe that Mrs. Forrester's generosity and her greed, her exquisiteness and her coarseness, her fidelity and her betrayal, are irreconcilable contradictions. He judges her harshly and keeps his distance from her. When Mrs. Forrester invites him to her dinner party, for example, he resists, arguing, "What do you want me for?" and later feels "angry with himself for having been persuaded" to accept; on the night of the dinner, he is "the last guest to arrive" (158). Yet against all rational preconceptions, at this dinner party Niel is still moved by Mrs. Forrester's "indomitable self," and his apprehension of her telling about first meeting Captain Forrester is one of the timeless moments of recognition at the heart of the novel (164–67).

Niel's conflict may be illustrated by the word "always," which runs through the novel and becomes a motif. Initially, "always" refers to apparent permanence within time—to rituals, for example, that by repetition seem constant. Captain Forrester's toast, "Happy Days," is such a ritual, "the toast he always drank at dinner." As a hostess, Mrs. Forrester carries out other such rituals: "she was always there" (12) to greet visitors; to the young Niel, she seemed "always the same" (39). Such rituals serve their function: they provide a sense of security and stability. But eventually the world of change exerts itself, and in retrospect, the apparent stability offered by rituals seems illusory. Captain Forrester falls from power; Mrs. Forrester is neither always there nor always the same. But even as Niel must accept the loss of Mrs. Forrester within the historical narrative (indeed, he must accept that he never possessed her, and never could have), he comes to realize her permanence on a symbolic level. "Always" runs through the symbolic elements of the novel also, referring to a permanence that exists outside of time. In the end, Niel is certain only that Mrs. Forrester "had always the power of suggesting things much lovelier than herself, as the perfume of a single flower may call up the whole sweetness of spring" (172).[19]

Significantly, Niel casts his reflection in the past tense— for him, Mrs. Forrester "*had* always the power of suggesting things"—and with this past tense, the reader departs from Niel. Niel's resolution comes with his subjective sense that Mrs. Forrester had the power to evoke a symbolic mode of perception; he has reached the point that he is no longer analyzing and judging—no longer holding it against her that "she was not willing to immolate herself, like the widows of all these great men, and die with the pioneer period to which she belonged, that she preferred life on any terms." Ironically, however, his resolution comes only after she, whom Niel believed "preferred life on any terms," has died, and we suspect that Niel's longing for permanence, forever frustrated in a world of change, ends with the secure distance and detachment of an experience "recollected in tranquillity."[20]

For the reader, however, Marian Forrester continues to live in the novel, for in reading we, like Niel with his uncle's books, meet "living creatures, caught in the very behavior of living" (81). As a result, it is impossible to settle Marian Forrester into a fixed meaning, to put her into the past tense and set one's mind to rest about her. Although she recedes in the reader's memory, she comes forward again with each rereading and, by continuing to exert her intense individuality, evokes fresh responses and forces the reader to expand his or her experience of her. In so doing, the reader takes up where Niel left off. Each reading contains moments of recognition and resolution in which Mrs. Forrester is seen as a whole, combining contrary qualities that are logically irreconcilable. Once read, the novel evokes questions which, in turn, lead back into the work. And each time we return to the novel, expansion continues. By offering "an expanding potentiality for formulating values, an expanding area of sympathy and insight out of which values of increasing refinement can emerge and to which they can return," *A Lost Lady* is a novel of experience. The reader is "always in the process of formulating values, although he never arrives at a final formulation."[21] As Karl Kroeber observes, experiences of symbolic meaning "are purely subjective and creative; they cannot be told about; we must . . . participate."[22] Unlimited opportunity for the individual to engage in personal experience, to formulate values, and to create anew—the description could be of *A Lost Lady*. For in *A Lost Lady*, Cather celebrates the constantly expanding possibilities of romantic symbolic art even as she laments the closed frontier of history.

9 *The Professor's House:*
A Book of Dreams

He seemed to be at the root of the matter; Desire under all desires, Truth under all truths.[1]

By 1923 Willa Cather's long struggle to find her way as an artist was in one sense over, for she was recognized as one of America's foremost writers. Struggle continued, of course, but now of a different kind—not to find her personal voice and develop her craft, but "to preserve the integrity of her life as an artist."[2] For the period in which Cather came into her own was also a time of intense pressures. There was the strain she felt over writing *One of Ours* and the exhaustion that followed it, the difficulty of writing *A Lost Lady,* which gave Cather more trouble than any of her other novels, and the public demands that, following her Pulitzer Prize, were so great Cather had to hire a secretary to handle her correspondence. She wrote to her friends of feeling tired and pressured, even of going to bed partly because she had a cold and a bad back, but also to find the solitude to play with an idea.[3] Finally, there were her profound concerns over world affairs. "The world broke in two in 1922 or thereabouts," Cather was to write later: the breaking of present from past, the individual from tradition, the subject from his world.[4] From these feelings Cather wrote one of her finest books, *The Professor's House.*

In her early novels Cather had written about how to know the outside world. In *O Pioneers!* and *My Ántonia,* for example, she celebrated the creative power of the imagination to transform her native Nebraska into a New World Eden and one of its pioneers into a mythic earth mother. Subsequently, Cather treated this relationship between the individual and the world—subject and object—as increasingly difficult. In *One of Ours* Claude Wheeler is adrift in a modern wasteland in which natural myths have been reduced to propaganda slogans, and in *A Lost Lady* Niel Herbert comes to realize that he can neither recapture a noble past nor imaginatively possess Marian Forrester. As if the world has fallen from grace, the land and its inhabitants no longer offer truths.

In *The Professor's House* Cather abandoned the search of her previous characters for value outside themselves and set Godfrey St. Peter on an internal quest for that which is real, through public roles to an original identity. The novel begins with external changes completed. "The moving was over and done," the first sentence reads. St. Peter and his wife have moved into a new house, yet he retains his third-floor study in the now-empty old one. As E. K. Brown and others have pointed out, the setting is symbolic.[5] The upper recess of an abandoned house is the only inhabited portion of a structure now empty and dead; similarly, a narrow intellectualism is all that is left of St. Peter's own life. By training his mind, like his stomach, to be active at a fixed time, he has lived two lives — teacher and scholar. In the process, however, he has neglected his personal life, until it has become as empty as his abandoned house. Scholarly habits have become fixed and intellect hardened, and his head is "more like a statue's head than a man's" (13).

Cather introduces St. Peter as a character who has suffered a romantic version of the Fall as a lapse in perception, from creative imagination to reason. She then sets him on a quest for redemption by which he must retrieve his real self. The narrative form has, as Stephen Tennant noted, a "profound symbolism" of gazing from the immediate to the timeless.[6] It does so through a series of frames, narrative open windows which promise something real, but which once entered reveal disorder and emptiness. As if standing with St. Peter outside his house, looking through a window at his wife and son-in-law inside, the reader begins with St. Peter's family, apparently successful and presumably happy. Upon moving inside the frame, however, she sees private lives of loneliness and jealousy, and turns to the freedom offered by another open window — that of Tom Outland's story. Once again there is the promise of something real, and once again she finds loss and betrayal. Finally, the window opens inward to St. Peter's original self.

The journey is from the public to the private, from external to internal. In "The Family" the apparent public success of the family — St. Peter and his wife are able to build a new house with proceeds from his book, one daughter is married to a popular journalist, the other to a successful businessman — gives way to a private reality of fragmentation and loneliness. The St. Peters maintain only the façade of their marriage; he is happiest away from his wife and afraid people will say they have separated. Similarly, he is deeply ignorant of the private fears and aspirations of others in his family and college: he is, for example, amazed to learn that the sewing woman, Augusta, had ever expected any future other than to grow old in the service of his family, surprised that his wife feels lonely at aging, shocked over Professor Crane's claim to share in proceeds from Tom Outland's invention.

In his new house, where he has his own bedroom and bathroom, St. Peter carries out his most personal activities alone, then uses the reflected image of a mirror to adjust himself for others. The idea of public selves runs through this section, which consists of encounters that remind St. Peter of outward responsibilities. His wife, Lillian, reminds him of what he owes to other people; his younger daughter, Kathleen, that his family will lose face if they don't make up Augusta's financial losses; Mrs. Crane, that others see clearly his obligations to them; his older daughter, Rosamond, that it is not fitting for him to remain alone in the old house. Each encounter presents to St. Peter a symbolic mirror of others' expectations; together their reflections multiply. Kathleen, for example, reminds her father of Rosamond's treatment of the Cranes, who believe themselves entitled to money from Outland's invention. It is as if St. Peter is caught in a maze of mirrors from which there seems no escape, each mirror demanding that he assume a pose—of concerned father, of sympathetic host, of brilliant scholar, of devoted husband. St. Peter's extreme fatigue suggests the toil of these demands and the question of the book: Where is the true or authentic self in it all?

By the end of "The Family" St. Peter has come to feel that "the university, his new house, his old house, everything about him, seemed insupportable, as the boat on which he is imprisoned seems to a sea-sick man" (150). He is ready to move through the next open window that promises freedom—his memory of Tom Outland. Outward connections are suspended: Mrs. St. Peter and the Marselluses sail for France, and St. Peter returns to a solitary life in his old house, where he plans to prepare Tom Outland's diary for publication. To do so, he must write an introduction, a task that evokes his memory of a story Outland told one rainy summer night. In turning to Outland for his second youth years ago, St. Peter had found a surrogate, and in evoking his memory now, he gives himself up to the memory so completely that the surrogate (Outland) and the speaker (St. Peter) merge.

Outland's story appears to offer the unalloyed happiness of pure imaginative experience. Exploring, Outland discovered the Cliff City of an ancient Indian tribe, a place of "immortal repose" and "the calmness of eternity" (201). There, "in a world above the world," he lived alone, feeling the religious emotions of wholeness and possession (240). But a troubling undercurrent of human values betrayed runs through the story. Outland appreciated the beauty and dignity of Cliff City; at the same time, he was a modern version of the "brutal invaders" who ravaged the ancient tribe (221). He hired workmen to clear a road to Cliff City, excavated the ruins, numbered specimens, each evening wrote of an account of his work in "a merchant's ledger," and eventually went to Washington for others to "dig out all its secrets" (211–12, 224). In the end he also betrayed Rodney Blake, the cowhand who befriended him.

"Tom Outland's Story" ends with a sense of loss, as Outland recalls his unsuccessful efforts to find Blake and the reader recalls that Outland himself, long dead, is no longer very real to those who once knew him (111). Again the quest for a real self is thwarted: Outland eludes others in death, and in recalling him, St. Peter is hidden beneath the surrogate he has adopted.

In the third section the window opens inward, allowing the buried life to be released. St. Peter discards the role he had assumed through his adult life, and his "original ego" (265) returns, a primitive that had long remained dormant. By relinquishing former duties, St. Peter is free to revel in his imaginative life "as if it were a new sense, arriving late" (263).

He seemed to know, among other things, that he was solitary and must always be so; he had never married, never been a father. He was earth, and would return to earth. When white clouds blew over the lake like bellying sails, when the seven pine-trees turned red in the declining sun, he felt satisfaction and said to himself merely, "That is right." Coming upon a curly root that thrust itself across his path, he said: "That is it." When the maple-leaves along the street began to turn yellow and waxy, and were soft to the touch, — like the skin on old faces, — he said: "That is true; it is time." All these recognitions gave him a kind of sad pleasure. (265–66)

This scene is at the heart of the book, the real thing found in the smallest of the Chinese boxes.[7] Released from the limiting reason of the scholar, St. Peter's perceptions are "recognitions" of truths. Beneath the public roles is an archetypal identity; with it, St. Peter merges with all life, human and natural. Through our deepest desires we make connections with nature, which is exhibiting similar desires for renewal and continuity. This is the primitive reality that "seemed to be at the root of the matter; Desire under all desires, Truth under all truths" (265).

As in her earlier books, Cather again wrote of nature. Yet there is a difference. Cather's earlier nature, like Wordsworth's, ministered to the individual: the Genius of the Divide bowed down to Alexandra Bergson, the stream in Panther Canyon was a graceful lover for Thea Kronborg, and the wise voice of nature murmured truths to Claude Wheeler. In *The Professor's House* nature is a nonhuman other, and the pull St. Peter feels toward it is *toward this otherness*. One scene illustrates the point. After swimming, St. Peter sometimes sat with unread letters in his hand, "but somehow never taking his eyes off the pine-trees, appliquéd against the blue water, and their ripe yellow cones, dripping with gum and clustering on the pointed tips like a mass of golden bees in swarming time" (270). Here nature is densely and sensuously complete in itself. It is because nature is full in its otherness that St. Peter yearns for it as "eternal solitude . . . a release from every obligation, from every form of effort" (272).

Here Cather's nature resembles not Wordsworth's but Frost's. As St. Peter stops to contemplate the pine trees, so Frost's speaker in "Stopping by Woods on a Snowy Evening" pauses to watch the dark woods fill with snow. Only with immense effort does each man pull himself away, back to the human world:

> The woods are lovely, dark and deep,
> But I have promises to keep,
> And miles to go before I sleep,
> And miles to go before I sleep.[8]

Frost wrote what Robert Langbaum discusses as "the new nature poetry," which attempts to "rescue nature, as it is in itself, from the outmoded concept" of the religion of nature. It offers both hope and danger. By it, one can reach an archetypal reality, a redeeming identity beneath fallen or artificial selves. The danger is that the pull toward this primal reality may become a temptation toward death. As Langbaum writes of Frost's poem, "The momentary insight into the nonhuman otherness of nature is salutary, but to prolong it is to seek unconsciousness, individual extinction, before your time."[9] Langbaum could be writing of *The Professor's House,* in which St. Peter's momentary insight into archetypal reality similarly threatens to become prolonged into death. As if powerless to resist, St. Peter approaches the end of his life. Reason has provided no stay against his yearning for annihilation; now instinct too proves insufficient. When St. Peter falls asleep in his study, then awakens to realize the room has filled with gas, instinct is strong enough to move him from his coffin-bed but not to save him.

St. Peter is saved, however. At midnight, suspended between life and death, time and timelessness, he awakens to see Augusta, who had appeared to pull him from the gas-filled room and open the windows that admit life-giving air. Her presence is the last narrative window: seeing her, St. Peter recognizes an everlasting folk wisdom that links men and women in nature, and Cather again resembles Frost, whose "poetry . . . place[s] us in contact with a survival-making eternal folk wisdom."[10]

Cather goes beyond Frost in one respect, however. While Frost wrote idylls suspended from time, Cather resembles those writers since the Romantic period "who have made us most aware of the historical moment, having themselves not merely known about but felt the conflicts of their age."[11] *The Professor's House* is about that historical moment when things broke apart: science from religion, thought from feeling, the present from the past. As a historian St. Peter can understand the tragedy of the time, and as a teacher he has a platform from which to speak. Cather gives him one of her most stirring indictments of modern materialism:

Science hasn't given us any new amazements, except of the superficial kind. . . . It's the laboratory, not the Lamb of God, that taketh away the sins of the world. You'll agree there is not much thrill about a physiological sin. We were better off when even the prosaic matter of taking nourishment could have the magnificence of sin. I don't think you help people by making their conduct of no importance — you impoverish them. As long as every man and woman who crowded into the cathedrals on Easter Sunday was a principal in a gorgeous drama with God, glittering angels on one side and the shadows of evil coming and going on the other, life was a rich thing. The king and the beggar had the same chance at miracles and great temptations and revelations. And that's what makes men happy, believing in the mystery and importance of their own little individual lives. It makes us happy to surround our creature needs and bodily instincts with as much pomp and circumstance as possible. Art and religion (they are the same thing, in the end, of course) have given man the only happiness he has ever had. (68–69)

St. Peter is the first of what was to be a gallery of Cather's characters to confront the modern threat of annihilation. He recognizes that we need aesthetics to provide order against the chaos of nature and the vastness of time. Nature gains from being arranged, he reflects, and we are happiest when ritual arranges our individual lives, so that each action occurs not in a void but within a larger meaning. Like Wallace Stevens, who in "Anecdote of a Jar" wrote of an object that when placed against a landscape provides a saving point of reference, Cather wrote that religion and art provide a saving sense of order.

In *The Professor's House* Cather asked what remains when aesthetics can no longer provide that order. Science has disproved religion, and rampant materialism has undermined art. As a result, outward connections "had become insupportable" (156), and St. Peter can save himself only by cutting loose from them. In doing so he confronts questions about the self basic to modern literature, and to which writers respond differently:

In attempting to liberate the individual from the social and moral categories that define him, literature somehow dissolved him out of existence. Writers nowadays, who want to face this problem, can . . . face it in two ways. They can deny the existence of a free and knowable self and—like Beckett, Sarraute and Robbe-Grillet in Paris—take soundings of characters only to make us hear the hollow ring within. Or they can—like Mann, Joyce, Yeats, Eliot, Lawrence—reaffirm the authenticity of the self by finding that individual identity emerges, like smaller Chinese boxes out of the larger, from an archetypal identity. [12]

We may add to the second group Willa Cather, for she found an archetypal identity beneath social roles and affirmed a symbolic method beneath a narrative one. In doing so, Cather rescued the imagination from individual caprice, for "a genuine archetype shows itself to have a life of its own, far older and more comprehensive than ideas belonging to the individual consciousness or to the sacred consciousness of individual communities." To use Philip Wheelwright's terms, we might say Cather turned from confrontative imagining to archetypal imagining. Both types acknowledge the importance of concrete universality, by which the universal and the particular are united. But whereas the confrontative imagination works by intensifying individual experience—by making a subjective perception so unique, sensuous, immediate, and intense that the particular unities with the universal, the archetypal imagination works by going "beneath" or "beyond" individual experience, to subjectivity that "has its origin somehow . . . beyond the confines of the individual."[13] In *The Professor's House* Cather sought that origin of subjectivity through dreams.

Like W. B. Yeats, who advised in *Collected Poems* that we leave the "Grey Truth" of science and return to dreaming, Cather found in dreaming a redemption for the human soul.[14] In letting go of ties to the external world and releasing the truths of his own heart, St. Peter reaches a dream state remarkably similar to what Gaston Bachelard discusses as reverie. The dreamer enters reverie by withdrawing into solitude. When, Bachelard writes, he "has swept aside all the 'preoccupations' which were encumbering his everyday life, when he has detached himself from the worry which comes to him from the worry of others, when he is thus truly the *author of his solitude,* when he can finally contemplate a beautiful aspect of the universe without counting the minutes, that dreamer feels a being opening within him." Time is suspended, and "the World is so majestic that nothing any longer happens there; the World reposes in its tranquility." There is no longer a separation of subject from object, for "the communication between the dreamer and his world is [so] close . . . it has no 'distance,' not that distance which marks the *perceived world,* the world fragmented by perception." In reverie, "*the cosmic image is immediate.*"[15]

The description could be of St. Peter, who by casting off everyday preoccupations and detaching himself from others' worries, becomes the author of his own solitude and feels a being opening within. In his daydreams St. Peter enjoys a timeless peace and a

communication with his world so close that he does not distinguish between himself and it. He was, Cather wrote, not a scholar
but a primitive, "only interested in earth and woods and water.
Wherever sun sunned and rain rained and snow snowed, wherever
life sprouted and decayed, places were alike to him. . . . he felt
satisfaction and said to himself merely: 'That is right'" (265). St.
Peter ceases to be a perceiver and his world ceases to be an other;
there is no distance. Instead he enjoys contemplation in which "the
cosmic image is immediate," for which Cather used what Bachelard called "a psychology of capital letters."

Such truths make worldly questions — what will happen next
and to whom — insignificant, a point Cather makes in the last
pages of her novel. Saved by Augusta, St. Peter returns to live out
his natural lifetime, yet in a mood of indifference. Death is no
longer frightening and life no longer contains ecstasy, so he has no
great reason to avoid dying or embrace living. He is changed —
that is the one thing that Cather makes clear — for he had let go of
something precious — the lover. Cather uses "lover" for the out-
ward-reaching impulse to unite with an object, the impulse that
was behind all St. Peter's relationships — with Lillian, with Outland, with his Spanish Adventurers, with nature: "The man he was
now, the personality his friends knew, had begun to grow strong
during adolescence, during the years when he was always consciously or unconsciously conjugating the verb "to love" — in society and solitude, with people, with books, with the sky and open
country, in the lonesomeness of crowded city streets" (264). Without that yearning St. Peter would be apathetic, but "at least, he
felt the ground under his feet. He thought he knew where he was,
and that he could face with fortitude [his family's return] and the
future." So ends The Professor's House.

This ending is, critics have long charged, unsatisfactory: it is
both grim and ambiguous. The grimness is perhaps inevitable
from the dilemma inherent in St. Peter's experience: to release his
original ego he cast off his public selves, yet the being he released
existed only in the most primitive form, certainly not enough developed to bring back to the world of dinner parties and student
papers. By discarding a modern sense of the self (identity developed through unique experience in the "real" world), Cather
reached archetypal truth; but it would not be until Death Comes for

the Archbishop that she would write of selflessness as a source of energetic life in the world.

The charge of ambiguity is another matter. Ambiguity lies at the heart of *The Professor's House,* and therein lies its brilliance. When we ask what, precisely, happened and why, precisely, did it happen, we are suffering from the same fall in perception that initially limited St. Peter. [16] To trace the release of her character from such questions, Cather used a symbolic method very like that of Lawrence. Settings, characters, action—all have only the slightest concern with circumstantial reality. St. Peter's study, the major setting of the book, is only incidentally a scholar's study which contains a dressmaker's dummies. These "forms" (Cather's word for them) are so powerful because any attempt to decode them linguistically is blatantly inadequate. To identify them as Augusta's dressmaker's dummies or to explain that they are St. Peter's way of dealing with his disappointments with women is to state the obvious and to miss the point. The "dead, empty house," the "dark den," St. Peter's skull-like head with its cavities for eyes—all are such forms. The action similarly strains against logic of the everyday world. To write that this is a book about a scholarly professor who, "reluctant to move into a new, more comfortable house . . . remains in the old room he has been used to working in, despite the protestations of his wife and daughters," is akin to saying *Lady Chatterley's Lover* is about an affair between a woman and a gamekeeper. [17]

From the beginning truths of the unconscious belie circumstantial surfaces of things, and scenes have a dreamlike quality: St. Peter's defense of the dressmaker's dummies, the apparitional visitors to his study, the dinner party. In the first major scene, St. Peter resolutely defends "his ladies" by blocking the door of his study against Augusta and declaring he will be "damned" if he lets the forms be removed. As Augusta recognizes, his action is absurd by the logic of ordinary reality, yet the truth of the matter is that St. Peter's salvation *does* lie in his protecting the forms that remain in the "dark den" of his unconscious.

The dinner party similarly has a surrealistic, dreamlike quality, with Louie Marsellus bubbling and babbling, dominating and possessing. Insensitive to people but responsive to food, he is "silenced during the soup," after which he romps ahead, then "paused long enough to have some intercourse with the roast." Manners barely cover the most outrageous actions. Marsellus announces his plan to name his home "Outland" as a living memorial to his wife's dead fiancé; McGregor reacts by lighting a big cigar at a table candle before the others have finished dessert; and the hostess invites her son-in-law to her bedroom (35–43). Here is the unreality of that other dream novel, *Alice in Wonderland;* through it all St. Peter, like Alice at the tea party, seems a bewildered onlooker to a world gone mad.

"The dream is specifically the utterance of the unconscious," Carl Jung wrote, which "may give expression to ineluctable truths, to philosophical pronouncements, illusions, wild fantasies, memories, plans, anticipations, irrational experiences . . . and heaven knows what besides."[18] In *The Professor's House* Willa Cather traced the redemption of her character's unconscious through expressions as richly diverse as those described by Jung. For Cather too recognized that the unconscious takes on different forms, and she used those forms to reflect its growing strength: initially it emerges as irrational disruptions of the ordinary world; then, gaining independence, as plans and memories; and finally as the fully realized archetypal truths of reveries. It is the pressure exerted by this growing unconscious that results in movement from one narrative "open window" to another, from "The Family" to "Tom Outland's Story" to "The Professor."

The unconscious truths of dreams appear first almost unobtrusively as disruptions to the rational surface of things. St. Peter ends his lecture, for example, with a philosophical pronouncement so personal and controversial his wife is ashamed and cautions him against "thinking aloud" (70). Elsewhere the surrealism of illusions and fantasies momentarily breaks through the ordinary: St. Peter watches his daughter actually turn green with envy, sees his wife's face become plasterlike, and watches his son-in-law (as if transformed into a predatory animal) "pounce" upon his possessions.

Gradually dreams assume the more independent form of memories that well up from St. Peter's past: of buying dahlias in Paris, of staying in France with the Thieraults, and of meeting Tom Outland. Pressure builds until St. Peter breaks connections to the outside world and retreats to his study. "Tom Outland's

Story" follows. An extended memory, "Tom Outland's Story" suggests how strong St. Peter's impulse to dream has become: with it the present is suspended and the memory of Outland *is* the reality. This memory prepares St. Peter for the next movement through the next narrative open window, for by rekindling St. Peter's youthful imagination, it anticipates the "new friendship" with "the original, unmodified Godfrey St. Peter" that follows.

Lying by the lake for hours, St. Peter most fully realizes the voice of his unconscious. He gives himself to "day-dreams" or reveries in which he has "recognitions" of archetypal truths. And "when he was not dumbly, deeply recognizing, he was bringing up out of himself long-forgotten, unimportant memories of his early childhood" (266). St. Peter's memories are of his grandfather's having once lost himself in dreams, as he is doing now; and he begins to understand what he had then ridiculed, when Old Napoleon Godfrey "used to go about lost in profound, continuous meditation" (266).

Today, "violently innoculated with Freud" (Cather's phrase), we look to dreams to unlock secrets of an individual's personality.[19] Willa Cather saw dreams differently. Before Freud introduced the subconscious into the English language there was the reality of dreams, she wrote to Dorothy Canfield Fisher; everyone knew of this reality from personal experience. Cather had recently had one such dream, so extraordinarily powerful and living that there had to be something in it—a sense of perfect harmony and accord and happy affection that persisted despite changed conditions. She had had six dreams like that, she wrote; they always pleased her, and afterwards she never felt she had been fooled. She supposed Freudians would have a glib explanation for what happened, but she preferred her own.[20] Cather wrote that letter in 1922, the period she later said the world broke in two. Unhappy with the present, Cather returned, we are told, to the permanent past; long before that, however, she turned to dreams as stays against loss and change.

Cather scorned the Freudians (or anyone else) who would reduce the mysteries of consciousness to scientific explanations, just as she was impatient with art that reduced meaning to a literal account. When, for example, in a conversation about Jungian analysis, Dr. William Alanson White praised O'Neill's *Strange In-*

terlude as "a fine dramatic experiment to put into words the split between what a character wanted to seem and what he actually was and felt," Cather responded sharply: "Every play that amounted to anything contained secret reactions, inner feelings that diverged from what was actually being said and done by a protagonist on the stage. That could be expressed by action, by facial expression, by tone — it did not need to be inserted as spoken dialogue."[21]

But Cather was not hostile to psychology per se. The same year *The Professor's House* appeared she wrote of delighting in Joseph Collins's book *The Doctor Looks at Literature,* subtitled *Psychological Studies of Life and Letters.*[22] She was especially impressed with his chapters on Lawrence (whom Collins praised for his verbal art and condemned for his "morbid sex consciousness") and on Proust (whom Collins greatly admired). But more important than her liking Collins's comments about specific writers, the fact that she enthusiastically recommended his book suggests that she approved of his general attitude toward psychology, that his attitude coincided with her own.

Collins recognized psychology as a valuable tool, but one that was in danger of becoming a cult, so popular that its limitations were being forgotten. Psychology is "an inexact science," he wrote, which "has no interest in the nature of the soul . . . or in the reality of ideas," but was concerned instead with "the facts of mental life and describing, analysing, and classifying them."[23] When we want to get a true picture of human life, Collins continued, we must turn to the novelist and historian, not the psychologist or physiologist. For their part, novelists might study psychology to sharpen their wits, "but after that the sooner they forget it the better. The best thing that fiction writers can do is to depict that problematic in life in all its intensity and perplexity, and put it up to the psychologists as a challenge."[24]

Within a background of Cather's romanticism, *The Professor's House* is a watershed book. In redeeming St. Peter's original self by dreams, Cather shifted the terms of identity from individuality developed empirically — through experience — to that which lies beneath experience and which is protected from the vicissitudes of time. Until *The Professor's House* she had written from the subject-object assumption of dualism, giving to her characters the responsibility for establishing or attempting to establish a meaningful relationship with the outside world. By the time Cather began writing *The Professor's House* she had taken that premise as far as she could, for she had reached the disillusionment characteristic of late romanticism, which sees the imagination fade and the outside world become corrupted. In *The Professor's House*, Cather found an alternative.

In her next book, *My Mortal Enemy*, Cather traced the casting off of a now-outmoded romanticism; following it, she was never again to write from a literary premise of dualism. *Death Comes for the Archbishop, Shadows on the Rock, Lucy Gayheart*, and *Sapphira and the Slave Girl*—all are books of symbolic forms in the manner of *The Professor's House*.

10 *My Mortal Enemy:* The Idolatry of Sentimental Romanticism

I began to understand a little what she meant, to sense how it was with her. Violent natures like hers sometimes turn against themselves . . . against themselves and all their idolatries.[1]

In *The Professor's House* Willa Cather had cast off outside connections and affirmed a unity that lay beneath them. She was, it would seem, ready to write *Death Comes for the Archbishop,* the book in which she would celebrate the new key of symbolism. Indeed, one would think that she did turn next to her southwestern narrative of two priests, for while critics have written copiously about both *The Professor's House* and *Death Comes for the Archbishop,* they generally have overlooked the novel that separates the two. Even Edith Lewis devoted only a single clause to *My Mortal Enemy,* noting, after an extended discussion of *The Professor's House,* simply that "the following Spring Willa Cather wrote the short novel *My Mortal Enemy* at 5 Bank Street."[2] Other writers have given the book only slightly more attention, calling it "a pure instance of Cather's theory of the ideal novel, the novel démeublé," then faulting it for being excessively stripped down and therefore "a difficult and intransigent book."[3] Seen within Cather's literary career, however, *My Mortal Enemy* seems a fitting conclusion to the first major phase of her writing, a freeing of storytelling from those aspects of romanticism that had reached a dead end.

In her early writing Cather had celebrated the imaginative power of the individual to convert her world into symbolic truth: in *O Pioneers!* the narrator imaginatively transforms Nebraska into a New World Eden; in *The Song of the Lark* Thea Kronborg takes experience into herself, then releases it again, transformed into great art; in *My Ántonia* Jim Burden comes to see an immigrant farm woman as an earth mother. The motive force behind each novel, as behind romanticism in general, is a yearning for connection with the outside world, a belief that the creative imagination is able to perceive the world as an organism in which the finite participates in the infinite.

But in his desire to perceive meaning, the romantic faces the danger of imposing his feelings upon objects that do not deserve them. When that happens, romanticism has degenerated into sentimentality, which is "an overindulgence in emotion, especially the conscious effort to induce emotion in order to . . . enjoy it; also the failure to restrain or evaluate emotion through the exercise of judgment."[4] It is a definition of sentimentalism, which Cather consistently distinguished from the romanticism she revered. In her earliest essays she attacked the one, which she identified with love, and extolled the other, which she identified with religion and art. Her 1899 review of Kate Chopin's *The Awakening,* for example, contains terms that anticipate *My Mortal Enemy:*

Edna Pontellier and Emma Bovary are studies in the same feminine type. . . . Both women belong to a class, not large, but forever clamoring in our ears, that demands more romance out of life than God put into it. . . . they are the victims of the over-idealization of love. . . . These people really expect the passion of love to fill and gratify every need of life, whereas nature only intended that it should meet one of many demands. They insist upon making it stand for all the emotional pleasures of life and art; expecting an individual and self-limited passion to yield infinite variety, pleasure, and distraction, and to contribute to their lives what the arts and the pleasurable exercise of the intellect gives to less limited and less intense idealists. So this passion, when set up against Shakespeare, Balzac, Wagner, Raphael, fails them. They have staked everything on one hand, and they lose. They have driven the blood until it will drive no further, they have played their nerves up to the point where any relaxation short of absolute annihilation is impossible. . . . and in the end, the nerves get even. Nobody ever cheats them, really. Then the "awakening" comes.[5]

The early review expresses Cather's lifelong view that romantic love is by definition sentimental, an excessive emotion for which death is the happiest ending. Had they lived, Bartley Alexander, Marie Shabata, Emil Bergson, and Claude Wheeler would have experienced their own awakenings, and at their deaths we feel relief at what they have been spared.

Consequences of romantic love are not so easily dismissed in *The Professor's House.* Godfrey and Lillian St. Peter were once absorbed in each other, and recollections of their youthful happiness together form a haunting backdrop to St. Peter's solitary discovery of his real self. That memory is made real by the continued presence of Lillian. Though her scenes are relatively brief, they establish her pain over losing that love: her jealousy when her husband begins taking Tom Outland to his study, talking with the boy as he had once talked with his wife; her loneliness when at breakfast she attempts to engage St. Peter in conversation; her thoughtful disbelief when she learns he will not accompany his family to France; her melancholy agreement that their living into middle age has been a mistake, for "we should have been picturesquely shipwrecked together when we were young."[6] Largely through Lillian, Cather evokes the question, How does it happen that "people who are intensely in love when they marry, and who go on being in love, always meet with something which suddenly or gradually makes a difference" (49)?

This is the question Cather addressed in *My Mortal Enemy*, the only novel she devoted to romantic love and the last time she included it at all in her major writing.[7] *My Mortal Enemy* is Cather's version of an awakening.[8] The book is structured by three meetings between the central character, Myra Driscoll Henshawe, and her narrator, Nellie Birdseye, each meeting beginning with a sentimental idea and ending when human reality disproves that idea. In the first the girl Nellie thinks of Myra Driscoll and Oswald Henshawe as timeless lovers giving the dare to Fate; her sentimental notions end when she finally meets Myra Henshawe, disappointingly not a legendary heroine but an aging woman. In the second a fifteen-year-old Nellie visits the Henshawes in New York, her sentimental ideas about marriage ending when she comes upon the couple in the midst of a quarrel. In the third, an adult Nellie finds the Henshawes in a West Coast apartment house, her notions of loyalty shaken when she glimpses Myra's bitterness about her life with Oswald.

The Henshawes' story is one we, like Nellie, have heard since we can remember anything at all. The stock situation of young lovers who defy the world is so firmly part of our cultural heritage that it has become synonymous with "romantic" in the popular use of the term. By Aunt Lydia's account, Myra Driscoll is a one-dimensional heroine in that story, an orphan who, brought up by her great-uncle in a manner worthy of a fairy tale, "had everything:

dresses and jewels, a fine riding horse, a Steinway piano" (12). She falls in love with the dashing Oswald Henshawe; the lovers meet the opposition of their elders (the result of "an old grudge of some kind" [13]), and though risking disinheritance, they secretly elope. The formula story ends, of course, with "they lived happily ever after," but Nellie refuses to allow the Henshawes to remain in a vague timelessness. Despite the fact that they were disinherited, have the lovers been happy? she asks. The rather offhand reply to her question—"Happy! Oh yes! As happy as most people"—elicits Nellie's reflection, "That answer was disheartening; the very point of their story was that they should be much happier than other people" (17).

In asking the same question—what is the point of the Henshawes' story?—we realize there is neither a single point nor a single story. Unlike an objective fact, a story changes each time it is told, for each teller and each listener contributes to its living personality. Who is telling a story and who is listening to it are as vital to its meaning as is its subject. And this first account of the Henshawes' story (there will be many more to follow) is a highly sentimental version, told to a young, impressionable girl by Lydia, Myra's friend and Nellie's aunt.

Lydia is one of those women in Cather's fiction who feed upon others, akin to the three guardians in "The Joy of Nellie Deane," Johanna Vavrika in "The Bohemian Girl," and Mrs. Anderson in *The Song of the Lark*. Tillie Kronborg, Thea's "addle-pated aunt" in *The Song of the Lark,* is Cather's most sympathetic portrait of the type. There is something touchingly generous about the sentimental spinster who tries to make a heroine of Thea, "adapting freely the latest novel she had read."[9] Aunt Lydia is Cather's harshest portrait of the same type, for her sentimentality is mean-spirited and meddlesome, even predatory. Under the guise of friendship she helps Myra deceive John Driscoll, then helps Oswald deceive Myra. Under the guise of giving her favorite niece advantages, Lydia tells the girl her mother doesn't appreciate her, confides that Myra is ruining Oswald, and insinuates he is justified in infidelity. Under the guise of affection she tells the Henshawes' love story to her niece, weaving a web about the girl as she—and others like her—once did about Myra.

This is, then, the first tale teller. In telling her sentimental version of the Henshawes' story to Nellie Birdseye, Lydia initiates the girl into the myth of female happiness through romantic love, of princes who appear to spirit away Sleeping Beauty and her literary cousins to everlasting happiness. For Nellie the old Driscoll place is a story given physical form, set in the middle of her otherwise ordinary hometown. As other adults have long ritualistically told fairy tales to the young, Lydia ritualistically took Nellie for walks about the old Driscoll grounds and told her "again about that thrilling night (probably the most exciting in her life)" when Myra and Oswald eloped. The power of the tale is great. When Nellie was older she often walked about the Driscoll place, independently dreaming the sentimental notions her aunt had taught her: "I thought of the place as being under a spell, like the Sleeping Beauty's palace; it had been in a trance, or lain in its flowers like a beautiful corpse, ever since that winter night when Love went out of the gates and gave the dare to Fate" (17).

But as Nellie is to come to understand, giving the dare to Fate is one thing in a legend and quite another in the real world. Fate for Sleeping Beauty and her prince consisted of circumstances of their birth — family position and class; because they dared to turn their backs on such worldly matters, they were rewarded by everlasting happiness. For them mortality or immortality is not a factor; in a fairy tale, all characters live forever. The question is whether they will do so happily. But for human beings, fate is something else altogether, involving not so much the circumstances of birth as birth itself — that is, the condition of mortality. The premise is of eventual death rather than everlasting life, and this is the fate that Myra and Oswald cannot leave behind. Continuing to live after the thrilling night they eloped, they wrinkle and grow stout, worry about shirt fronts and train schedules. They gradually age; they slowly die. As Nellie recognizes upon first meeting Myra, human reality belies any sentimental story. The heroine Myra Henshawe is ageless youth; at forty-five "the real Myra Henshawe" is "a short, plump woman in a black velvet dress," sadly sensitive to her double chin (19).

First simply by being herself, later by speaking directly of her life, Myra Henshawe emerges as the teller of her own tale, a human story that contrasts dramatically to Lydia's sentimental one. At the time of their second meeting, for example, Myra directly questions the morality of advancing others in love. In a classically romantic setting—a moonlit night, a tower in the distance, a young girl dreaming of love—Myra comments on the human consequences of such dreams: "See the moon coming out, Nellie—behind the tower. It wakens the guilt in me. No playing with love; and I'd sworn a great oath never to meddle again. You send a handsome fellow . . . to a fine girl . . . and it's Christmas eve, and they rise above us, and the white world around us, and there isn't anybody, not a tramp on the park benches, that wouldn't wish them well— and very likely hell will come of it!" (31).

As if learning the lessons Myra is teaching, Nellie ends her adolescence with two revelation scenes. In the first Nellie glimpses the power of art when she hears Madame Modjeska sing "the Casta Diva aria, which begins so like the quivering of moonbeams on the water" (47) and sees "Myra, crouching low beside the singer, her head in both hands, while the song grew and blossomed like a great emotion" (47–48). This is valid romanticism, and as Nellie realizes, it reveals Myra's finest potential, "mysteriously related to something in her nature that one rarely saw, but nearly always felt; a compelling, passionate, overmastering something for which I had no name, but which was audible, visible in the air that night, as she sat crouching in the shadow" (48). The second revelation is a dark one in which Nellie glimpses the pain possible in marriage. Coming upon the Henshawes in the midst of a quarrel, Nellie feels fear, as if she had fallen "from security into something malevolent and bottomless" (51). Her sentimental notions of marriage shattered, Nellie leaves the Henshawes.

At the time of their third meeting ten years later, realism is dominant, inescapably revealed in both setting and action. The setting is "a sprawling overgrown Westcoast city which was in the throes of rapid development—it ran about the shore, stumbling all over itself and finally tumbled untidily into the sea" (57). Here Nellie by chance finds the Henshawes living in a shabby rooming house. Physical changes extend to the Henshawes, who by now appear specters of their former selves. Oswald has "thin white hair and stooped shoulders" and "the tired, tired face of one who has utterly lost hope" (61). But no such simple description could portray Myra Henshawe, who "sat crippled but powerful in her brilliant wrappings. She looked strong and broken, generous and tyrannical, a witty and rather wicked old woman, who hated life for its defeats, and loved it for its absurdities" (65).

In these last scenes Oswald and Myra offer to Nellie alternate stories, much as Lydia and Myra had done earlier. On the one hand Oswald is "a sentimentalist, always was; he can look back on the best of those days when [he and Myra] were young and loved each other, and make himself believe it was all like that"; on the other Myra recognizes "it wasn't. I was always a grasping, worldly woman; I was never satisfied" (88). When Myra speaks so directly of her own life, the effect is dramatic. It is as if a character from a fairy tale—Sleeping Beauty or Snow White—were to take on human form, step forward, sigh, and say, "Let me tell you what it was really like." With painful honesty Myra explains to Nellie, "People can be lovers and enemies at the same time, you know. We were. . . . A man and woman draw apart from that long embrace, and see what they have done to each other . . . when [the feeling] remains so personal . . . something gives way in one. In age, we lose everything; even the power to love" (88–89).

The Henshawes' story has become more personal with each telling. Lydia's sentimental legend gives way to Myra Henshawe's account of her own life, personal truth so painfully honest that, after telling it, she sends Nellie away. Surely, one thinks, this is the most private version possible. Yet in dying Myra speaks yet more intimately, "scarcely above a whisper . . . a soul talking" directly to its god. Her cry, "Why must I die like this, alone with my mortal enemy," has the truth of a deathbed confessional, unsoftened for any human ear.

Nellie initially turned away with a shudder from such private truth. But gradually she grows calmer until she "began to understand a little what [Myra] meant. . . . Violent natures like hers sometimes turn against themselves . . . against themselves and all their idolatries." With these words the scene ends. Nellie offers reassurance that understanding is possible, for she has begun to understand. But she doesn't interpret. In *My Mortal Enemy* understanding is something each person must seek alone. And so we are left to ask, What are these false gods against which Myra Henshawe has turned? and to realize that they are the idolatries of a modern age, in which people seek meaning from an object, satisfaction from the world. Myra Henshawe's tragedy is that she expected a lover to gratify her every need; her triumph is that she turned from her idolatries to the truths of religion. Father Fay, the Catholic priest who attends Myra Henshawe in her last days, prepares the reader for that turn.

It is not unusual for a priest to attend the dying, but here it is the priest who is instructed by his parishioner rather than the reverse. Father Fay recognizes that Myra Henshawe is "a most unusual woman," compares her to saints of the early Church, and contrasts her to sensibilities to his own time. "She's not at all modern in her make-up, is she?" he asks (93). Unlike those who seek meaning from the world, Myra Henshawe speaks of value in quite other terms. Like a marble sphinx, so close to death she seems to have left the mortal world, Myra utters the truth she has reached: "Religion is different from everything else; *because in religion seeking is finding*" (94). Nellie is there to comment: "She seemed to say that in other searchings it might be the object of the quest that brought satisfaction, or it might be something incidental that one got on the way; but in religion, desire was fulfillment, it was the seeking itself that rewarded" (94).

The idea runs through Cather's writing (one need only recall Daniel Forrester's belief that "a thing that is dreamed of in the way I mean, is already an accomplished fact", [10] but it is especially important to the three books in which she was affirming possibilities for imaginative truth in a world broken in two—*The Professor's House, My Mortal Enemy,* and *Death Comes for the Archbishop.* Like Myra Henshawe after him, Godfrey St. Peter realized the futility of seeking satisfaction from an object. Since adolescence he had consciously or unconsciously conjugated the verb "to love" with people, nature, books, and finally with Lillian. His despair in middle age resulted from awakening to the futility of any quest that looks to an object—any object—to satisfy the soul. Myra Henshawe takes his awakening one step further, to identify in religion a different kind of love, one in which "seeking is finding . . . desire was fulfillment." Cather's next major characters—Fathers Latour and Vaillant—were to live by that love.

The Professor's House and *My Mortal Enemy* are pivotal books. Until the early 1920s Cather had affirmed continuities of art and nature, beside which death seemed a little thing. Alexandra will live on in the land she awakened, Ántonia in the races that sprang from her, and even Marian Forrester in her effect upon those she introduced to life. Cather offered no such assurances in *The Professor's House,* where she asked what alternatives remain when continuities are broken and the world cannot satisfy. Godfrey St. Peter confronts extinction and returns not so much to live as to await death. In *My Mortal Enemy* Cather went on with ideas that appeared in *The Professor's House;* she wrote not so much about how people live as about how they die. She established, in other words, a "tragic sense of life."[11] Death frames the book: in the opening scenes, that of John Driscoll; in the final ones, that of Myra Henshawe. As John Driscoll died, so shall his niece, for despite the yearnings of their immortal souls, human beings are doomed to failure by their mortality. Mortality is Fate; the measure of an individual is how he or she meets that inevitable end.

Myra Driscoll's love story is set against this backdrop. In comparison to it the sentimental notion of everlasting love — giving the dare to Fate by romantic passion — is pathetically inadequate. Even when a girl, Nellie Birdseye was disappointed in meeting Myra and Oswald and felt that John Driscoll had got "the more romantic part" after all, for his death seemed a triumph over mortality. When the church went to his coffin, surrounding, receiving, assimilating into its body his body, he seemed translated "with no dark conclusion to the pageant, no 'night of the grave.'" To Nellie it seemed he went "from the glory of the high altar . . . straight to the greater glory, through smoking censers and candles and stars" (18–19). By such a measure the Henshawes' life together is painfully disappointing, a drawn-out conclusion to one thrilling night. But by the same tragic measure, Myra Henshawe's death is triumphant. Like her uncle before her, she gets the more romantic part in the end.

Myra dies by a carefully conducted ceremony in which she officiates over her own rites. She first sees that candles are burning about her body in her room, then she removes her body to a cliff, a natural high altar where she might first receive absolution and then see the dawn by which she is translated into heavenly glory. There are neither human priests nor human mourners at this ceremony; Myra's life has been a refining of personal truth, and she meets death alone. But she has described the moment in advance. When she first visited the cliff where later her body would be found, Myra spoke of the place in terms strikingly reminiscent of her uncle's funeral: "I'd love to see this place at dawn. . . . That is always such a forgiving time. When that first cold, bright streak comes over the water, it's as if all our sins were pardoned; as if the sky leaned over the earth and kissed it and gave it absolution. You know how the great sinners always came home to die in some religious house, and the abbot or the abbess went out and received them with a kiss?" (73). Myra Henshawe's is an audacious ceremony, more magnificent than any church could perform, for it is the sky that bends over her, the dawn that receives her, and nature itself that gives her absolution.

The novel does not end with Myra's death. In the last pages Cather again tempts Nellie with sentimentalism. Faced with the disparity between his memory of a youthful Molly Driscoll and the dying woman beside him, Oswald sacrifices the woman to the memory, and he asks Nellie to do the same: "I don't want you to remember her as she was here. Remember her as she was . . . when she was herself, and we were happy. Yes, happier than it falls to the lot of most mortals to be" (103). His reference to mortals recalls Myra's dying description of him as her mortal enemy; his aspiration to be happier than most mortals suggests the hubris of the sentimentalist, who arrogantly prefers his emotions to all else. Then, in what I consider the most chilling line of the novel, Oswald reveals how far his sentimentalism has taken him: "These last years it's seemed to me that I was nursing the mother of the girl who ran away with me. Nothing ever took that girl from me" (104). Oswald's fierce devotion to the girl he remembers has blinded him to the woman she became; he is the enemy of her mortality. Again Cather uses contrasting scenes to make the moment dramatic. Oswald's wish to remember a girlish Myra "when she was herself" echoes an earlier scene in which Nellie came upon the dying woman in the shabby room and felt the delight of recognizing "she was . . . she was herself, Myra Henshawe."

Nellie Birdseye tells Myra's story not as Lydia or Oswald would have it, but as Myra Henshawe taught her. In doing so Nellie completes her own awakening to a sentimentality that insists people fit themselves into simplistic roles. By the end of *My Mortal Enemy* the once moon-struck girl has become the narrator who combines compassion and objectivity to tell of Myra Henshawe in

all her contradictions—her combination of meanness and greatness, worldliness and spirituality, hatred and love.

Myra Henshawe's story warns against exalting "a common
feeling into beauty," and Nellie Birdseye is profoundly affected by
it—that much is clear. But when we begin to interpret that effect,
we run into difficulty. To argue, as some critics have done, that
Nellie is tragically disillusioned with life is to exercise the reduc-
tive sentimentality that Cather exposes, one which would "expect
the passion of love to fill and gratify every need of life." Only the
Aunt Lydias and Oswald Henshawes of this world would equate
romantic love and life, Cather seems to say. Yet even when we
grant that such love is inadequate and that Myra Henshawe's death
is triumphant, the novel remains troubling. Cather has disproved
conventions about love, then offered sphinxlike riddles in its place:
Myra Henshawe's apparently loving husband is her "mortal enemy"; people are "lovers and enemies at the same time"; in religion
"seeking is finding."

In stripping away conventions to reach a meaning so individual that each character—and each reader—must discover it for
himself or herself, Cather anticipates later writers who similarly
work toward questions rather than answers. Somewhat surprisingly, for example, *My Mortal Enemy* resembles John Fowles' *The
French Lieutenant's Woman*. Like Sarah Woodruff, Myra Henshawe
may have reached her own truth, but she remains elusive to the
reader; and like Charles Smithson, Nellie Birdseye is freed from
conventions, but her freedom is by definition uncharted. In reading Fowles we call such freedom existential; in reading Cather we
are left hanging, for we have come to expect from her something
quite different.

That sense intensifies because *My Mortal Enemy* invites comparison with *My Ántonia* and *A Lost Lady,* novels of aesthetic and
thematic resolution. In 1926 Cather once again used a young narrator to tell the story of an older woman, the classic romantic narrative structure by which a perceiving mind experiences an object.
But Nellie Birdseye is significantly different from her predecessors. Never does she reveal Jim Burden's desire to make Ántonia
his or Niel Herbert's wish to force Marian Forrester to reveal her
truth to him; never does she reveal the familiar tension of a romantic imagination attempting to convert an object into a symbol.

Nellie Birdseye is a highly sensitive recorder rather than a creator, and she is telling Myra Henshawe's story rather than making that story her own. As if beginning where Godfrey St. Peter had left off when he discarded the secondary person he had become, Nellie is not troubled by a romantic ego which projects its desires upon an object, then feels fulfilled or not to the extent that those desires are met. The last of Cather's first-person narrators, Nellie points ahead to subsequent major characters—Fathers Latour and Vaillant, Cécile and Euclide Auclair, Sapphira Dodderidge Colbert.

Part IV. Romanticism in a New Key

In Red Cloud with her parents, Charles F. and Mary Virginia Boak Cather, and her brother Douglass, ca. 1926

11 *Death Comes for the Archbishop:*
A Miracle of Symbolic Sight

Miracles . . . rest . . . upon our perceptions being made finer, so that for a moment our eyes can see and our ears can hear what is there about us always. [1]

Until 1923 or thereabouts, Willa Cather was asking the literary question basic to romanticism: how do subject and object meet? [2] Her responses formed a pattern characteristic of the romantic: in her early books she had celebrated the power of the individual imagination to discover symbolic truth in the outside world, and in later ones she had explored the tragedy of irresolution, asking what is left when imagination fades and nature is corrupted. One wonders what Cather might have written had she continued to address this literary problem: stories of exhausted protagonists vainly searching for their lost youth, or satires blasting a decadent world, perhaps.

But Cather never found negation creative. Having taken the subject-object bifurcation as far as she could, she sought an alternative to it, turning to resources she had long been laying in store. She had written of the Southwest in her 1909 story, "The Enchanted Bluff," before first visiting there in 1912, and she was to go back again and again—in her visits of 1914, 1915, 1916, and in her writing. For Cather the Southwest was a place of beginnings, where one could find truths of human consciousness that reside beneath the complexities of a modern world. As she wrote in a 1916 essay, immediately following her first visit to the Mesa Verde,

The Mesa Verde is not, as many people think, an inconveniently situated museum. It is the story of an early race, of the social and religious life of a people indigenous to that soil and to its rocky splendors. It is the human expression of that land of sharp contrasts, brutal contrasts, glorious color and blinding light. The human consciousness, as we know it today, dwelt there. . . . One has only to go down into Hopiland to find the same life going on today on other mesa tops; houses like these, kivas like these, ceremonial and religious implements like these—every detail

preserved with the utmost fidelity. When you see those ancient, pyra-
midal pueblos once more brought nearer by the sunset light that beats on
them like goldbeaters' hammers, when the aromatic pinon smoke begins
to curl up in the still air and the boys bring in the cattle and the old
Indians come out in their white burnouses, you begin to feel that cus-
tom, ritual, integrity of tradition have a reality that goes deeper than the
bustling business of the world.[3]

In her fiction, too, Cather wrote of the Southwest as offering a
reality beneath "the bustling business of the world." By going into
the earth in Panther Canyon and rising above it on the Blue Mesa,
Thea Kronborg and Tom Outland left behind "the stream of
meaningless activity," and both reached understandings that
"were not expressible in words."[4] Thea Kronborg found remnants
of pots beautifully decorated with geometrical patterns — a crested
serpent's head, a band of white cliff-houses on a black ground —
and her heart went out to those Indian women who, by expending
care upon vessels that would not carry water better because they
were decorated, expressed their desire for something other than
mere survival. Similarly, Tom Outland found in the architecture
of Cliff City the "distinct feeling for design" of an ancient people
who, on their mesa above the world, "lived for something more
than food and shelter."[5] Both Thea and Tom responded to this
feeling with reverence, for "wherever humanity has made that
hardest of all starts and lifted itself out of mere brutality, is a sacred
spot."[6] Both were renewed, even consecrated, by the experience.

In 1925 Cather returned to the Southwest and, like her characters, found renewal. Since those first trips twelve years earlier, she
had come to feel "that the story of the Catholic Church in that
country was the most interesting of all its stories. The old mission
churches, even those which were abandoned and in ruins, had a
moving reality about them; the hand-carved beams and joists, the
utterly unconventional frescoes, the countless fanciful figures of
the saints, no two of them alike, seemed a direct expression of some
very real and lively human feelings."[7] Her curiosity had focused
upon Father Lamy, first archbishop of New Mexico, whose life was
a dramatic example of the dilemma Cather had written of with
Claude Wheeler, Niel Herbert, Godfrey St. Peter, and Myra Henshawe. Here indeed was a sensitive individual caught in an alien
world, and Cather wished to learn about "the daily life of such a

man in a crude frontier society." When she came upon William Joseph Howlett's *The Life of the Right Reverend Joseph P. Machebeuf,* the story of Fathers Machebeuf and Lamy told partially by Machebeuf's letters inserted into the narrative, she found what she needed, "the mood, the spirit in which they accepted the accidents and hardships of a desert country, the joyful energy that kept them going." And there in Santa Fe, "in a single evening . . . the idea of *Death Comes for the Archbishop* came to her, essentially as she afterwards wrote it."[8]

Like Thea Kronborg's epiphany in Panther Canyon, Cather's was a coming together of long-held materials in a revelation about art. Thea had asked, "What was any art but an effort to make a sheath, a mould in which to imprison . . . life?"[9] Now it was as if Cather had taken Thea's question one step further, to ask what if that feeling were not a *means* to convert life (lived experience in the "real" world) into art; what if that feeling *were* the reality? She would write a book in which "the mood is the thing—all the little figures and stories are mere improvisations that come out of it."[10]

That literary problem was profoundly different from the one Cather had posed in her earlier books. In *O Pioneers!* she had asked, What can one make of the Nebraska land by seeing it imaginatively? and in *My Ántonia,* What can one make of a pioneer woman? In *Death Comes for the Archbishop,* she wrote of another reality—not of a place or person, but of a mood independent of the physical world. It was a new starting point, enabling Cather to discard the dualism that had become debilitating and to celebrate literature in a new key—that of symbolism.[11] Cather stayed four months during that visit of 1925, traveling about the country, talking with its people, reading. When she returned to New York and the apartment at 5 Bank Street, she began writing her new book "like a happy vacation from life."[12]

With the first pages of *Death Comes for the Archbishop,* Cather announced that here was something different from the romantic and American western traditions in which she had previously written, with their preoccupation upon individual sensibility, will, and imagination.[13] The prologue presents cardinals in the Sabine hills above Rome, like gods in heaven rather indifferently directing the lives of mortals far distant from them. The effect is to contradict any notion of the heroic individual determining his own and the world's fate: by the end of the prologue, his superiors have decided that Jean Latour, a young parish priest in Canada, will be sent to found an apostolic vicarate in New Mexico. As for the young priest, he is as of yet ignorant of this decision regarding him.

Cather makes the contrast explicit in the first scene of the narrative proper. The opening sentence is familiar to any reader of western American literature: "One afternoon in the autumn of 1851 a solitary horseman, followed by a pack-mule, was pushing through an arid stretch of country somewhere in central New Mexico. He had lost his way, and was trying to get back to the trail, with only his compass and his sense of direction for guides" (17). The individual against the wilderness—it is the staple of the novelist of the American West. Convention has it that the traveller will search in the distance until he sees a landmark—in Cooper's *Pathfinder* four wayfarers glimpse a wreath of smoke circling up against a far ridge; in *The Virginian* the tenderfoot steadies himself against the vast expanses of cattle country by sighting Medicine Bow behind him and Bow Leg Mountains before him. Behind this tradition is the assumption that the individual can successfully pit himself—and it is usually a man who is making his way through an unknown territory—against the physical world.

Latour's reaction is another matter altogether. Cather doesn't show him charting his way physically by the sun or his compass; instead, he orients himself spiritually by a symbol—a juniper shaped in the form of the Cross. His actions contradict rational calculations: he dismounts before the tree, bares his head, and kneels, further exposing himself and his mare to the murderous desert sun. Yet "when he rose he looked refreshed" (19). Similarly, when he becomes disoriented by the heat, he doesn't exert himself one more time, as the conventional western hero would do; instead, "empowered by long training, the young priest blotted himself out of his own consciousness and meditated upon the anguish of his Lord. The Passion of Jesus became for him the only reality; the need of his own body was but a part of that conception" (20).

This early withdrawal from the physical world establishes the pattern for the rest of the book. Unlike western heroes who impose justice and order upon the frontier, Fathers Latour and Vaillant characteristically turn away from worldly matters. They ride from a woman in distress with the knowledge she has been abused cruelly by her husband and will undoubtedly be punished horribly for aiding them. Vaillant prepares a Mexican boy to be hanged, though he knows the sentence is unjust. Latour does not intervene in Martinez's corrupt ministry, nor does he assist Sada in escaping her oppressive employers or interfere when his friend, Carson, persecutes his other friends, the Navajos.

Incongruities aren't unusual in Cather's writing, but her treatment of them here is. Cather gave to Jim Burden, Niel Herbert, and Nellie Birdseye the responsibility for reconciling disparities, or at least attempting to do so. She placed no comparable responsibility on a character in *Death Comes for the Archbishop;* instead she maintained an attitude of acceptance. The friendship between Fathers Latour and Vaillant, for example, the core relationship of the book, is a coming together of such different natures that each is unable to comprehend the other rationally. After working with Father Joseph for twenty-five years, Latour muses of his friend: "He could not reconcile the contradictions of [Father Joseph's] nature. He simply accepted them, and . . . realized that he loved them all" (226). Father Joseph is similarly unable to reconcile contradictions of the Bishop's life, thinking his friend's refined sensibilities would seem better suited elsewhere. Vaillant recognizes that Latour exhibits personal pride, seen most clearly in his vanity concerning his cathedral; and Latour, that the generous Vaillant seems at times materialistic, badgering his parishioners out of good wine, down mattresses, and prized white mules.

Yet the friendship of the two priests is one of great love, the major example of the mood that unifies the narrative and the miracles that run through it. In the book's key passage, Father Latour says, replying to Father Vaillant's view of miracles as "something we can hold in our hands and love":

Where there is great love there are always miracles. . . . One might almost say that an apparition is human vision corrected by divine love. I do not see you as you really are Joseph; I see you through my affection for you. The Miracles of the Church seem to me to rest not so much upon faces or voices or healing power coming suddenly near to us from afar off, but upon our perceptions being made finer, so that for a moment our eyes can see and our ears can hear what is there about us always. (50)

In this passage Cather distills the most important single idea she took from Catholicism—divine love or *agape*. With it, she found in religion the means to continue her lifelong commitment to vindicate imaginative thought in a world threatened by materialism.

The theological virtue of love is the third and greatest of the divine virtues enumerated by Saint Paul (1 Cor. 13:13); it is called charity (*caritas*) or *agape,* and defined as "a Divinely infused habit, inclining the human will to cherish God for His own sake above all things, and man for the sake of God."[14] Divine love is distinct from human love, or *eros,* which is given in response to attractiveness in an object. Eros is the love that Jim Burden felt for Ántonia and Niel Herbert for Marian Forrester. Unlike human love, divine love has its source in God's love and is "divinely infused" into the individual. Because it "has its prototype in the Agape manifested by God . . . it must be spontaneous and unmotivated, uncalculating, unlimited, and unconditional"; it is "the love which loves despite even the repulsiveness of its object."[15]

From the core friendship between Fathers Latour and Vaillant, a joyful mood extends outward, in what appears to be indiscriminate envelopment. Indeed, David Daiches wrote, "it might almost be said that the moral pattern in *Death Comes for the Archbishop* is deficient because the author is warmly sympathetic to everybody."[16] Yet this sympathy *is* the moral pattern. In writing of "human vision corrected by Divine love," Cather follows Catholic teaching that "whosoever sees in his fellow-men, not the human pecularities, but the God-given and God-like privileges, can no longer restrict his love . . . but must needs extend it . . . to all the units of the human kind . . . and *even to enemies.*"[17]

This is not to say that conflict and struggle are absent. Latour recognizes human failings, at times so intensely he feels revulsion, but he moves beyond them to see God-given and God-like privileges. He reflects that though Father Gallegos was impossible as a priest, "there was something very engaging about Gallegos as a man" (84), and though he feels horror at the Indians' ceremonial cave, he liked "their veneration for old customs," which was similar to veneration in his own religion (135). The disorder of Padre Martinez's house was almost more than his fastidious nature could bear, but Latour recognized he "had never heard the Mass more impressively sung than by Father Martinez" (150).

As dramatically, the power of divine love is illustrated by the setting, a desert where "the water holes were poisonous, and the vegetation offered nothing to a starving man. Everything was dry, prickly, sharp; Spanish bayonet, juniper, greasewood, cactus; the lizard, the rattlesnake, —and man made cruel by a cruel life" (278). Here is realism in its most extreme form, rendered in a scene that resembles Cubism in art. Like the Cubist, who eschews a human perspective that organizes objects into forms, Cather created a landscape characterized by the breakdown of form into flattened shapes.[18] When he enters New Mexico Territory Latour is lost in a "geometrical nightmare" in which shapes are repeated so often that the distinction between "featureless" and "crowded with features, all exactly alike" is meaningless. Hills cease to be hills and are flattened cones of a uniform red; the junipers on them cease to be trees and are simply smaller cones of a uniform yellowish-green; finally, even the depth of the cone is lost, and what is life is "the intrusive omnipresence of the triangle" (18).

Yet Fathers Latour and Vaillant find that "their way through the wilderness . . . blossomed with little miracles" (279). There are the obvious miracles—and the book is filled with them. When Latour was lost, a cruciform tree appeared, and when he was near death from thirst, he came upon hidden water. But more important there is the miracle of a mood that defies setting and characters. In a country so alien that it would try the strength of giants, there emerges a sense of greaty beauty, and among people made cruel by a cruel land, there is a feeling of fellowship.

To tell of a harmony that defies time and place, Cather gave to her book only the most cursory chronological structure. She followed Father Latour's life from the time he entered the Southwest as a young priest in 1851 until his death in 1889, and she arranged his experiences in an ascending historical order: early episodes involve ancient Indian rituals, later ones involve Mexican religion and culture, still later ones involve Spanish American culture. But historical time, with its connotations of progress, means little. In the end, though a cathedral has been built, gardens planted, a railroad introduced, such physical changes are relatively insignificant; for as Father Latour "often said, . . . his diocese changed little except in boundaries. The Mexicans were always Mexicans, the Indians were always Indians" (286).

The truths Cather celebrated confound understanding in historical time, and to write of them she followed not a mimetic but an allegorical mode, superbly suited to the religious conceptions excluded from mimetic stories:

In allegory plots are either ritualized or symmetrical, and for these we need another principle of combination of parts, something other than Aristotle's "probability." It will have to be a type of magical causation, for the following reason. Whenever fictional events come about arbitrarily through the workings of chance ("accidents") or are brought about by the supernatural intervention of a superior external force ("miracles"), this accident and this intervention have the same origin, in the eyes of religion and poetic tradition. [19]

Magical causation by accidents, the supernatural, miracles— Cather included them all in the most heterogenous mix of episodes and characters, stories, myths, and legends. Chance or the supernatural intervenes in the picaresque wanderings of the two priests, and a wildly varied gallery of storytellers appear to tell a never-ending litany of tales. The result could be the most awkward combination, yet these parts, so apparently disparate from one another, are seamlessly joined. Cather uses formal correspondences of doubling to unite them, following a principle by which "any two systems of images put in parallel, and kept parallel, will appear to be magically joined—as readers . . . assume a primitive attitude and ask how two levels could fail to be united by occult affinity, if they are thus drawn together by formal correspondence."[20] Doubling is seen first in the central characters, Fathers Latour and Vaillant. Despite their different natures, the two priests seem as one, joined by twinning imagery: their similar clothing; their common history, language, culture; their union in rituals of praying, eating, working; their two white mules.

From her two priests, Cather extends doubling by analogy. Bishop Latour, using the sacramental power of symbolization, recognizes God's work by simile. Apparently alien forms participate in Christian fellowship, as the enveloping miracle of divine love extends to the physical world. The juniper is shaped like a cross; smoke of burning pinion logs is like incense rising to Heaven; the noxious datura produces blossoms like Easter lilies; the rock of Ácoma is like a physical form of Christ's morning. The earth mirrors the sky, for "every mesa was duplicated by a cloud mesa, like a reflection" (95); the people mirror the land and each other. Latour recognizes that "travelling with Eusabio was like travelling with the landscape made human" (232); he and Jacinto are alike in their good manners, he and Eusabio in their nobility. The people mirror the saints, and a priest's life is like Christ's.

Similarly, doubling joins places and cultures. Father Latour recognizes that the settlement of Agua Secreta "was his Bishopric in miniature" (32); his country estate north of Santa Fe recalls a French orchard; his Midi Romanesque cathedral reflects the Old World in the New, and its gold rock reflects the desert country from which it was made. Episodes too mirror one another. A young Father Latour comes upon Agua Secreta, is greeted by shepherds, shares their supper, and afterward reads prayers; his story mirrors that later told by Father Junipero of lost travellers who came upon an oasis, were greeted by shepherds, "sat at their table and shared their supper, and afterward read the evening prayers" (281). The first miracle story of Our Lady of Guadaloupe, who arranged flowers in a shepherd's mantle to create a painting of the Blessed Virgin in robes of blue and rose and gold, is doubled in that of the wild flowers that Father Latour domesticates, a miraculous portrait in blue and rose spread over a desert hillside. Finally, episodes are framed by parallel details. The prologue's setting, in which "waves of rose and gold throbbed up the sky from behind the dome of the Basilica" (13) is doubled by the bishop's golden hill: "The base of the hill before which they stood was already in shadow, subdued to the tone of rich yellow clay, but the top was still melted gold—a colour that throbbed in the last rays of the sun" (244). The Old World heaven at the beginning is mirrored by a New World one at the end.

The effect is of a magical world in which correspondences link heaven and earth, past and present, history and legend. Here is none of the tension by which Jim Burden perceived Ántonia, Niel Herbert worshipped Marian Forrester, or Nellie Birdseye recalled Myra Henshawe. Instead, Cather said, she wrote *Death Comes for the Archbishop* "in the style of legend, which is absolutely the reverse of dramatic treatment," for she wished to write a narrative without accent, as if all human experience measured against the supreme spiritual experience—divine love—were one.[21] For her models, she turned to saints' lives like *The Golden Legend* and to Puvis de Chavannes' frescoes of Saint Genèvieve.

In narrative method Cather's book resembles the saints' lives, which eschew historical reality for devotional mood. When we read the saints' legends we do not ask if a saint was really like that; we are not concerned with questions about individuals living in the physical world. Indeed, "if we are to judge the 'Golden Legend' from an historical standpoint, we must condemn it as entirely uncritical." It is, however, "a complete success" as a book of devotion, "adapted to the simple manners of the common people."[22] This adaptation comes in subject matter, of course, but perhaps even more in the narrator's attitude toward that subject matter. As Père Delehaye writes of saints' lives, the curious thing about legends, hagiographical or otherwise, is that

behind the ultimate author who puts them down in writing, there is a hidden "author," anonymous and manifold, whose memory stretches back through generations: this "author" is the masses, the people themselves. The true matter of the legend is fashioned by the mind and soul of the people, and added to, or even at times substituted for, what is authentically known of the saints. The legends of the saints show us not so much the particular personalities and deeds of a certain number of individuals, as the ideals of the people from whose heart the legends sprang.[23]

Cather's narrator is in the manner of the saints' lives—and quite unlike anything she had previously created. Here is not the rhapsodic universal voice of the speaker in *O Pioneers!*, the individuality of Jim Burden, or the ironic complexity of Nellie Birdseye. Instead, the narrator of *Death Comes for the Archbishop* speaks with reassuring directness, expressing the ideals of a people and offering the security of common values. There is no pronoun in English to represent this narrative voice, a collective yet personal voice into which "he" and "she" are subsumed.

"One summer evening in the year 1848," the narrator begins the story, immediately placing the reader in the comfortable position of hearing a story often told before—"Once upon a time." From the beginning the narrator interprets, selects, resolves. Using foreknowledge, he provides the perspective of a lifetime to introduce a specific moment. In describing Father Vaillant, for example, he writes, "The wiry little priest whose life was to be a succession of mountain ranges, pathless deserts, yawning canyons and swollen rivers, who was to carry the Cross into territories yet unknown and unnamed, who would wear down mules and horses and scouts and stage-drivers, tonight looked apprehensively at his superior and repeated, 'No more, Jean. This is far enough'" (41). Similarly, in an aside about dinner, he anticipates Friar Baltazar's downfall, remarking "The roast was to be a wild turkey, superbly done—but that, alas, was never tasted" (109).

This narrator has the authority of knowledge, which he freely shares. Here are no surprises, no ironic twists or double meanings. When he evokes an expectation, it is often by a direct question which he immediately fulfills by a similarly direct answer. For example, after describing the solitary priest entering the desert, he asks, "How, then, had Father Latour come to be here in the sandhills?" and then immediately answers his question by saying "On his arrival at Santa Fe, this was what had happened" (23). Following the account of the Indian resistance to government persecution, the narrator reports that Manuelito resolved, "I will never cross the Rio Grande," then immediately provides the long view: "He never did cross it. He lived in hiding until the return of his exiled people. For an unforeseen thing happened,"—and tells the story of Manuelito (296). As much as the friendship between Latour and Vaillant, the narrator establishes the happy mood of the book: he takes the reader with him as a companion on a journey of storytelling.

Like the saints' legends, Puvis de Chavannes's frescoes do not evoke questions about experience as it is lived. *Sainte Geneviève en Prière*, for example, includes a shepherd family—father, mother, child—in the right foreground, looking upon Saint Geneviève kneeling with uplifted face before a rudimentary cross protruding from the side of a tree. In the background sheep are clustered to the right and left, and a man watches the kneeling saint from behind a tree. The background and foreground are flat and one-dimensional, so that all parts share an equal importance.[24] The figures are simplified in line, the shepherd and his family suggesting strength in their stylized muscular bodies and classically draped clothing, the kneeling saint suggesting otherworldly holiness in her delicate profile and her flowing hair joining her flowing garment. The effect is allegorical. Each figure represents an idea: the shepherd family the common people, the kneeling saint holiness. Questions the painting may pose (why does the family pause?

why does the kneeling Genèvieve pray?) evoke responses that are allegorically abstract (the family pauses before holiness; Genèvieve prays because she is saintly). There is no cause-effect, no before and after. Like Puvis de Chavannes's figures, the men and women whom Cather's priests meet on their picaresque journey tend to be allegorically simplified: Father Martinez is carnal lust; Father Lucero is miserliness; Friar Baltazar is gluttony; Dona Isabella is childish vanity. As Father Latour recognizes, "each of these men not only had a story, but seemed to have become his story" (183).

As he used simplified lines, so Puvis de Chavannes uses an abbreviated color scheme to unify. A single tone (usually a light, cool one) characteristically infuses his paintings, suggesting that parts share an essential unity. Similarly Cather gave scenes the harmony of single colors or hues: the road to Mora by a lead, slaty gray, Laguna by yellow, Arroya Hondo by pastels, the church scene with Sada by the soft white of the moon on winter snow. Running through the entire narrative and connecting individual episodes are "waves of rose and gold"—colors that throbbed from behind the dome of the basilica (13), touched the hidden treasure of the golden chalice (207) and the golden brown of Madelena's cheeks (210), then lit Latour's golden hill and golden cathedral. And red is poured over scenes by the sun sinking, reflecting a "flash of copper" on St. Peter's (4), a "beautifying light" over the houses of Agua Secreta (31), "a copper glow over the pine-covered ridge of mountains" behind Pecos (119). For this red, especially, Cather uses synaesthesia. Red, the Sangre de Cristo, "liquefies upon occasion" (273) and pulsates through the narrative, joining its parts in a living body of Christian fellowship. It is the pulsating, throbbing red of a beating heart.

The saints' lives and allegorical frescoes, Catholicism and ancient Indian art—these are subjects and modes identified with the past. And at first glance one is tempted to assume Cather retreated from modern tensions to traditional religion and allegorical art. But if one were to classify *Death Comes for the Archbishop*—admittedly a dangerous endeavor with Cather's writing, for it resists classification—it would not be as Catholic or allegorical, but as symbolist. In it, correspondences suggest the sacred quality of symbolization, by which "religion is a gradual envisagement of the essential pattern of human life" to which "almost any object, act, or event may contribute."[25] Trust in that pattern enables divine love and all that follows it—allegorical correspondences, magical causation, talismanic objects.

Cather also used language in the manner of the symbolist, released from discursive logic and empirical reality. When, for example, she wrote of Latour's love for New Mexico, language *is* the conceptualization:

[There is] this peculiar quality in the air of new countries . . . [which] one could breath . . . only on the bright edges of the world, on the great grass plains or the sage-brush desert.

That air would disappear from the whole earth in time, perhaps; but long after his day. He did not know just when it had become so necessary to him, but he had come back to die in exile for the sake of it. Something soft and wild and free, something that whispered to the ear on the pillow, lightened the heart, softly, softly picked the lock, slid the bolts, and released the prisoned spirit of man into the wind, into the blue and gold, into the morning, into the morning! (275–76)

The language entices the spirit to join it by parallelism which hypnotically flows, seductively caresses, until it bursts into ecstatic freedom with the repeated "into the morning." It is irrelevant to ask what the words stand for; the passage will not translate as signs for the physical world. Instead, it follows its own law of generation and has its own movement. Initially emphasis is on the subject, "the air," straining away from physical reality when repeated as the indefinite "something." Release begins when the subject is dropped and the focus shifts to verbs acting on indirect and direct objects ("whispered to the ear . . ., lightened the heart, . . . picked the lock, slid the bolts, . . . released the prisoned spirit"). Finally, the language soars when the focus shifts to prepositional phrases, "into the wind, into the blue and gold, into the morning, into the morning!"

Such language is a highly sophisticated form of symbolization, that impulse for design, pattern, and meaning which distinguishes humanity from mere brutality. But "it is foolish convention that we must have everything interpreted for us in written language," Cather maintained. "There are other ways of telling what one feels": designs on water pots, rituals of cookery, manners of a culture, decorations on churches.[26] She paid tribute to the common impulse behind them all as something sacred, to be treated reverentially. Claude Wheeler learns of the "almost holy traditions" of making German Christmas cakes; Godfrey St. Peter spoke movingly of the saving power of religious rituals; Tom Outland believed that wherever that impulse for design first appeared "is a sacred spot."[27]

In *Death Comes for the Archbishop* Cather wrote of a highly developed power of symbolization which provides meaning to the most ordinary acts and the most disparate objects: a wooden parrot, a desert rock, a tamarisk tree. When the young Latour is lost, he finds his way by recognizing the image of the Cross in a juniper, and he kneels before it; the scene dramatically illustrates the saving power of conceptualization. Later an older Latour again is lost, spiritually rather than physically; he feels himself "an alien," believes "his prayers were empty words," and his soul "a barren field" (211). He is again saved by the power to conceptualize. Kneeling beside the poor servant Sada before "the image of the Virgin, the figures of the saints, the Cross," Latour felt "the beautiful *concept* of Mary" pierce his heart, a "miracle" of love (217–18; my emphasis). Latour's gift to Sada, the figure of the Virgin on a medal, is an unsophisticated but similarly precious symbol of love: "a treasure to hide and guard, to adore while her watchers slept. Ah, he thought, for one who cannot read — or think — the Image, the physical form of Love!" (218–19).

Yet as Cather presents the sacramental quality of symbolization, she suggests also its limitations. *Agape* accompanies trust in a world that is God's word; conversely, anything outside this pattern poses an immense threat. As Susanne Langer writes, symbolic man has "the burden of understanding" by which "he must conceive a world and a law of the world, a pattern of life, and a way of meeting death." Langer goes on: "Now, he can adapt himself somehow to anything his imagination can cope with; but he cannot deal with Chaos. Because his characteristic function and highest asset is conception, his greatest fright is to meet that which he cannot construe — the 'uncanny,' as it is popularly called."[28] This is the horror Cather includes in *Death Comes for the Archbishop* — of a world that includes powers of darkness which taunt the believer, tempting him to abandon faith. For the American Southwest presents enormous risks; physical hardships, of course, but far more important, spiritual temptations of materials that predate form and of a people who exist outside Calvary's sacrifice.

In the prologue is the warning that "the desert down there has a peculiar horror," for "the very floor of the world is cracked open into countless canyons and arroyos, fissures in the earth" of great depths, announcing the horror that extends through the book — of a world untouched by the Creator's hand (7). In the Southwest Latour found a plain of such antiquity and incompleteness that it was "as if, with all the materials for world-making assembled, the Creator had desisted, gone away and left everything" (95). And at Ácoma, Latour felt "a sense of inadequacy and spiritual defeat," for he again confronts something outside his religion: "something reptilian . . . a kind of life out of reach, like the crustaceans in their armour" (100, 103). In the church, "more like a fortress than a place of worship," Latour's feelings were intensified: "He had never found it so hard to go through the ceremony of the Mass. Before him, on the grey floor, in the grey light, a group of bright shawls and blankets, some fifty or sixty silent faces; above and behind them the grey walls. He felt as if he were celebrating Mass at the bottom of the sea, for antediluvian creatures; for types of life so old, so hardened, so shut within their shells, that the sacrifice on Calvary could hardly reach back so far" (100).

Latour experiences this horror most fully when, seeking refuge from a storm, he is taken by his Indian guide into a cave. Initially Latour attempts to construe the cave into symbolic patterns he knows. He perceives the opening as "mouthlike," the surrounding rock as "two great stone lips," and the entryway as "the throat of the cave"; inside, he compares the lofty cavern to a Gothic chapel. But underworld darkness takes him backward through time — to primitive cultures when he feels a vibration that "hummed like a hive of bees, like a heavy roll of distant drums," and then to an even earlier time when he hears from a crack below him "one of the oldest voices of the earth" and realizes that it is "a flood moving in utter blackness under ribs of antediluvian rock . . . moving with majesty and power" (127–30). It is one of the most forceful scenes in Cather's writing. Confronted with "utter blackness" — the nothingness that obliterates physical sense — and "antediluvian rock" — the vastness that obliterates time — Latour meets the abyss, and he turns from it with a shudder. His resolve not to enter a cave again is deeply human and profoundly humble. With it, Cather suggests how vulnerable humanity is to the threat of annihilation.

Cather only touches on such scenes and then passes on. In *Death Comes for the Archbishop* she maintains the joyful energy that she had recognized in the two priests who were her models. She recalled after completing her book that she did not have "much difficulty in keeping the pitch. I did not sit down to write the book until the feeling of it had so teased me that I could not get on with other things. The writing of it took only a few months, because the book had all been lived many times before it was written, and the happy mood in which I began it never paled."[29] She did not leave behind the threat of annihilation, however. For it was to loom increasingly large in her final novels.

12 *Shadows on the Rock:*
The World of the Mind

These coppers, big and little, these brooms and clouts and brushes, were tools; and with them one made, not shoes or cabinet-work, but life itself.[1]

Willa Cather wrote *Shadows on the Rock* at a time of personal upheaval. In 1927 her apartment was to be demolished and she was forced to leave 5 Bank Street, "where she had had fourteen years of the happiest work and living."[2] Always deeply rooted in place, Cather found the move painful. "She felt like a turtle that was losing its shell," Elizabeth Sergeant wrote; "the psychic pain of stripping off this protective integument was unbearable; she was exposed and miserable."[3] Undecided what to do next, she moved with Edith Lewis into temporary quarters in the Grosvenor Hotel, where they would remain for nearly five years. During this time many of Cather's belongings were in storage, and she lived without them in rooms she found dark and cramped.

Cather returned to her family, going to Nebraska for Christmas with her parents. But there too she faced loss. Her father had an attack of angina while she was in Red Cloud, and he died in March, soon after she had returned to New York. His death "was a great shock to her—not only the personal loss, but her realization of the changes it foreshadowed."[4] Cather returned to Red Cloud for the funeral, and there she helped make plans for her mother to go with Douglass, Willa's brother, to California for a rest. But Mrs. Cather suffered a paralytic stroke in December, at which time Cather went to California to be with her. Again, arrangements had to be made for Mrs. Cather, this time for nursing care. Mrs. Cather's illness was long and, for a person of her strong-willed nature, especially painful: "In Willa Cather's long stays in Pasadena, where her mother was cared for in a sanatorium, she had to watch her continually growing weaker, more ailing, yet unable to die. It was one of those experiences that make a lasting change in the climate of one's mind."[5] Finally, during this period Isabelle McClung began the long illness that would end in her death.

Writing *Shadows on the Rock* provided for Cather the center and stability that seemed so missing from the rest of her life. Edith Lewis described it as "a great release" from difficulties, and Elizabeth Sergeant, as "a kind of underground place, to which she could retire for a few hours of concentrated work."[6] Cather's subject also seemed a release: she wrote about "a kind of feeling" about life and fate she admired, "a mental complexion inherited, left over from the past, lacking in robustness and full of pious resignation."[7]

The narrative centers on one year in the lives of the apothecary Euclide Auclair and his young daughter, Cécile, colonists in late-seventeenth-century Quebec; it proceeds by the slight incidents of life itself. Cécile obtains shoes for her friend, Jacques; the two children go sledding; the Auclairs and their friends unwrap a Christmas box sent from France the previous spring; Cécile, soon to be thirteen, receives her first long dress; she goes with their friend Pierre Charron to visit a family on a nearby island; Charron invites Cécile and her father to a supper party, where she hears a parrot talk; the Auclairs' patron, Count Frontenac, dies, and Charron comes to comfort them. In an epilogue the narrator reveals that fifteen years later Cécile is married to Charron and the mother of four sons. Euclide Auclair prepares to leave his shop to join them for dinner.

A twelve-year-old girl living in a remote settlement during the seventeenth century, preserving a pious mood inherited from another age—such materials suggest that Cather was retreating from the twentieth century into the past. Yet through the broader setting within which she placed those materials, Cather addressed modern themes of alienation, loss, despair, and annihilation.

Quebec is built upon a grey rock in the midst of distances that exceed human comprehension. The rock is apparently linked to the larger world by the St. Lawrence river, which is "the one thing that lived, moved, glittered, changed,—a highway along which men could travel, taste the sun and open air, feel freedom, join their fellows, reach the open sea . . . reach the world, even!" (7). Yet this promise of connection is illusory. Across the river is a black pine forest, "the dead, sealed world of the vegetable kingdom"; the river itself ends in the sea, equally threatening with its "mountains of waves" that make up a "wilderness of hostile, never-resting water" (6, 208). Finally, across the ocean lies France, in its decadence as savage and cruel as nature's wildernesses.

In France, where the ruling class was as dark, closed, and hostile as the sealed forest, the Auclairs had lived in their apothecary shop, "a narrow wedge . . . built in next to the carriage court of the town house of the Frontenacs." The Frontenacs' mansion was as remote as Browning's dark tower: it "had only a blind wall on the street and faced upon its own court," where "nothing ever changed." Auclair passed his childhood looking out on the "same stillness" of a tomb, upon "shuttered windows behind their iron grilles, the steps . . . green with moss . . . , the empty stables at the back, the great wooden carriage gates that never opened" (17– 18). Beneath this tomblike surface was further death, a society whose members were strangling in slow agony. By the time he was an adult, Auclair's business had "contracted steadily, so that . . . he scarcely knew where to turn" (30), and he "had seen taxes grow more and more ruinous, poverty and hunger always increasing. People died of starvation in the streets of Paris, in his own parish of Saint-Paul, where there was so much wealth. All the while the fantastic extravagances of the Court grew more outrageous" (32).

Though apparently so different, the forest, ocean, and France pose a common threat. The "suffocation, annihilation" of the forest is similar to "the wastes of obliterating, brutal ocean" (7, 25), and both are similar to a France where one class is preying upon another. They make up the most hostile context of any of Cather's writing, in its metaphysical implications far exceeding the brutality of the first Nebraska stories, where Cather had pitted her early pioneers against a harsh but comprehensible nature. In "On the Divide," for example, she wrote of Canute Canuteson's ten-year battle with his land as one he would not win, yet she knew that future generations *would* succeed, and she enabled Canute in the meantime to at least understand his adversary. Canute "knew by heart every individual clump of bunch grass in the miles of red shaggy prairie that stretched before his cabin"; from his cabin he looked out onto landmarks that were individualized, even named. He lived on a stretch of land in Nebraska known as "the Divide," and by Rattlesnake Creek. A few cottonwoods and elms grew along Rattlesnake Creek, further particularizing the land— enough, Cather wrote, to prevent the settler from shooting himself.[8]

There is no such particularity in *Shadows on the Rock.* The forest across the river is sealed and remote, powerful enough to be a vegetable *kingdom,* but one from which civilized human beings are excluded. It is "an uncharted continent" without symbolic forms, where "European man was quickly swallowed up in silence, distance, mould, black mud, and the stinging swarms of insect life that bred in it" (6−7). The ocean, too, is indescribably vast and powerful; it too is incomprehensible. Like predators stalking their prey, the forest crouches waiting across the river, darkness encircles the settlement, "the grip of still, intense cold tighten[s] on the rock as if it would extinguish the last spark of life" (26), winds blast the rock, and sleet scratches against the colonists' windows.

The colonists can never hope to subdue, adapt to, or even understand such forces. Qualifiers emphasize the unequal terms of the struggle: on the one hand there is nature's immensity, with its wastes of ocean and its unending forest; on the other hand, the diminutives of human endeavour—a little household, a slight apothecary, his young daughter, members of a small colony perched on a tiny rock, supplied annually by little wooden boats. Mere survival seems admirable, and survival with order, decency, and beauty miraculous. And this is the miracle of the Auclairs, "an orderly little French household that went on trying to live decently, just as ants begin to rebuild when you kick their house down."[9]

The marvel is that Cather convinces us of "the strength that came out of flesh and blood and goodwill, doing its uttermost against cold, unspending eternity" (208−9). She does so by presenting the power of domestic ritual. At the center of the book is Auclair's combination shop and home, within which is Cécile's kitchen. From it extend domestic actions that knit together the colonists and enable them to survive. While she is dying, Madame Auclair instructed her daughter about the linen that, properly cared for, would last a lifetime. The legacy she contained in that lesson was "a feeling about life that had come down to her through so many centuries and that she had brought with her across the wastes of obliterating, brutal ocean" (25). Similarly, she taught her daughter to cover the parsley in winter, and in doing so to defy the "grip of still, intense cold [that in winter] tightened on the rock as if it would extinguish the last spark of life" (26).

By such simple actions Cécile maintains an order to which others are drawn. Though the Auclairs cannot conquer the wilderness, they can take in exiles from it. Jacques, child of a prostitute, carries the "bad blood" (52) that threatens to make him an outcast, as Frichette carries inside him the wound he suffered in the wilderness, a rupture that "for a woodsman that was almost like a death-sentence" (138). Blinker too contains within him that which he would flee. In France destined to be one of the king's prison torturers, he sought refuge in the New World, yet he could not escape the memories that haunt him.

Through no fault of his own each of these characters is an unfortunate; each comes scarred to the Auclairs', bearing signs of his past. Blinker appears as a scratching at the window, initially indistinguishable from the savage winds that also scratch there; Frichette comes bearded and dressed as a woodsman, so disguised the Auclairs do not recognize him; Jacques, ragged and dirty from neglect, initially is watched suspiciously. In these characters Cather presented our most basic human fears of being lost, abandoned, tormented; then she traced how each is healed. Brought into the Auclairs' home, Jacques is washed, clothed, and instructed; Frichette is fed; and Blinker is solaced. Most important, each participates in rituals of story telling, by which individual lives are joined to timeless legends.

Tales of hardship and brutality, told in the warmth of the Auclair household, become varicolored designs interwoven with domestic details into a tapestry.[10] *While eating the soup prepared by Cecile,* Blinker tells of the recluse's visit from the angels; later, *after her father stoked the fire,* Cécile repeats the story to him, and during that winter *"by many a fireside* the story of Jeanne Le Ber's spinning-wheel was told and re-told with loving exaggeration" (136; my emphasis). Always there is the fire toward which people draw close. As Blinker told of his past torture, Auclair "poured him a glass of spirits and *put some more wood into the stove"* (159), and when Frichette came to the apothecary's door, Auclair "took the poor fellow back into the sitting-room and gave him his own arm-chair *by the fire"* (138; my emphases).

When repeated, these most ordinary of actions establish the rhythms by which individuals become a family and colonists a community. Domestic activities order the Auclairs' days: awakening to Bishop Laval's bell, then drinking chocolate in the morning, eating soup at noon, visiting with neighbors in the afternoon,

walking in the evening, and, always, telling stories. Seasonal
rhythms weave together the days: each spring ships and swallows
return to the rock and Cécile cares for the linen; each autumn Auclair prepares wood doves. In the forest Pierre Charron "shot up
and down the swift rivers of Canada"; he comes from it to enter,
then leave the Auclairs' home (171). Rhythms run through the
most casual of meetings: When Cécile greets Pierre, "he stood
laughing, holding both her hands and swinging them back and
forth in a rhythm of some sort" (171); when they visit Bishop
Laval, Cécile and Pierre find him "walking up and down the
sanded paths" (175); crossing the river with Pierre, Cécile hears
"from the water itself . . . a deep rhythmic sound" (186). Finally
for years the ships "had been beating back and forth between Canada and the Old World," and stories of the fleet's hardships "were
told over and over in Quebec" (208).[11]

   Thus human rhythms become as reassuringly familiar as natural ones. The mystery is that they occur on a tiny rock in the
wilderness, seemingly lost in darkness, space, and time:

Why, the priest wondered, were these fellows always glad to get back to
Kebec? Why did they come at all? Why should this particular cliff in the
wilderness be echoing tonight with French songs, answering to the
French tongue? He recalled certain naked islands in the Gulf of the St.
Lawrence; mere ledges of rock standing up a little out of the sea, where
the sea birds came every year to lay their eggs and rear their young in the
caves and hollows; where they screamed and flocked together and made a
clamour, while the winds howled around them, and the spray beat over
them. This headland was scarcely more than that; a crag where for some
reason human beings built themselves nests in the rock, and held fast.
(225–26)

Cather has posed the riddle of life itself, to which no answers are
forthcoming. She then deepens the mystery with characters who,
faced with perpetual uncertainties, make vows of perpetual stability. The missionary Chabanel did so because he suffered "an almost
continual sense of the withdrawal of God" (152); then, inspired by
his example, Father Hector made a similar vow. Such loyalty is not
limited to the religious; it occurs in an apothecary's constancy to
his patron, a mother's unswerving fidelity to domestic traditions,
and a daughter's fidelity to her mother's wish.

Loyalty occurs too in the colonists' devotion to the household objects they carried with them into the wilderness. Cather had long used domestic objects to suggest respect for tradition: one thinks of Mrs. Shimerda's goosedown blankets, Mahailey's quilts, the Henshawes' plum-colored curtains. In the Canadian wilderness, such objects seem talismans. Euclide carried with him to Canada his medicinal paraphernalia; as important, he carried a stuffed baby alligator purchased long ago from a sailor by Auclair's grandfather to consecrate the ancestral shop, as it now consecrates Euclide's own in Quebec. And as the stove containing its sacred fire is the center of the Auclairs' kitchen, so the red sofa brought from Paris is the center of their salon, preserved with as careful attention. Madame Auclair lay upon it when she instructed Cécile about the household; after her death, it is as precious to her husband and daughter as the crèche they receive from France. They make a place for the crèche, but off to one side, for "they found the thought of moving the sofa, where Madame Auclair used so often to recline, unendurable" (106). When after the Count's death Pierre Charron accepts Auclair's invitation, "often extended, but never before accepted, of spending the night here and sleeping on the sofa in the salon" (267), the action symbolizes his assumed authority in the Auclair family.

Other objects similarly have sacred qualities. For Jacques, Cécile's silver cup engraved with her name is a chalice. As if before taking communion, before drinking chocolate Jacques "liked to hold [the silver cup] and trace with his finger-tips the letters that made it so peculiarly and almost sacredly hers" (87). The alligator of the apothecary, Madame Auclair's red sofa, Bishop Laval's glass fruit, Cécile's cup—each will remain as a testimony to the people who owned them; each contains a story to be repeated as a priest recites a liturgy. "Even if you died," Jacques says of Cécile's cup, "it would still be there, with your name" (87). [12]

These objects and the domestic rituals they represent ward off chaos, and human beings abandon them at great risk. For her first trip off the Rock, Cécile is taken by Pierre Charron to visit the Harnois family on an island that from Quebec looked pastoral: there the soil was richer, the air more perfumed, the climate more favorable; there the best produce was grown and the most eels were caught. Yet for Cécile it is as if she has been taken by Charron over the river Styx. The Harnois live poorly, perilously close to savagery; Cécile feels revulsion at their dirty bed linen and oppressively closed rooms and, more important, feels a "chilling fear of the night" in such a place (194). Without domestic order to protect her, annihilating darkness is terrifying.

When she returns to the Rock, she makes her own vow of perpetual stability to Canada. As if in the ceremony marking the end of a novitiate, Cécile wishes to kneel down and kiss the earth; as if putting on her habit and taking up her rosary, Cécile puts on her apron and "began handling her own things again":

[Yet] it all seemed a little different. . . . She did not feel like a little girl, doing what she had been taught to do. She was accustomed to think that she did all these things so carefully to please her father, and to carry out her mother's wishes. Now she realized that she did them for herself, quite as much. . . . These coppers, big and little, these brooms and clouts and brushes, were tools; and with them one made, not shoes or cabinet-work, but life itself. One made a climate within a climate; one made the days, — the complexion, the special flavour, the special happiness of each day as it passed; one made life. (197–98)

This is Cécile's epiphany; it marks the end of her youth. Following it, secondary characters bear witness to her maturity: her father remarks, "You are your mother over again" (213), and her aunt sends to her from France a package filled with the fine things of a lady. By making the Auclairs' exile permanent, succeeding scenes almost immediately translate Cécile's commitment into the action. The Count de Frontenac dies, and without his patron, Euclide "felt for the first time wholly and entirely cut off from France; a helpless exile in a strange land" (263). The void is filled when Pierre Charron comes from the woods to comfort the Auclairs, a Canadian to provide the security they previously had felt from their French patron. In an epilogue fifteen years later the isolation that had been threatening has become comforting, and Euclide at last looks forward, believing himself "fortunate to spend his old age here where nothing changed; to watch his grandsons grow up in a country where the death of the King, the probable evils of a long regency, would never touch them" (280).

It would appear that the colonists have resisted change by transplanting French culture to Quebec, yet the irony is that *off* the

Rock nothing has changed—the forest remains unending, the ocean obliterating, and France corrupt—and on it life is *unlike* that of Old France. As if only exiles know the full joys of fidelity, the colonists live more elementally and intensely than others. "There is no other place in the world where the people are so devoted to the Holy Family as here in our own Canada," Madame Pommier says; "I never knew its like at home" (101). As so often, Cather uses nature to make her point. Cécile, fearing she will have to return to France, is more than ever sensitive to the beauty about her: "The glorious transmutation of autumn had come on: all the vast Canadian shores were clothed with a splendour never seen in France; to which all the pageants of all the kings were as a taper to the sun" (228). Transmutation—the change of substances, forms, and conditions from one state into another—is at the heart of *Shadows on the Rock*. And that is the other irony: though nothing is changed off the Rock, on it transmutations have taken place, for from routine actions and ordinary objects the colonists have made life.

Two major symbols convey this idea—the Rock and fire. By 1931 the rock was familiar to readers of Cather, for it had appeared in "The Enchanted Bluff," "Tom Outland's Story," and "The Mass at Ácoma." In her description of Ácoma, Cather explained the symbol. The rock is a sanctuary

very different from a mountain fastness; more lonely, more stark and grim, more appealing to the imagination. The rock, when one came to think of it, was the utmost expression of human need; even mere feeling yearned for it; it was the highest comparison of loyalty in love and friendship. Christ Himself had used that comparison for the disciple to whom He gave the keys of His church. And the Hebrews of the Old Testament, always being carried captive into foreign lands, —their rock was an idea of God, the only thing their conquerors could not take from them. . . . The Ácomas, who must share the universal human yearning for something permanent, enduring, without shadow of change, —they had their idea in substance. They actually lived upon their Rock; were born upon it and died upon it. There was an element of exaggeration in anything so simple![13]

In *Shadows on the Rock* it was as if Cather had moved onto the Rock, with those who had loyalty in substance, and presented the creative potential of such a life. She did so by her second major image—fire.

Fire, "the agent of transmutation,"[14] is at the core of this book, physically and symbolically. Inside Cécile's kitchen is the fire she tends and toward which others draw near, sacred because it transmutes substances, forms, and conditions from one state into another. By it wood from the merciless forest is changed into life giving heat; the material world is changed into the rich odors of fowl roasting and bread baking; fears of chaos are transformed into feelings of comfort; a hostile world becomes a shelter. When Cécile is sick, she remains in bed beside the fire, "dreamily conscious of [the town's] activities and of the lives of her friends; of the dripping grey roofs and spires, the lighted windows along the crooked streets, the great grey river choked with ice and frozen snow, the never-ending merciless forest beyond. All these things seemed to her like layers and layers of shelter, with this one flickering, shadowy room at the core" (157–58). A fire casts shadows that people a bare rock with figures of legend.

The ideas of loyalty and transmutation come together in Cécile Auclair, by whose loyalty the sacred fire is tended and life is created. At first glance Cécile seems a young version of those widely diverse women in Cather's writing who create art from life: Ántonia Cuzak, Marian Forrester, Myra Henshawe, Mrs. James T. Fields. Yet none compares to Cécile, who at ten began making "the ménage for her father," responsible not only for maintaining a comfortable home but for upholding the exacting standards of French culture (10). Cécile is younger, yet more competent and committed than her predecessors: she has the selflessness of her mother (who while dying worried about her husband's delicate appetite and sensitive skin), which she charges with a passionate dedication to domestic details (her eyes darken with concern over a poulet and flush with excitement over a roast; she awakens in the night to cover the parsley). Surely no child was ever as obedient, loyal, and good as Cécile, and if we judge her characterization from a historical standpoint, we must condemn it as completely uncritical.[15] Yet Cather makes no pretense at presenting childhood as it is lived in the real world; instead, in *Shadows on the Rock* she wrote a saint's life to tell of the apotheosis of a French girl into a Canadian Holy Mother.

In essentials Cécile's life could be that of the Virgin Mother, who except in fulfilling her vocation as Mother of Christ remained in the background of events; who was preeminent in purity and obedience, sinlessness, perpetual virginity, mediatorship; and who moved through stages toward sainthood: acceptance of vocation, purification, apotheosis.[16] Signs of Cécile's vocation were evident in her youth, recognized by her mother when she looked into the girl's eyes and said to herself, *"Oui, elle a beaucoup de loyauté,"* and later by Mother Juschereau, who searched in Cécile's face for religious vocation and recognized that Cécile's calling lay in this world (25, 40). Her vocation would be apparent without direction from secondary characters, however; she is unfailingly tender, dutiful, loyal. The only defiant words she utters are a further testimony to her loyalty, for she replies to her father that she will never abandon Jacques in her heart.

As was the Virgin Mother's, Cécile's youth is a time of purification, which "at the higher religious levels [denotes] . . . any of various disciplines or rituals for the moral or spiritual cleansing."[17] Caring for linen, preparing food, tending the fire (in itself a symbol of purification)—all are spiritually cleansing disciplines, repeated until they have become rituals which prepare Cécile for assuming Motherhood.[18]

Most important, Cécile tenderly cares for Jacques, identified by Bishop Laval with the Infant Savior. As the Virgin Mother is a mediator for all living, Cécile is a mediator for the boy: she intercedes for him with her father and Bishop Laval, introduces him to the saints and Jesus, prepares a fête of the crèche especially for him. And like the Virgin Mother, Cécile has a special mediatorship in her concern for both human well-being and for spiritual grace. Cécile declares fervently that she shall always pray for Jacques; at the same time, she recognizes he needs "someone in this world" to watch over him and, when he is dirty, wash his face (231–32).

Scene after scene emphasizes the connection. When, for example, Cécile and Jacques stand before the Blessed Virgin and Child, the human figures seem to mirror the holy ones; and when they go sledding they are surrounded by a splendor that anticipates Cécile's apotheosis:

When Jacques and Cécile ran out into the cold . . . , from the houses along the tilted street the evening candlelight was already shining softly. Up at the top of the hill, behind the Cathedral, that second afterglow, which often happens in Quebec, had come on more glorious than the first. All the western sky, which had been hard and clear when the sun sank, was now throbbing with fiery vapours, like rapids of clouds; and between, the sky shone with a blue to ravish the heart, — that limpid, celestial, holy blue that is only seen when the light is golden.

"Are you tired, Jacques?"

"A little, my legs are," he admitted.

"Get on the sled and I will pull you up. See, there's the evening star — how near it looks! Jacques, don't you love winter?" She put the sled-rope under her arms, gave her weight to it, and began to climb. A feeling came over her that there would never be anything better in the world for her than this; to be pulling Jacques on her sled, with the tender, burning sky before her, and on each side, in the dusk, the kindly lights from neighbours' houses. . . . On a foreign shore, in a foreign city . . . would not her heart break for just this? For this rock and this winter, this feeling of being in one's own place, for the soft content of pulling Jacques up Holy Family Hill into paler and paler levels of blue air. (103–4)

Cécile's tender care of Jacques, the colors of holy blue and gold, the echo of "celestial" (heavenly) with "Cécile" and "clair" (light) with Auclair, the halo-like afterglow behind the figures, the ascent "into paler and paler levels of blue air" — all link Cécile to the Virgin Mother.

Purification continues through "The Long Winter" and climaxes with Cécile's glimpse of darkness on the Île d'Orléans followed by her personal vow of loyalty upon returning to her home, prepared to enter womanhood. And that presents a most interesting problem, for it is as difficult in fiction as in religion to maintain a woman's virginity while commemorating her motherhood. Cather does so by narrative strategy. In the story proper Cather tells of Cécile at twelve and newly thirteen, still wearing the cropped hair and short dresses of her youth and apparently unconscious of her approaching womanhood. When her aunt sends to her the fine things of a lady, she asks, "What did it mean?" (213)

Cather suggests what it means by imagery that further links Cécile to the Virgin Mary. Among her new clothes are two items described in detail: a long, very fine blue silk dress and a gold broach. The long dress of a woman, the colors of the Holy

Mother—they are now Cécile's to don. In seeing them Jacques regards Cécile as previously they had regarded the Blessed Mother and Child: in his eyes, Cécile has become "the loveliest of all the Virgins in Kebec, a charming figure of young motherhood, —oh, very young, and radiantly happy, with stately crown, and a long, blue cloak" (65). Jacques clasps his hands together as if in prayer and looks at Cécile in adoration. "'Oh, Cécile,' he breathed, 'you will be so beautiful'" (214). But Cécile puts on her blue dress only in the privacy of her bedroom, replacing it with a familiar jersey before rejoining her father and friends. The story proper ends with Pierre Charron assuming authority in the Auclair household, not yet married to Cecile.

Cather maintains this virginity by passing over the years of Cécile's marriage, conceptions, and births to an epilogue telling of Cécile fifteen years later, now the mother of four sons. As though she has ascended beyond this world, Cécile lives in the Upper Town beyond the Ursuline convent, where Cather does not present her directly. Instead, Cather describes her mediating effect. As the French girl who married the woodsman, Cécile is the means by which the Old World has joined with the Canadian wilderness. From their union came "the Canadians of the future, —the true Canadians" (278). Implicitly from her love for Canada comes the peace of the epilogue, so unlike the mood of the story proper, with its backward look of homesickness for the Old World and its terror over annihilation in the new one.

Like Cather's other writing, *Shadows on the Rock* is a vindication of imaginative thought in a world threatened by materialism. In it, Cather wrote in the symbolist mode of *The Professor's House* and *Death Comes for the Archbishop*. Settings, characters, incidents—all have the reality of an idea for which capital letters are appropriate: Cécile is Mother, Jacques is Child, the Rock is Loyalty, and the wilderness beyond it Annihilation. Circumstantial reality is largely irrelevant.

It is a far cry from Cather's early writing, in which she began with individuals living in a specific place and time, then presented an imagination interacting with an outside world, awakening a response from it, converting it into meaning. She began with the premise that the outside world was real, then posed the literary

188 ROMANTICISM IN A NEW KEY

question of how to interact with it meaningfully. Her metaphors for her relationship to her subject are telling. In a 1913 interview about *O Pioneers!* Cather recalled her "introduction" to the country, then her desire to be true to it in her writing.[19] Imagery here, as in the novel, suggests that the country is real, responsive, valuable: it sleeps, awakens, stretches. Nearly two decades later Cather described her relationship to another subject for another book, and she uses significantly different metaphors. In writing *Shadows on the Rock* she had "taken [a] seat in the close air by the apothecary's fire," she recalled, and the rest came from that.[20] Inside the shop, by the fire—from such a position one can forget the outside world, and that is precisely the point Cather makes. Our only world is that of the mind, Cather wrote in *Shadows on the Rock* (97). By such a premise life in exile on a rock suspended in time and space is a highly refined human truth, for there can be no illusion that the outside world can supply meaning. One of the most vivid descriptions of Quebec is from Cécile's point of view when she is in bed, her mind working like the flickering fire beside her to cast shadows, people the Rock, create a shelter, purify experience.

To my mind, however, the most interesting questions posed by *Shadows on the Rock* concern the wildernesses Cécile has no comprehension of or curiosity about: the chaos of the forest, the wastes of the ocean, the corruption of France. Cather invests them with intense emotional energy. Who, for example, could forget the forest crouching beyond Quebec?

On the opposite shore of the river, just across from the proud rock of Quebec, the black pine forest came down to the water's edge; and on the west, behind the town, the forest stretched no living man knew how far. That was the dead, sealed world of the vegetable kingdom, an uncharted continent choked with interlocking trees, living, dead, half-dead, their roots in bogs and swamps, strangling each other in a slow agony that had lasted for centuries. The forest was suffocation, annihilation; there European man was quickly swallowed up in silence, distance, mould, black mud, and the stinging swarms of insect life that bred in it. (6–7)

Such a passage leaves one asking about the chaos he glimpses: What is it, and what is it to experience it? These are literary questions Cather posed in her final novels. But first she returned to childhood memories in the volume she called *Obscure Destinies*.

13 *Obscure Destinies:* Unalterable Realities

Wonderful things do happen even in the dullest places.[1]

In the decade before *Obscure Destinies* appeared in 1932, it seemed that Willa Cather had turned from Nebraska as resolutely as had her characters Claude Wheeler and Niel Herbert. After *One of Ours* and *A Lost Lady,* she had written novels about other places (Michigan, the Southwest, Quebec), distant times (the mid-nineteenth century, the seventeenth century), and historical people (French priests in New Mexico and immigrants to Canada). But for the three stories included in *Obscure Destinies,* Cather returned to memories of Red Cloud and Webster County. Childhood friends reappear—Annie Pavelka's husband (along with memories of Charles Cather) as the prototype for the Bohemian farmer Anton Rosicky, Grandmother Boak for Mrs. Harris, Margie Anderson for Mandy, Mr. Richardson and Mr. Miner for Mr. Trueman and Mr. Dillon, and young Willa for Vickie Templeton and the narrator of "Two Friends."[2]

Any such identification of prototypes is useful only up to a point, however. In a letter to Carrie Miner Sherwood, Cather wrote that her stories came from emotion, not from the faces and arms and legs of people she knew.[3] And though Cather did return to early materials for her 1932 volume, her emotions about those materials were different from those of *O Pioneers!* and *My Ántonia.* In her early Nebraska novels Cather's exceptional individuals fulfilled their destinies by rising above the common lot, and her sensitive observers strained to grasp immortal truths in the material world: Alexandra Bergson, to see the beauty of the land; Jim Burden, to see Ántonia as an earth mother; Niel Herbert, to get at the secret of Marian Forrester. Her characters proved their worth by escaping the ordinary—or by attempting to do so; their happiness was, as Jim Burden realized, being "dissolved into something complete and great."[4] The phrase echoes in "Neighbour Rosicky," but with an important difference, for in her story of a Bohemian farmer Cather wrote of happiness not in greatness but in a simple life that was "complete and beautiful." Whereas Cather formerly had pulled away to transcend mortality by converting life into art, she now wrote of accepting life as it is.

As so often, Cather's personal life inspired her art. Beginning in late 1927, events revealed the vulnerability of the places and people which youth takes for granted. Within four years Cather lost two homes (she left her Bank Street apartment in 1927; the next year her parents' Red Cloud home was closed) and both her parents (her father suffered a heart attack in 1927, then died in 1928; her mother suffered a stroke in 1928, became increasingly incapacitated during the next two years, and died in 1931). The two books Cather wrote during this period—*Shadows on the Rock* (1931) and *Obscure Destinies* (1932)—at first glance so different, are thematically complementary: both are about loss, one of home through exile, the other of persons through death. Each contains what the other lacks. In *Shadows on the Rock,* place comes alive, so that Cécile's kitchen seems the living idea of domesticity and the Rock that of faith. By comparison characters seem flat. Because they represent ideas rather than take on lives of their own, they are absolved from the mortal world of change, and death is a distant thing. Madame Auclair is preserved in memory; Euclide Auclair is "scarcely changed at all" by time; Cécile is apotheosized into a Canadian Holy Mother. *Obscure Destinies* is about this subject missing from *Shadows on the Rock.* It is the single volume in Cather's canon about dying (a different subject from death), and it contains Cather's most mature, satisfying treatment of human relationships.

Obscure Destinies opens with a death sentence on its first major character, Anton Rosicky:

> When Doctor Burleigh told neighbour Rosicky he had a bad heart, Rosicky protested.
> "So? No, I guess my heart was always pretty good."

The scientific diagnosis is accurate: within the year Rosicky will die. But the story demonstrates how limited that diagnosis is, and how Rosicky does have a good heart in that which matters—the ability to love. The central tension of "Neighbour Rosicky" involves Rosicky's hunger "to feel sure [his boys] would be here, working this very land, after he was gone," and his fear that his married son, Rudolph, will take a job in the city: "To Rosicky that meant the end of everything for his son. To be a landless man was to be a wage-earner, a slave, all your life; to have nothing, to be nothing." That danger is heightened because the Czech Rudolph has married Polly, an American town girl whose suspicion of country life is evident in her plucked eyebrows, her bobbed hair, and her formal ways with Rudolph's family. "'Good evening, Mr. Rosicky,'" she says when her father-in-law comes. "She never called him father, or Mary mother."

Rosicky cannot stop the drought that is making farming hard for the young couple, nor can he give to them material goods, for he is not a wealthy man. What he has is "a special gift for loving people," offered in quiet, unobtrusive ways. He arranges that Polly and Rudolph will have the family car on Saturday nights; he cleans the kitchen for Polly; he tells of living in London—the most painful time of his life and a subject still so sore it scarcely bears touching—and he does so in English, a "bothersome" language for a long story, so that Polly can hear. Most important, he gives the example of his own contentment.

Cather presents the contentment of her character in the story's slow pace and calm mood. Rosicky quiets those about him by reminding others to talk softly and asking them to withhold questions until after a meal. He slows conversations by drinking coffee from time to time, pausing to take another piece of apple cake, filling his pipe. Alone, he follows the same calm pace. After seeing Polly and Rudolph off to the picture show, Rosicky "took his own time with the dishes. He scoured the pots and pans and put away the milk and swept the kitchen. He put some coal in the stove and shut off the droughts, so the place would be warm for them when they got home late at night. Then he sat down and had a pipe and listened to the clock tick." Simple words and careful details maintain the slow rhythm of the passage. As scenes flow into each other with the same rhythm, their calm seems a preparation for death. After cleaning up at Rudolph's and Polly's, Rosicky walked home and "stopped by the windmill to look up at the frosty winter stars and draw a long breath before he went inside. That kitchen with the shining windows was dear to him; but the sleeping fields and bright stars and the noble darkness were dearer still."

By such pauses Cather presents Rosicky's contentment; by shifting point of view she demonstrates its power. Doctor Ed, a hard-pressed professional who appreciates the welcome of a warm home, pauses to remember breakfast at the Rosickys', and Mary, once a rough farm girl, watches her husband drink coffee and thinks about the gentleness of their life together. These are unconventional materials for fiction, for here important moments are quiet ones when action is suspended, and the most powerful character is one who does little, in the ordinary sense of things. The story's most dramatic scenes occur when action is stopped and Rosicky does nothing. Polly awakens to life while she sits quietly beside her sleeping father-in-law, and Doctor Ed awakens to the beauty about him while he sits silently beside the graveyard where Rosicky lies buried.

Nevertheless, "Neighbour Rosicky" is about power—the power of a man who, like Christ, changes the world by inspiring others to love. Anton Rosicky is a priestly intermediary between flesh and spirit, life and death. Two features, especially, suggest his effect: Rosicky's queer eyes twinkle, so that light surrounds him as if a halo; and his warm touch heals, as if by a laying on of hands. The eyes and the hand, light and warmth, appear in the most casual moments—in the twinkling smile of Rosicky's eyes as he puts more coal in the fire or talks to Mary; in the warmth of his hand as he extends a fee and a handshake to Doctor Ed, an extra ration of oats to his workhorses, an evening in town to Polly. Casual moments, yes, but ones that convey the magical, even sacred power of love. The story's climatic scene is about this power. When Polly sees Anton Rosicky double over in pain, she runs toward him and cries, "Lean on me, Father, hard." In so doing Polly acknowledges Rosicky as her worldly father (shortly thereafter she reveals she is pregnant and, implicitly, will take her place in the Rosicky family) and her spiritual one. When his pain has gone, Polly takes his hand and opens herself to the grace of love:

His hand pressed hers. She noticed that it was warm again. The twinkle in his yellow-brown eyes seemed to come nearer.

"I like mighty well to see dat little child, Polly," was all he said. Then he closed his eyes and lay half-smiling. But Polly sat still, thinking hard. She had a sudden feeling that nobody in the world, not her mother, not Rudolph, or anyone, really loved her as much as old Rosicky did. It perplexed her. She sat frowning and trying to puzzle it out. It was as if Rosicky had a special gift for loving people, something that was like an ear for music or an eye for colour. It was quiet, unobtrusive; it was merely there. You saw it in his eyes, — perhaps that was why they were merry. You felt it in his hands, too. After he dropped off to sleep, she sat holding his warm, broad, flexible brown hand. She had never seen another in the least like it. . . .

Polly remembered that hour long afterwards; it had been like an awakening to her. It seemed to her that she had never learned so much about life from anything as from old Rosicky's hand. It brought her to herself; it communicated some direct and untranslatable message.

Polly's awakening completes the ironic reversal begun in the story's opening exchange: Rosicky dies of a "bad" heart, content in having seen into Polly's good one. His last thoughts are an extended play upon the meanings of "heart," by now used exclusively for the capacity to love: "Girls nowadays didn't wear their heart on their sleeve. . . . Either a woman had that sweetness at her heart or she hadn't. . . . if they had that, everything came out right in the end." Medical distinctions between good and bad hearts are finally irrelevant; as physical organs, all hearts will fail. The important meaning of "heart" concerns the capacity to love, by which continuities are possible—endings with beginnings, one person's dying with new life forming.

Assured about the future of his family, Rosicky feels "the cramp" (not "heart attack") begin again in his chest, and rises, "to get to his bed if he could." Again a play on words presents continuity between life and death, for the bed Rosicky reaches is the grave. As comfortable with death as he was with life, he is ready to rest in "the sleeping fields." Cather prepared for this death by following Rosicky's thoughts as he passed the graveyard, then— something only a highly skilled writer could make work—as he imagined himself lying within it. Upon his death the passage echoes in the reader's mind, as if from the grave Rosicky describes his continuing contentment:

A man could lie down in the long grass and see the complete arch of the sky over him, hear the wagons go by; in summer the mowing-machine rattled right up to the wire fence. And it was so near home. Over there across the cornstalks his own roof and windmill looked so good to him. . . . it was a comfort to think that he would never have to go farther than the edge of his own hayfield. The snow, falling over his barnyard and the graveyard, seemed to draw things together like. And they were all old neighbours in the graveyard, most of them friends; there was nothing to feel awkward or embarrassed about.

For the conclusion Cather moves outside the Rosicky family to Doctor Ed, who again provides a long perspective. As Polly earlier had sat quietly beside the bed where Rosicky slept, Doctor Ed "stopped his car, shut off the engine, and sat there for a while" by the graveyard where Rosicky lay. Like Polly, Doctor Ed has an awakening:

A sudden hush had fallen on his soul. Everything here seemed strangely moving and significant, though signifying what, he did not know. Close by the wire fence stood Rosicky's mowing-machine, where one of the boys had been cutting hay that afternoon; his own work-horses had been going up and down there. The new-cut hay perfumed all the night air. The moonlight silvered the long, billowy grass that grew over the graves and hid the fence; the few little evergreens stood out black in it, like shadows in a pool. The sky was very blue and soft, the stars rather faint because the moon was full.

For the first time it struck Doctor Ed that this was really a beautiful graveyard. He thought of city cemeteries; acres of shrubbery and heavy stone, so arranged and lonely and unlike anything in the living world. Cities of the dead, indeed; cities of the forgotten, of the "put away." But this was open and free, this little square of long grass which the wind for ever stirred. Nothing but the sky overhead, and the many-coloured fields running on until they met that sky. The horses worked here in summer; the neighbours passed on their way to town; and over yonder, in the cornfield, Rosicky's own cattle would be eating fodder as winter came on. Nothing could be more undeathlike than this place; nothing could be more right for a man who had helped to do the work of great cities and had always longed for the open country and had got to it at last. Rosicky's life seemed to him complete and beautiful.

In contrast to the quiet, even the stasis, of the previous scenes, this final one bursts with movement — of horses pulling the mowing machine, of new-cut hay perfuming the air, of wind stirring and neighbors passing. And in contrast to the previous focus on one person's life, specifics here join the universal: a little square of grass is "forever stirred" by the wind; one family's fields run into endless sky; a single man has merged with all of nature. This is a graveyard that is part of life, where the fence separating the living from the dead is hidden with grass, where some neighbors lie inside and other neighbors pass on their way to town. "It is not chaos or death—it is form, union, plan—it is eternal life—it is Happiness": Whitman's words from "Song of Myself" describe Cather's story.[5]

"Neighbour Rosicky" is as Whitmanesque as was *O Pioneers!* In 1913 Cather announced the affinity with her title and then spelled it out with her conclusion—"Fortunate country, that is one day to receive hearts like Alexandra's into its bosom, to give them out again in the yellow wheat, heat, in the rustling corn, in the shining eyes of youth!"[6] In 1928 the affinity is relaxed, natural, unobtrusive—yet nonetheless present as powerfully as ever. Like Whitman, Anton Rosicky bequeathed himself to the dirt to grow from the grass he loved.[7]

In a 1936 essay on Katherine Mansfield, Willa Cather praised the "virtuosity" of Mansfield's short stories, then noted that "it was usually Miss Mansfield's way to approach the major forces of life through comparatively trivial incidents."[8] Cather could have been writing of her own "Old Mrs. Harris," her finest story. It is a simple story, of a woman who has come with her daughter's family from Tennessee to Skyline, Colorado, where she keeps house for them. Here are none of the dramatic incidents of the conventional writer, but instead the seemingly unimportant ones that make up the daily lives of ordinary people: a neighbor brings a coffee cake for Mrs. Harris; a cat dies; the family attends a church supper; fifteen-year-old Vickie wins a scholarship; Victoria Templeton learns she is pregnant; old Mrs. Harris dies. Through such "comparatively trivial incidents," Cather approached "the major forces of life."

The story begins with Mrs. Rosen, the Templetons' cultured, learned Jewish neighbor who tries "to get . . . to the real grandmother" by laying siege to the Templeton home: she spies until she sees Victoria leave, then marches over with her coffee cake to catch Mrs. Harris unawares. But a person can't be "got" that easily. Troubled with the irregular visit, Mrs. Harris is on her guard, and Mrs. Rosen leaves disappointed. The scene establishes the rhythm that continues through the story, between outside and inside, expectation and reality. Before she met the Templetons, Mrs. Rosen was inconsolable, fearing a racket from their children and flies from their livestock; upon coming to know them, she was drawn to their pleasant ways and natural friendliness. She expected Mrs. Templeton as a southern woman to be "willowy or languishing," then found her to be high-spirited, direct, and warmly genuine. She expected the Templeton parlor to be cluttered, then found it neat and comfortable; she expected the Templeton children to be ill-mannered, then found they were most courteous.

Mrs. Rosen's expectations are remarkably similar to a reader's, if my students are representative. Like Mrs. Rosen, these students feel impatience with Vickie, horror at Victoria ("she is a monster," one said), and pity for Mrs. Harris. Yet even as they talk, they move beyond such easy generalizations: someone remarks that the self-centered Vickie is good about minding the baby and thoughtful in buying presents for her brothers; another that the selfish Victoria is loving (she gives her children "a real smile" when she sees them) and generous (without being patronizing, she includes the outcast Maude children in an ice-cream social). And another says that despite her loneliness and her exhaustion, Mrs. Harris is profoundly happy.

By shifting point of view from character to character, Cather maintains this rhythm between outside and inside, expectation and reality. Mrs. Rosen's thoughts about her neighbors are followed by Mrs. Harris's own thoughts, Victoria Templeton's, and Vickie's, until the story resembles a many-faceted gem.[9] The technique resembles that of "Neighbour Rosicky," but its effect is quite different: in "Neighbour Rosicky" points of view come together in a central character, while in "Old Mrs. Harris" individuals seem painfully lonely, each living a secret life which she keeps hidden. Mrs. Rosen does not discuss her sorrow over being childless; Victoria goes into her bedroom and closes the door when she is unhappy; Vickie thinks everyone is an enemy; Mrs. Harris speaks neither of her regret for Tennessee nor of her knowledge she is dying.

Shifting points of view, then, present intensely private lives of very different people; yet even while each individual is solitary, each is part of a family. To read "Old Mrs. Harris" is to experience a double life, "every individual . . . clinging passionately to his individual soul" and, at the same time, participating in a group life.[10] The night Mrs. Harris is dying, we focus upon her, but we know where the others are and what they are feeling: Victoria is in her room, unhappy over her pregnancy; Mr. Templeton is at his farm, where he has enjoyed a chicken dinner and anticipates sleeping in the clean guest bed; Vickie is at her father's office, engrossed in reading; the twins are outside playing with the neighbors; Mrs. Rosen is in Chicago, celebrating her niece's wedding.

Not surprisingly, the contrasts that are fundamental to "Old Mrs. Harris"—the expected versus the unexpected, the interior life of an individual versus the group life of the family—produce irony. There are incidental ironies: one woman desperately wishes for children while another desperately wishes she were not again pregnant, and a man moves his family west to improve their fortunes, only to find reduced circumstances. There are humorous ones: Mrs. Rosen's plump body belies her ideal of a responsibly restrained life, and her actions undercut her thoughts (she accepts a second piece of chocolate cake even as she suffers from tightly bound stays and envies Victoria Templeton's figure). Finally, there are the most profound ironies of human existence: people living in a crowded household are lonely; youth is thoughtless and old age solitary; the miracle of life results in the tragedy of death; as one life is ending, another is beginning.

Though individuals in "Old Mrs. Harris" *feel* these ironies, no one understands them. No one has the keen perception of Anton Rosicky; no one experiences awakenings as did Polly and Doctor Ed. Sometimes characters turn to the folk wisdom of cliché: "[Life] is not at all fair!" (Mrs. Rosen); "Nothing comes easily in this world" (Vickie); "Life hadn't used her right" (Victoria); "Everything that's alive has got to suffer" (Mrs. Harris). Usually, however, individuals don't articulate truths at all; instead they simply rise above discrepancies by loving generosity. One scene serves as an example. When she sees Victoria Templeton nursing the baby, Mrs. Rosen "could not help admiring him and his mother. They were so comfortable and complete. . . . 'What a beautiful baby!'

[Mrs. Rosen] exclaimed from her heart. And he was. A sort of golden baby. His hair was like sunshine, and his long lashes were gold over such gay blue eyes. There seemed to be a gold glow in his soft pink skin, and he had the smile of a cherub." It is a moment of unexpected beauty, in which the woman Mrs. Rosen had thought selfish seems a Madonna with child. And it is one of great generosity—that of a mother feeding her child from her own body, and that of a woman who, bitterly aware she has no children, admires another woman's baby.

Such generosity ignores limitations of age, culture, education, and personality. Victoria regrets her youthful figure and freedom, yet she couldn't resist her twins the moment she saw them, and most surely she will love her new baby as readily. Traditionally southern in her belief that girls should be foolish and romantic, Mrs. Harris cannot comprehend her granddaughter's desire for an education; yet she sees that Vickie has the money to attend the university. Mrs. Rosen is deeply critical of the Templeton's improvident ways, yet she unhesitatingly arranges an unsecured loan to Vickie. Despite their youthful restlessness, the twins sit with their grandmother; and despite her exhaustion, old Mrs. Harris continues to work for her daughter's family. The mystery at the heart of this story is that the family from which individuals are fleeing offers freedom from individuality, and the children who mean unending work for an old woman bring to her youth:

The moment she heard the children running down the uncarpeted back stairs, she forgot to be low. Indeed, she ceased to be an individual, an old woman with aching feet; she became part of a group, became a relationship. She was drunk up into their freshness when they burst in upon her, telling her about their dreams, explaining their troubles with buttons and shoe-laces and underwear shrunk too small. The tired, solitary old woman Grandmother had been at daybreak vanished; suddenly the morning seemed as important to her as it did to the children, and the mornings ahead stretched out sunshiny, important.

Generosity such as this springs from compassion, from sharing in the suffering of another and giving aid or support; it appears in the most dramatic scene in the story. In the hushed stillness of night and by the soft light of an old lantern, Mandy "performed one of the oldest rites of compassion" by rubbing Mrs. Harris's feet. Less dramatic but similarly significant acts of compassion inform the most ordinary of days. The most powerful scene for me is that of Mrs. Harris's young grandson caring for her as she lay dying. Albert gets a wooden crackerbox as a bedside table, puts a clean napkin on it, pumps water until it runs cold and exchanges the tin cup for a glass tumbler; he then gets one of his linen handkerchiefs for his grandmother, loosens the curtains over the windows, and reads to her. Should Mrs. Rosen have visited her neighbor that night, she undoubtedly would have seen the ordinary objects and mean surroundings as signs of neglect, yet each was an expression of the most tender, thoughtful love. "Grandmother was perfectly happy," Cather wrote of her last hours.

Understanding Mrs. Harris's perfect happiness means putting aside pity and feeling compassion. The distinction is central to the story, one toward which shifts in perspective (expectation and reality, outside and inside) and point of view (Mrs. Rosen, Victoria, Vickie, Mrs. Harris) lead. Pity comes from concern or regret for an inferior, and "to be pitied was the deepest hurt anybody could know." Pity is the outside view of Mrs. Rosen or my students when they judge Victoria selfish and believe Mrs. Harris neglected. Compassion is shared suffering, which means shared humanity, for as Mrs. Harris knows, "Everything that's alive has got to suffer." Compassion means realizing that the narrator, describing youth coming closer to age, includes each of us:

Thus Mrs. Harris slipped out of the Templetons' story; but Victoria and Vickie had still to go on, to follow the long road that leads through things unguessed at and unforeseeable. When they are old, they will come closer and closer to Grandma Harris. They will think a great deal about her, and remember things they never noticed; and their lot will be more or less like hers. They will regret that they heeded her so little; but they, too, will look into the eager, unseeing eyes of young people and feel themselves alone. They will say to themselves: "I was heartless, because I was young and strong and wanted things so much. But now I know."

"Two Friends" has an even less conventional plot than the other stories in *Obscure Destinies*: a narrator recalls a friendship that ended with a quarrel over politics. But as Cather explained privately, "Two Friends" was not meant to be about the two men at all, but about a picture they conveyed to a child.[11] She indirectly makes the same point in her story. Beginning it, the narrator muses that "even in early youth . . . we yet like to think that there are certain unalterable realities, somewhere at the bottom of things. These anchors may be ideas; but more often they are merely pictures, vivid memories, which in some unaccountable and very personal way give us courage." Seagulls are seemingly free and homeless, yet "at certain seasons even they go back to something they have known before; to remote islands and lonely ledges that are their breeding-grounds." And like the gulls, people too have retreats. "Two Friends" tells of such a retreat that was lost, a picture that was distorted.

"Long ago . . . there lived two friends," in a time as distant as youth is to the adult. Their friendship was exactly contemporary with the narrator's childhood: it began the year she was born; she knew the two men from the time she was ten; she saw them separate when she was thirteen, on the threshold of becoming an adult. In writing her story Cather told how things seemed to her as a child, who didn't notice certain things and exaggerated others, who looked up at her world and, especially, at the two men she admired. R. E. Dillon was the biggest banker of the community and the proprietor of its large general store; he owned farms "up in the grass country." J. H. Trueman was "a big cattleman" with "a high sense of honour," who "was large . . . about money matters." Together they travelled "to big cities" in the wide world beyond their community, and together they represented "an absence of anything mean or small."

Largeness was, it seemed, the one thing the men had in common. They were opposites in almost everything else. Dillon was Irish, Trueman American; Dillon's face was bony and his body wiry, Trueman's face solid and his body heavy; Dillon was a banker and Trueman a cattleman; Dillon lived a regular life, Trueman an irregular one; Dillon talked well, Trueman was usually silent; Dillon was a Democrat, Trueman a Republican. Such differences were unimportant, however, so long as the two men were alike in essentials, both "successful, large-minded men who had made their way in the world when business was still a personal adventure."

To the child who knew them, the friends seemed as constant as nature itself. "Every evening they were both to be found at Dillon's store," in cold weather inside playing checkers, in spring and summer outside in two armchairs. Gestures and rhythms catch their constancy — the poised and resting hands of each man, the cigar that seemed to belong in Mr. Trueman's hand, "like a thumb or finger," the relaxed rhythms of their good talk and the comfortable silences of their friendship.

Details such as these contribute to the picture at the heart of the story: on moonlit summer nights two friends sit outside Dillon's store, a blind wall behind them and a dusty road before them. A simple picture, yes, but something quite remarkable happens in it. By an outpouring of moonlight and silence, sensations melt together — sound, touch, sight, and taste — and then the two men were most "largely and positively themselves." To the child they seemed celestial bodies in space, catching the white light of the moon and casting dark shadows upon earth:

One could distinguish their features, the stripes on their shirts, the flash of Mr. Dillon's diamond; but their shadows made two dark masses on the white sidewalk. . . . Across the street, which was merely a dusty road, lay an open space. . . . Beyond this space stood a row of frail wooden buildings. . . . These abandoned buildings, an eyesore by day, melted together into a curious pile in the moonlight, became an immaterial structure of velvet-white and glossy blackness, with here and there a faint smear of blue door, or a tilted patch of sage-green that had once been a shutter.

The road, just in front of the sidewalk where I sat and played jacks, would be ankle-deep in dust, and seemed to drink up the moonlight like folds of velvet. It drank up sound, too; muffled the wagon-wheels and hoof-beats; lay soft and meek like the last residiuum of material things, — the soft bottom resting-place.

After such a moment the narrator scarcely needs to explain that "wonderful things do happen even in the dullest places — in the cornfields and the wheatfields." When she goes on to recall, "sitting there on the edge of the sidewalk one summer night, my feet hanging in the warm dust, I saw an occultation," she could be describing the two friends, who "seemed like two bodies held steady by some law of balance, an unconscious relation like that between the earth and the moon." The occultation of Venus that the three saw one night seems a heavenly affirmation of the mysterious balance between the two friends.

That picture of two friends sitting together is one of those "vivid memories" by which we realize "certain unalterable realities, somewhere at the bottom of things"—the purity of high ideas and the constancy of large natures. On such memories we rest our faith that if the material world were distilled, its "last residuum" would be not mere matter but an idea. They are "truths we want to keep."

Friendship between the two men ended, however, when Mr. Dillon returned from a Democratic convention afire with the populism of William Jennings Bryan, so simplistically held that a child could grasp it immediately: "that gold had been responsible for most of the miseries and inequalities of the world; that it had always been the club the rich and cunning held over the poor, and that 'the free and unlimited coinage of silver' would remedy all this." History, politics, religion—all combined in arousing emotions about false ideas, based on nothing at all. "Dillon declared that young Mr. Bryan had looked like the patriots of old when he faced and challenged high finance with: 'You shall not press this crown of thorns upon the brow of labour; you shall not crucify mankind upon a cross of gold.'" High-sounding phrases that, when examined, are nonsensical. Dillon's populism is as comically naive as that of Lou Bergson, another follower of William Jennings Bryan, who argued that populist responsibilities included blowing up Wall Street. [12]

When Dillon became a man obsessed with ideas Trueman held in contempt, their friendship was doomed. Trueman withdrew his money from Dillon's bank, and the rupture was complete. Without the other, each man lost the balance that had made him seem larger than the ordinary: Dillon's talk became shrilly sarcastic; Trueman's silence, heavily grim. Each seemed to become smaller; then each disappeared: Dillon unexpectedly died; Trueman silently left town. From San Francisco came another picture of Mr. Trueman, a sad parody of the largeness and harmony of his former friendship with Dillon. Trueman had taken "an office in a high building at the top of what is now Powell Street," and there he "used to sit tilted back in his desk chair, a half-consumed cigar in his mouth, morning after morning, apparently doing nothing, watching the Bay and the ferry-boats, across a line of wind-racked, eucalyptus trees."

What was lost for the narrator was a picture of equilibrium, a memory of harmony. She is left with the uneasiness of seeking a retreat that no longer exists:

The breaking-up of that friendship between two men who scarcely noticed my existence was a real loss to me, and has ever since been a regret. More than once, in Southern countries where there is a smell of dust and dryness in the air and the nights are intense, I have come upon a stretch of dusty white road drinking up the moonlight beside a blind wall, and have felt a sudden sadness. Perhaps it was not until the next morning that I knew why, — and then only because I had dreamed of Mr. Dillon or Mr. Trueman in my sleep. When that old scar is occasionally touched by chance, it rouses the old uneasiness; the feeling of something broken that could so easily have been mended; of something delightful that was senselessly wasted, of a truth that was accidentally distorted — one of the truths we want to keep.

The breaking of that friendship "has ever since been a regret," Cather wrote, using again a word that in *Obscure Destinies* expresses the deepest losses: Mrs. Harris regrets her home in Tennessee, Victoria Templeton regrets her youth, and Vickie will regret that she heeded Mrs. Harris so little. In "Two Friends" the narrator too regrets a loss, made more painful when unexpectedly she comes upon "a dusty white road drinking up the moonlight." The description of the earth and the moon pouring their energies into each other is as passionate as any Cather wrote, yet here the experience is of beauty without truth, balance without harmony, sound without meaning.

When I began writing about *Obscure Destinies* I responded most intensely to "Neighbour Rosicky" and "Old Mrs. Harris," tacitly agreeing with critics who regard "Two Friends" as a lesser story. I now believe "Two Friends" belongs in the volume, is one of Cather's strongest stories, and is among the most disturbing of her writing. In this, apparently the most impersonal story in the volume, Cather wrote her most personal account of loss. By recalling a vivid memory that she once thought an unalterable reality "somewhere at the bottom of things," then telling how it was "accidentally distorted," Cather questioned the foundations of the romantic's faith. Truth in the sense Cather meant lies beyond accident (the transcendental romanticism of her early writing) or be-

neath accident (the archetypal symbolism of her later writing); because it is unalterable, it provides an anchor, a retreat, a breeding
ground, "a soft bottom resting place." By considering in "Two
Friends" the possibility that this truth can be distorted and lost,
Cather anticipated the dark romanticism of her final novels.

Part V. Dark Romanticism

In New York with S. S. McClure, May 1944, when Cather received the Gold Medal for Fiction of the National Institute of Arts and Letters.

14 The Shadows of Evil:
Willa Cather and Gothicism

As long as every man and woman . . . was a principal in a gorgeous drama with God, glittering angels on one side and shadows of evil coming and going on the other, life was a rich thing.[1]

One characteristic of Willa Cather's romanticism, as of all romanticism, is a faith in the imagination as a means of transcending dualities of human existence. The most memorable passages of Cather's novels present moments of transcendence which affirm that universal truths exist and that through the imagination we can experience them: Alexandra Bergson joining with the Genius of the Divide, Thea Kronborg uniting with art in Panther Canyon, and Jim Burden recognizing Ántonia as a mythic earth mother. When, in the single scene most widely recognized as Cather's, Ántonia emerges from a fruit cave followed by her children, Jim does not see her simply as she appears—a woman with grizzled hair, calloused hands, and missing teeth—but also as a symbol of fertility and goodness. Later Jim reflects that such an experience is one "we recognize by instinct as universal and true," in which "a look or gesture . . . somehow revealed the meaning in common things."[2]

But the extreme intensity of the romantic impulse toward resolution suggests a fear that final revelations may be denied and universal truths unattainable. These two impulses compose two sides of romanticism—the optimistic movement toward resolution in a higher order, and the pessimistic impulse seen when resolution is thwarted and irreconcilables triumph. As G. Richard Thompson notes, "The Gothic is the dark counterforce to optimistic Romanticism" because it "begins with irreconcilable dualities and, as a form, acknowledges the triumph of paradox and ambiguity—the impossibility of ultimate synthesis."[3] Acknowledgement of irresolution underlies the classic Gothic effect of reversal, which appears in the low Gothic of Monk Lewis as well as in the high Gothic of Brontë, Poe, and James: apparent safety is revealed to be illusory, beauty to be grotesque, and good to be evil. The heroine of the Gothic romance, fleeing from the dark villain, sees ahead the cloak of a rescuer and runs toward him in relief, only to see him turn (or drop his hood) and realize that she has approached the villain in disguise; the spectator of a medieval church sees carving that from a distance appears graceful, but on closer view realizes it consists of writhing snakes and demons; the viewer of a Piranesi prison scene sees stairs that appear to offer escape, but on following them finds they lead nowhere.[4]

Such reversals are basic to Cather's writing, initially in ghost and horror stories, later in Gothic themes of "the shadows of evil coming and going." "The Fear That Walks by Noonday" (1894) tells of a football team defeated by the opponent's dead player. It is a highly conventional ghost story, presenting the intrusion of the supernatural into the normal world. The Marathon College football team is playing a rival team whose star player has recently died. As they play, team members begin to fight the wind and to shiver, though bystanders are untouched by the wind or the cold. Like the weather, plays are mysterious: a ball eludes their grasp, a punt that no one made sails eighty yards, and players fall to the ground "for no visible reason."[5]

Two major characters are Horton, the dreamy romantic poet who is a member of the team, and Reggie, the pragmatic team captain. Horton is affected first. Running for a touchdown, he inexplicably throws his arms into the air and falls, "his eyes . . . wide open and full of unspeakable horror and fear, glassy as ice, and still as though they had been frozen fast in their sockets." Marathon loses the game, and the narrator's attention turns to Reggie, who at the postgame banquet sits stiffly correct at the head table, his white face and tense manner revealing his nervousness. Finally even Reggie acknowledges and salutes the supernatural. He proposes a toast "to the twelfth man, who won the game," tips his glass to the empty air "as though touching glasses with some one," begins to laugh, and then, while everyone else flees, falls "to the floor, cursing and struggling and grappling with the powers of darkness."

"The Fear That Walks by Noonday" is crude in conception and execution. It works by the most rudimentary elements of the ghost tale: the strange predominates over the commonplace and the supernatural over the natural; melodramatic terror results from an arbitrary intrusion of the supernatural into the natural. Yet because it *is* crude it is also clear and therefore useful in pointing to something important in Cather's writing: her acknowledgement that human experience contains dark mysteries, inexplicable by ordinary rules of logic but nonetheless there.

Following "The Fear That Walks by Noonday," Cather continued to write ghost stories. "The Affair at Grover Station" (1900) again contains a supernatural being verified by external reality. The narrative frame of the ordinary world encloses within it a ghost tale that disproves the ordinary. Like the Wandering Jew, "Terrapin" Rodgers must tell another his story to relieve his mind: "It's a grewsome tale, and someway we don't like to be reminded that there are more things in heaven and earth than our systems of philosophy can grapple with. However, I should like to tell the story to a man who would look at it objectively and leave it in the domain of pure incident where it belongs. It would unburden my mind, and I'd like to get a scientific man's opinion on the yarn."

Characters and action are conventional: the genial, handsome, and popular Larry O'Toole, a railway man, is murdered by the dark, brooding Freymark, his rival for the favor of Helen Masterson, the beautiful schoolteacher. Freymark deserves comment, for with him Cather begins her gallery of villains, "always the most complex and interesting character in Gothic fiction, even when drawn with a clumsy hand."[6] Of Asiatic descent, Freymark is

a wiry, sallow, unwholesome looking man, slight and meagerly built, and he looked as though he had been dried through and through by the blistering heat of the tropics. His movements were as lithe and agile as those of a cat, and invested with a certain unusual, stealthy grace. His eyes were small and black as bright jet beads; his hair very thick and coarse and straight, black with a sort of purple luster to it, and he always wore it correctly parted in the middle and brushed smoothly about his ears. . . . His hands, of which he took the greatest care, were the yellow, wrinkled hands of an old man, and shrivelled at the finger-tips, though I don't think he could have been much over thirty. The long and short of it is that the fellow was uncanny. You somehow felt that there was that in his present, or in his past, or in his destiny which isolated him from other men.

Romantic echoes abound: of De Quincey's horror over the incomprehensible vastness of time represented by the Asiatic in *Confes-*

sions of an Opium Eater and of Poe's horror of the uncanny—the preternatural aging, the old features in the young body, and the inexplicable mixture of human and inhuman natures in stealthy human beings who resemble cats.

The story develops by intrusions first of evil and then of the supernatural into the ordinary world. When Larry O'Toole does not appear to escort Helen to a ball, his friends try to carry on as usual. The narrator, then a young man, escorts Miss Masterson; Freymark (identified throughout by his red lips) arrives suspiciously late. The ball continues until Larry's wounded dog enters and falls howling at Freymark's feet. The façade of order is broken, the music stops, people mill about, and the narrator departs for Grover Station, where Larry was railway cashier, to seek out the explanation for his absence. In Larry's sleeping room upstairs, signs of disorder and violence heighten the narrator's fears. At last, however, he sleeps, only to awaken to see "a man standing with his back to me, chalking something on the bulletin board." Cather is comically explicit in describing the ghost, with his stiff movements, chalky face, colorless jellies for eyes, and mouth stuffed with white cotton. Upon the ghost's departure, the narrator realizes that he has written on the board the number of a railway boxcar. The narrator has the car traced, and Larry's body is inside, his mouth stuffed with white cotton and blue chalk on his fingertips.

As is apparent from even a brief synopsis, "The Affair at Grover Station" evokes two levels of response. First, as in "The Fear That Walks by Noonday," there is simple terror at a ghost's intrusion into the ordinary world. On this level, terror is accounted for and the mystery resolved when the corpse is found with chalk on its fingers. But the story is far more interesting in the response it evokes to Freymark, in whom Cather carefully crafted the threat of the uncanny. Freymark's catlike grace suggests an inhuman inner nature masked by a human appearance; his Asiatic ancestry suggests an ancient, barbarous time and "a race without conscience or sensibilities." The ambiguities that Freymark presents are not resolved; in the end he simply vanishes, leaving open the possibility of reappearance.

Other early stories present other Gothic ideas. "The Profile" (1907), for example, is an early version of doubling. Aaron Dunlap, a young artist, is intrigued by the contradictory faces of Virginia, a young woman he has been commissioned to paint. One side of her face is a girlish loveliness, the other a "grotesque mask" which "had evidently been caused by a deep burn, as if from a splash of molten metal. It drew the left eye and the corner of the mouth; made of her smile a grinning distortion, like the shameful conception of some despairing medieval imagination." The two halves of the face "absolutely contradict" one another, and while in his portrait Dunlap can ignore one by painting his subject in profile, he cannot reconcile the two.

On her part, Virginia seems oblivious to her disfigurement. It is never spoken of to her, and she never alludes to it. Gradually Dunlap comes to love her not despite but because of the scar, believing that love might heal her by comforting her when she can throw off her mask, recognize it, and weep over it. More important, he recognizes that behind the contradiction there exists a "perfect creature . . . the soul of tragic serenity and twofold loveliness."

Following their marriage, however, Virginia's absorbing interest in the material world and her "feverish admiration of physical beauty" intensifies, while Dunlap's life with her becomes increasingly false. The birth of a child exacerbates rather than heals the split. Eleanor is a sickly baby, with a "wan, aged little face" and "skeleton fingers," and Virginia responds to her daughter as she does to other aspects of the tragic side of existence, ruthlessly ignoring the child as she ignores one half of her own face.

Without the healing power of truth tempered by love, the splitting effect continues. A second Eleanor comes to visit, the beautiful older cousin of the child Eleanor. Eleanor the elder is a true mother to Eleanor the younger, the two drawn to one another as two halves of one nature. In contrast to their loving harmony, Dunlap feels increasing tension with his wife: when he sees her, he sees only her scar—which seems to have grown over her whole countenance—and the "shocking perversity" of her manner.

Finally Dunlap speaks of the scar. Like Geraldine in Coleridge's "Christabel," Virginia goes through death throes when confronted with the truth: her face grows crimson, then gray, she begins to shudder convulsively, and then she disappears. Before she leaves, however, she extends doubling, by placing an explosive in the alcohol lamp of her young cousin, Eleanor. The young woman's face is scarred when the lamp ignites, as Virginia's own face had been scarred years earlier. Immediately after his divorce from Virginia, Dunlap marries Eleanor Vane, apparently able at last to reconcile the tragic disparities of human existence.

"The Profile" is a crude but interesting story. Before now Cather had characteristically presented the grotesque as something external that intruded into human lives, to be exorcised or suffered. In "The Profile" she wrote of a "twofold loveliness," beauty coupled with ugliness, joy with pain; and she proposed that salvation resides in the power of love to reconcile the two. These were ideas that were to reappear in the novels, reaching their fullest development in *Death Comes for the Archbishop*.

In "Consequences" (1915) Cather again used the double to present contradictory sides of human nature, but this time she made the conflict internal. As in earlier stories she moves the reader from the ordinary to the supernatural by a sequence of story tellers: the objective observer, a middle-aged lawyer, Henry Eastman, tells the story he heard from his neighbor, Kier Cavenaugh. Cavenaugh is a Dorian Gray character, for his striking good health and high spirits defy the dissolute life he is living. It is an appearance that belies a dark secret, however; Cavenaugh is pursued by a "haunt," an old gentleman who becomes more ominous with each appearance. Initially he seems strange but hardly gruesome; it is only later that Cavenaugh realizes how lined his face was, how skull-like his head, how dead his hair. The horror that the haunt brings is psychological: he knows everything about Cavenaugh, and throws a bad light on it all. Cavenaugh fights against the haunt's attempts to "establish identity," but in spite of himself feels toward the old man a begrudging compassion and responsibility that make escape impossible, and he commits suicide.

In "Consequences" Cather presented alternative attitudes toward the shadows of her character's past. The feeling of loathing and despair that drives Cavenaugh to suicide is the more obvious one; yet Cavenaugh unexpectedly feels also compassion and responsibility for the haunt, and he will not cast off the grotesque reminder of his past. As so often, the unexpected is that which deserves attention: here an attitude Cather includes in an early story evokes a question about her later treatment of disappointments and shortcomings, those feelings that haunt a person and make her see herself as monstrous by presenting her past in the worst possible light.

What we find is that there is almost no guilt and self-hatred in Cather's writing, and remarkably little self-destructiveness. She created characters who accept responsibility and forgive shortcomings; they recognize that life is hard and bear disappointments with dignity. Alexandra Bergson was blind to the love that led to her brother's and closest friend's deaths, yet she is able to forgive herself and them; Thea Kronborg didn't return to her dying mother's bedside, yet both she and her mother understand that her decision was necessary, and neither interprets it as a failure of love; Victoria Templeton was insensitive to her mother, yet the narrator ends "Old Mrs. Harris" with the knowledge that understanding will come. In looking at the Gothic strain in Cather, we should note what it does not include as well as what it does. It does not include what Ellen Moers noted in the Female Gothic: "the self-disgust, the self-hatred, and the impetus to self-destruction that have been increasingly prominent themes in the writing of women in the twentieth century."[7]

Dark reversals and doubling, grotesques and the uncanny, horror and fear—these are Gothic elements Cather experimented with in her early stories, then integrated into the broader themes of her novels. In *O Pioneers!* Alexandra's ecstasy on the Divide is followed by the Marie-Emil love story, an American version of Keats's Gothic poem, "The Eve of St. Agnes," to which Cather has added a living corpse and a dark graveyard storm scene. As Cather noted in her 1932 preface to *The Song of the Lark,* that novel resembles Oscar Wilde's *The Picture of Dorian Gray,* a story of a psychological double in which an initially desirable new self grows to monstrous proportions and threatens to devour a former one. In *My Ántonia* the apparently idyllic frontier town of Black Hawk contains Wick Cutter, who threatens Ántonia with rape in action strongly reminiscent of the stock gothic thriller. In *One of Ours* Claude Wheeler searches for "something splendid" and finds himself in a nightmarish world of trench warfare, where swimming holes contain corpses and hands reach out from the grave. And in *A Lost Lady* the noble pioneer Captain Forrester is replaced by one of the purest grotesques in American fiction, the reptilian Ivy Peters, as the man who wields power over Marian Forrester.

My Ántonia serves as an example of the irrational that runs through these plains books. One of Cather's sunniest novels, *My Ántonia,* nevertheless contains Wick Cutter, a small-town Gothic villain. Like the Old World castle of countless Gothic tales, the Cutter house is an extension of its owner, a suspended world in which power is unchallenged. Though situated in Black Hawk, the house is "buried in thick evergreens" and secluded. The brooding horror over what occurs within it is heightened because, located in the middle of a thoroughly familiar American small town, its very presence refutes our assumptions about the security of ordinary human existence.

Together the Cutters are a composite monster type of the grotesque, in whom realms usually separated are fused.[8] Wick Cutter erases distinctions between male and female habits (he brushes his whiskers as a woman brushes her hair), human and inhuman (his face contains teeth so white they appear "factory made"), virtue and vice (he is "fastidious and prim about his place," yet "dissolute with women"). As Jim recognizes, "it was a peculiar combination of old-maidishness and licentiousness that made Cutter seem so despicable" (210–11). Mrs. Cutter, the physical manifestation of her husband's monstrous nature, has an appearance wildly incongruous with her habit of painting china: "She was a terrifying-looking person; almost a giantess in height, raw-boned, with iron-grey hair, a face always flushed . . . prominent, hysterical eyes," and Draculan "long and curved" teeth (211).

Because the Cutters exist outside human laws and restraints, it is appropriate that Cather deals with them by the extraordinary measure of exorcism, first the "intellectual exorcism" of comedy,[9] then by the rituals of demonology and art. To save Ántonia from rape, Jim takes her place in her bed at the Cutter house. The ensuing scene is one of the funniest in Cather's fiction, the humor of displacement heightened by a Gothic base narrative in which Jim is the victim-heroine. An edited version of the scene reveals how firmly Gothic it is:

The next thing I knew, I felt someone sit down on the edge of the bed. I was only half-awake. . . . I held my breath and lay absolutely still. A hand closed softly on my shoulder, and at the same moment I felt something hairy and cologne-scented brushing my face. . . . the detestable bearded countenance . . . was bending over me. . . . The hand that held my shoulder was instantly at my throat. The man became insane; he stood over me, choking me with one fist, and beating me in the face with the other, hissing and chuckling and letting out a flood of abuse. (248)

Here laughter turns away the threat of Wick Cutter. Later Cather uses other rituals to lay the Cutters to rest. Wick Cutter shoots his wife through the heart in a manner similar to that prescribed for vampires, then turns his gun on himself; and Ántonia tells their story to her children, like a fairy tale in which the deepest human fears are embodied, made safe by the art of the telling.

Exorcism frees victims from evil; it does not, however, resolve that evil, and in the end the Cutters remain paradoxes to all we consider human. In her mature writing Cather seldom resolves moral ambiguities and contradictions: Claude Wheeler dies, leaving behind a world grotesquely transformed by grasping materialism; Niel Herbert and Marian Forrester leave Sweet Water, now controlled by Ivy Peters.

"The demons of the Gothic—real, imagined, or fabricated—represent a sudden revelation of the uncontrolled forces of the mind as they are reified in the seemingly ordered, real world," writes Maximillian Novak. [10] Before *A Lost Lady* Cather characteristically placed the irrational in external events and people: a constantly evil Wick Cutter threatens a constantly good Ántonia. But beginning with *A Lost Lady* Cather presents within characters capacities for transformation: Marian Forrester's lovely laugh could suddenly become mocking, and beneath her gracious manner lay uncontrolled passion. Irrational possibilities are central in Cather's next book, *The Professor's House,* where beneath the familiar appearance of a middle-aged professor, St. Peter conveys the dark, brooding mystery of the Faustian Gothic hero. His physical characteristics are hallmarks of the type—dark coloring, a hawk nose, black eyebrows, and, especially, piercing eyes: "His wicked-looking eyebrows made his students call him Mephistopheles—and there was no evading the searching eyes underneath them" (13). The description could be of Ann Radcliffe's satanic Italian, Father Schedoni.

Like the Gothic hero, St. Peter has created a distinct world of his own. He isolates himself in his "dark den" beneath which "there was a dead, empty house"; he works there at night, stays until after midnight, surrounded by his "forms," including "a headless, armless female torso, covered with strong black cotton" (15–17). He is lonely and isolated; when he descends to the human world, he seems an alien, on the fringes of society, where he prowls "like a restless leopard" (38).

In the best Gothic tradition by which the hero is also victim, Cather presents St. Peter as a man of humanity, sensitive to the world in which a grotesque materialism threatens to replace that which is fine. Academic standards are giving way to a market mentality, and Tom Outland's legacy is being transformed into an "orgy of acquisition" (154). Frightening transformations are occurring too in his own family. The face of his wife changes, softening when she laughs and hardening when she encounters opposition. Kathleen had attempted repeatedly to sketch her mother, but the monstrous type always appeared: "She tried again and again, but the face was always hard, the upper lip longer than it seemed in life, the nose long and severe, and she made something cold and plaster-like of Lillian's beautiful complexion" (64). Kathleen and Rosamond also undergo bewildering transformations. Most people are aware only of Rosamond's fine beauty, but Kathleen, like Christabel fearful of Geraldine's serpent eyes, sees her sister as predatory, saying that when Rosamond approaches, "I feel hate coming toward me, like a snake's hate!" Under her sister's influence, the ordinarily generous Kathleen becomes jealous: as her father fearfully observes, her pale skin goes through an "ugly, painful tranformation" and literally takes "on a greenish tinge" (85–86).

Confronted with transformations about him in his family, his university, and the world, St. Peter retreats further, to his dark study, to his memory of Tom Outland, and to his former self. This boy's return to St. Peter is as fine an integration of a ghost story into a psychological novel as occurs in American literature. The boy who offers such promise also tempts St. Peter to embrace death, the temptation heightened by Gothic uses of setting and weather. Like Byron's Manfred in his tower, St. Peter is alone in his abandoned house when a storm comes up, further isolating him by its cold rain and heavy wind. Confronted with moral ambiguities he cannot resolve, he falls unconscious. Saved by Augusta, St. Peter lives, but with a modern curse upon his soul: he must live the rest of his days in lonely isolation.

This idea of the irrational breaking through civilized order, making those we love terrifying, is central to *My Moral Enemy*. Though she idealizes Myra Henshawe, Nellie Birdseye is always a little afraid of her, for her charming manner could become suddenly sarcastic, and her tender mouth could become "entirely different, . . . curl and twist about like a little snake." As Nellie realized, "Letting herself think harm of anyone she loved seemed to change her nature, even her features."[11]

When intensified, the experience can be that of opening mysterious veils to glimpse horror so total it obliterates everything. Such dark revelations occurred in Cather's early fictions: in Ivar's cry, "It has fallen," upon the discovery of Marie and Emil's bodies; in the glimpse of Wick Cutter's depravity, the horror of trench warfare, and the sinister threat of Ivy Peters. Yet in these works horror was absorbed by a general mood of positive romanticism: major scenes conveyed transcendent values, or at least the illusion of such values. In *My Mortal Enemy* major revelation scenes are dark reversals. Coming upon Oswald and Myra Henshawe in the midst of a quarrel, Nellie experiences the classic Gothic effect of fear when the ordinary suddenly falls away. The room, which formerly had seemed secure and inviting, seemed suddenly "in ruins" and tomblike: "The air was still and cold like the air in a refrigerating-room. What I felt was fear; I was afraid to look or speak or move. Everything about me seemed evil. When kindness has left people, even for a few moments, we become afraid of them, as if their reason had left them. When it has left a place where we have always found it, it is like shipwreck; we drop from security into something malevolent and bottomless" (51). Later the experience is repeated when Nellie hears the dying Myra Henshawe ask, "Why must I die like this, alone with my mortal enemy?" She felt her "hands grow cold and [her] forehead moist with dread," and it was only later that she grew calmer and began to understand (95–96).

After the dark *My Mortal Enemy*, Cather wrote *Death Comes for the Archbishop*, a book she later recalled writing as "like a happy vacation from life, a return to childhood, to early memories."[12] Even in this sunniest of her books, however, Cather included a Gothic undercurrent. Father Latour and his Indian guide, Jacinto, set out for a village in the Pecos mountains, where Father Joseph had fallen ill with the dreaded black measles. On their way, they were caught in a blizzard, and Jacinto led the way to shelter in a remote cave, used for ancient Indian religious rituals. When he follows Jacinto "through the orifice, into the throat of the cave," Latour "found himself in a lofty cavern, shaped somewhat like a Gothic chapel, of vague outline, — the only light within was that which came through the narrow aperture between the stone lips."[13] Though his need for shelter was great, upon entering the cavern Latour "was struck by a reluctance, an extreme distaste for the place. The air in the cave was glacial, penetrated to the very bones, and he detected at once a fetid odour, not very strong but highly disagreeable." In the cave he heard "the sound of a great underground river, flowing through a resounding cavern. The water was far, far below, perhaps as deep as the foot of the mountain, a flood moving in utter blackness under ribs of antediluvean rock. It was not a rushing noise, but the sound of a great flood moving with majesty and power. 'It is terrible,' he said at last" (127–30).

Latour was a witness to the uncontrolled forces that reside beneath the ordinary, and the experience affected him profoundly. He never spoke of the cave to anyone, and though it had probably saved his life, he remembered it "with horror. No tales of wonder, he told himself, would ever tempt him in a cavern hereafter." For inside he glimpsed forces outside any order as he knew it. This is a scene of high Gothic indeed.

Similar tensions are present in that other remarkably serene book, *Shadows on the Rock*. The gentle domestic order of Cécile and Euclide Auclair exists on a rock precariously suspended amidst primordial darkness, into which they venture only at great risk. Like Father Latour, who felt inexplicable horror in Jacinto's cave, Cécile feels terror when she travels to an island on the fringes of civilization. And as Latour left his cave with horror, so Cécile flees the island in panic to avoid again confronting darkness in such a place. In fleeing, Cécile pays tribute to possibilities basic to the Gothic: that order will disappear to reveal barbarity, that the familiar will drop away into emptiness. In her last two books, *Lucy Gayheart* and *Sapphira and the Slave Girl,* Cather too paid tribute to them.

15 *Lucy Gayheart:* A Female Gothic

Some people's lives are affected by what happens to their person or their property; but for others fate is what happens to their feelings and their thoughts — that and nothing more.[1]

When in the spring of 1933 Willa Cather began writing *Lucy Gayheart,* both her parents had died and the Cather home in Red Cloud had been sold. Though Cather had not lived permanently in Red Cloud since she had gone to Lincoln to attend the university in 1890, it had remained the place to which she returned frequently. These visits had been the focus of her year, as writing each morning was of her days, and the loss of the one profoundly affected the other. At Grand Manan for the summer, Cather was able to work on her new novel only at intervals: the first, uncharacteristically wooden parts of *Lucy Gayheart* reveal her strain.[2] It was not until she was at Jaffrey, New Hampshire, in the autumn that she finally hit her stride; there she wrote the last part "as fast as her pencil could move across the paper."[3] Yet again loss followed. In the months during which Cather was typing and revising her copy, there occurred what Edith Lewis described as "the greatest working calamity of her career":

Her . . . wrist began to be painfully swollen; and when she went one day to the doctor with it, he diagnosed it as a serious inflammation of the sheath of the tendon, and said the hand must be completely immobilized. From this time on she was never free from the threat of this disability, which attacked sometimes her right hand, and less frequently her left. Often for months together she had to wear the steel and leather brace . . . devised for her; it immobilized her thumb, but left her fingers free, so that she was able with some difficulty to sign her name, or to trace a few words at the end of a dictated letter. All this meant that for long periods she was unable to do any writing — she could not even typewrite. She never tried to dictate a piece of creative work. She felt it to be, for her, a psychological impossibility.[4]

Willa Cather's life was changed in other ways. In 1927 she had moved from her beloved Bank Street apartment, difficult to heat and in other ways inconvenient, but the place where she had lived during her most productive years. After living for almost five years in the Grosvenor Hotel, in 1932 she and Edith Lewis had moved into a Park Avenue apartment. There "she enjoyed a comfort and quiet, a protection from outside intrusion, she had never known before; freedom from any care about money; ease and prestige and consideration, and great pleasure in friendship. But she did not get back that power to work which comes from the sense of limitless reserves of strength, to use or throw away."[5]

The novel that came out of these situations and emotions was *Lucy Gayheart*. In it Cather returned imaginatively to the Nebraska home she had lost in her life and to memories of a youth now far behind her. She based her central character upon two girls she had met while living there. From her early years Cather remembered Sadie Becker, who with her family had moved to the small town from New York, where she had accompanied the singer Findley Hypes. In Red Cloud Sadie Becker was known for her skating, her vivacious manner, and her romance with a local boy. The pair met parental opposition, however; he married another, and eventually Sadie Becker left to study music. Cather remembered especially her eyes, and after completing her novel wrote to Carrie Miner Sherwood, asking what their color was; she had written of them as golden-brown, but after finishing her book wondered if they had been grey. Cather's second model was from a later period. After she was graduated from the university, Cather returned to Red Cloud ("Siberia," she postmarked a letter from this period). It was a depressing time, relieved when she attended a dance at another small town, Blue Hill, and talked about the classics and French literature with a Miss Gayhardt, "a fine, delicate, sensitive creative who seemed to her pitiably unsuited to teach school in that remote rough village."[6] The idea of feminine youth wasted remained with Cather, appearing in a short story long before it took final form in her novel.

"The Joy of Nelly Deane" (1911) is an early version of the novel.[7] Like Lucy Gayheart, Nelly Deane is the "gayest" girl in her small community, constantly in motion and flashing with youthful vitality. Cather's 1911 narrator recalls "how, the winter through, we all enjoyed seeing Nell skating on the river or running about the town with the brown collar turned up and her bright cheeks and her hair blowing out from under the round cap"; in an even more explicit parallel, "twice [Nelly] broke through the ice and got soused in the river because she never looked where she skated or cared what happened so long as she went fast enough."[8]

And Nelly Deane, like Lucy Gayheart, is imprisoned in a woman's world. In the early story Cather provides the external trappings of female culture through three women constantly hovering about Nelly—Mrs. Dow, Mrs. Freeze, and Mrs. Spinny. Their apparently good-natured attention has sinister implications in their repressive allegorical names and similarly repressive actions. In the opening scene, these three are preparing Nelly for her role in a theatrical production, fluttering about her until "it seemed as though they would never leave off patting Nell and touching her up." They do not leave off, as it turns out. As Nelly matures, her girlish dreams of marrying a traveling salesman and going with him "to live in Chicago, and take singing lessons, and go to operas, and do all those nice things—oh, everything!" come to naught, and she succumbs to the role she has been groomed for. She teaches school, though she is temperamentally unsuited for the job; she joins the Baptist church and marries the dour Scott Spinny, both of which she is also unsuited for; and she dies from unnecessary complications of childbirth. With each step she is surrounded by her "three guardians," the women who act as fates directing her in the roles she is destined to play.

These fates are overwhelmingly female. In this story women ostensibly serve as attendants for male characters; actually men, undeveloped in their own right, act as a backdrop to women's culture. Thus, although Nelly is pursued by Scott, she is courted by Scott's mother, one of the three guardians; though she is immersed in baptism by the minister, she is brought to the pool by the three women and, following the ceremony, enveloped and taken away by them; she is married to Scott, but in marriage turns to Mrs. Spinny for everything; while dying she sees a doctor but is attended first by Mrs. Spinny and then by all three women.

Setting and action further suggest the female culture that surrounds and engulfs Nelly Deane. Her room, for example, appears in two scenes. In the first, the overall impression of a comforting, secure refuge is undercut by diminutives that suggest the unreality of a child's fairy tale: the room contains "a tiny, white fur rug . . . and the prettiest little desk. . . . It was a gay little room." In the second scene, the room is clearly oppressive, and the narrator feels fear for Nelly, who "sat in that room with all her trinkets, the foolish harvest of her childhood." Action too presents engulfment, imaged in a series of metaphorical drownings: the young Nelly's breaking through the ice while skating, her disappearing beneath the dark water of her baptism, and her dying by complications of the womb. Finally, the structure of the story is that of enclosure by the three women who have surrounded Nelly Deane through her life. After her daughter-in-law's death, Mrs. Spinny takes Nelly's son and daughter, and the last paragraph the three women are again clustered around children who, as Nelly was at the outset, are glowing with "the flush of new beginnings."

"The Joy of Nelly Deane" is a chaste story in which a young author uses a young narrator to tell of girlish dreams, and as such it resembles *Lucy Gayheart* in subject and action more than in tone. In her novel, it was as if a mature Cather had asked, What would have happened to Nelly Deane had she not married but instead had left Riverbend and gone to Chicago to take music lessons? What would have happened to her childish vitality once it was awakened to a woman's passion? Her answer might by Lucy Gayheart, a character of sensitivity and spirit but one who lacks the fierceness of soul and clarity of vision for independent action.

As so often with Cather's writing, plot is apparently conventional. Lucy leaves home to study music in Chicago; falls in love with the singer Clement Sebastian; goes into decline upon his death; returns to her hometown, where on Christmas Eve her life instinct reawakens; and drowns in a skating accident. What Cather does with this plot is not conventional, however. Unexpectedly informing this story of youthful love and loss are echoes of Gothicism, in which a brooding sensitivity to death rules a suspended world, and awakening sexuality is a time of fearsome vulnerability.

As the soul-weary artist, Clement Sebastian is a descendent of the Gothic Byronic hero, a lonely figure beneath whose sophisticated manner lies a secret renunciation of life. In many ways more interesting than Lucy, he recalls Cather's other melancholy, middle-aged characters, Bartley Alexander and Godfrey St. Peter. But while they look to youth to awaken their original selves, Sebastian turns to Lucy because he knows his former self *cannot* be revived. In one of those dark revelations that appear so frequently in Cather's later writing, Sebastian feels the classic Gothic effect of reversal, his experience an early version of the drownings that run through the novel. Following the death of a boyhood friend, Sebastian realizes his own youth is "forever and irrevocably gone" (77). The apparently safe, normal world about him drops away, and "everything . . . had suddenly become unfamiliar and unfriendly" (78). All else follows from this revelation. To save himself Sebastian looks for "one lovely, unspoiled memory" (79), but to compound his horror, he is unable to recall anything worth remembering. It is then that he turns to Lucy.

Lucy Gayheart is unspoiled youth, and Sebastian clings to her as desperately as (though more elegantly than) his accompanist Mockford will later cling to him. In doing so he immerses Lucy in emotions for which she is unprepared: his own terror of emptiness and "love as a tragic force . . . passion that drowns like black water" (31). Love and passion are, indeed, dark, a mesmerizing possession through which runs an ambiguous sexuality. Lucy is aroused by Sebastian's appearance before she hears him sing. At a concert when he comes upon the stage, she responds to his "large, rather tired eyes," the hallmark of the Gothic hero, and to his body, described in sexual imagery as an oval shape sheathed in a black coat with a white waistcoat, that solidly fills the space it occupies. The arousal becomes possession when Lucy hears Sebastian sing "Der Doppelgänger," a song which casts over her a spell, in which she struggles "with something she had never felt before." Lucy lapses into unconsciousness, unaware of Sebastian's exit, only later to realize "there was nobody left before the grey velvet curtain but the red-haired accompanist, a lame boy, who dragged one foot as he went across the stage" (29–31).

From this scene on, Cather's story resembles nothing so much as *Dracula,* Bram Stoker's 1897 tale of dark possession and threatening sexuality.[9] Stoker's Lucy is in some ways the familiar Gothic character, a young unmarried woman, sexually attractive and therefore vulnerable to the dark master of the castle, who is crudely but powerfully presented as an elegantly charming count who at night turns into a huge wolf that breaks through the window of Lucy's bedroom. But Stoker does something most curious in developing this Gothic plot, for he makes his Lucy both victim and villain. She is the classic victim, whose innocence Stoker protects by making sex (thinly disguised as a vampire's possession) something that happens to her while she is asleep, about which she has no memory. But she is also villain, for once initiated, she preys upon others. In her Stoker suggests awakened female sexuality as monstrous, all the more terrifying because hidden beneath an appearance of virginal innocence. Against it the conscious will is powerless; Lucy herself is as unaware of feeling desire as of sleep-walking through the countryside to offer herself again to the dark figure who first possessed her. Similarly, superstition and religion are inadequate: accidents remove the garland of garlic from her neck and the crucifix from her lips. The only way to save her soul, Stoker's men agree, is to dismember her corpse.

But these characters give only lip service to saving Lucy, who is lost to this world from the moment of her seducer's first kiss, and whose immortal soul is at best a secondary concern. Instead, Stoker's characters seek to save themselves *from* her. For *Dracula* is a story of terrifying female sexuality told from a male point of view. Stoker's women are characteristically unconscious or dead; his action focuses on the men, who must recognize and protect themselves from female temptation lurking beneath the purest of appearances. As Lucy's fiancé, Arthur Holmwood is the person most directly threatened by the hideously sexual Lucy, whose kiss means possession. As Holmwood's friend and the man engaged to Lucy's friend, the narrator Jonathan Harker loves a woman as apparently innocent as Lucy once was, but implicitly with a similar capacity to become monstrous. With two doctors, one for the body and the other for the mind, these men form a human pack to confront female sexuality, which, once awakened, is so rapacious that even death will not still it. Only by driving a stake into the heart of Lucy's corpse, cutting off her head, and stuffing her mouth with garlic can the men in Stoker's tale make themselves safe from her insatiable desires.

In *Lucy Gayheart* Willa Cather retells Stoker's tale from a woman's point of view. Here is no male narrator telling about Stoker's Lucy, a character whose feelings we almost never hear about, even at second hand. Instead, this is Lucy's story of awakening desire, vulnerability, and possession. We are, for example, with Lucy when she first sees Sebastian, and we learn about her feelings when she first hears him sing (appropriately, the song of possession is "Der Doppelgänger"). And we remain with Lucy when she lapses into unconsciousness, later finding herself again in her familiar bedroom, but now "tired and frightened, with a feeling that some protecting barrier was gone—a window had been broken that let in the cold and darkness of the night" (32). Had Stoker allowed his Lucy to speak, she might well have described her own first possession in precisely those terms.

In subsequent action Cather presents the paradox that confronts the newly awakened woman, for whom sexuality announces adult desire which she may satisfy only by remaining childlike. Her womblike room violated and her developing self aborted, Lucy returns to an infantile, then presexual state. For what Sebastian does is not to awaken passion in her, but to draw it from her, feeding himself from her as surely as does Stoker's character from his Lucy. As Sebastian embraces Lucy Gayheart, he grows stronger, fresher, younger, while she becomes increasingly passive and dependent. Her pulsating energy gives way to timidity, uncertainty, and bewilderment, until she gives herself up to embraces in which Sebastian's "soft, deep breathing seemed to drink her up entirely" (87). Ultimately, her comfort is that of the womb. Lying in the dark against his shoulder, "she felt herself drifting again into his breathing, into his heart-beats" (89).

Cather further suggests Sebastian's ominous effect by secondary characterization and setting. She provides a background of Sebastian's past relationships with youth discarded or prematurely aging: the "nice young boy" he took into his house, then sent away when his wife became jealous, and the uncanny figures who attend him, the valet Guiseppe and the accompanist Mockford. Both seem boyish yet aged, as if youth had been drained from them, leaving them unnaturally old. And when Sebastian takes Lucy into his studio, it is as to a place as isolated, remote, and strange as Count Dracula's mountaintop castle. With him there, Lucy is "shut away from the rest of the world. It was as if they were on the lonely spur of a mountain, enveloped by mist" (75). Cather further envelops their relationship in mystery by writing almost nothing about Lucy's playing for Sebastian and little about art. Art, like love, provides the façade beneath which age seeks to stave off death by feeding upon youth. Like Stoker's Lucy, Lucy Gayheart seems largely unconscious when with Sebastian; she is happiest when, back in her own room at night, she recalls the day.

It is this loss of a self that is most chilling in Lucy's relationship to Sebastian, for as he draws life from her, he leaves her with emptiness and estrangement. After their first embrace, in which he took from her youthful love and gave to her his renouncement of life, she felt "far away from herself . . . as if everything were on the point of vanishing." Henceforth, her life submerged in his, Lucy ceases to be herself; she recognizes that by sending her away, "he could sweep her existence blank" (87–88).

That is precisely what happens. When Lucy hears Sebastian will go on tour, she feels "an enormous emptiness had opened on all sides of her" (116). The scene echoes Sebastian's revelation of emptiness and anticipates both characters' later physical drowning. In stressing Lucy's enforced passivity, Cather writes a female version of this classic Gothic effect: "It was strange, to feel everything slipping away from one and to have no power to struggle, no right to complain. One had to sit with folded hands and see it all go" (117–18).

Taking her youth with him, Sebastian leaves Lucy with his cast-off loneliness and sorrow. She returns to his empty study, where "all her companionship with him was shut up" (131), and she visits the church where she had seen him at a funeral, "a place sacred to sorrows she herself had never known; but she knelt in the spot where he had knelt, and prayed for him" (136). Later when she learns of Sebastian's death, she returns to Haverford, a pale, lifeless ghost of her former self. Her estrangement from the human world is such that she dreads to touch anything in her own house, lies tense even in her own bed, and sometimes is afraid of sleep, for "there had been nights when she lost consciousness only to drop into an ice-cold lake and struggle to free a drowning man from a white thing that clung to him. His eyes were always shut as if he were already dead; but the green eyes of the other, behind his shoulder, were open, full of terror and greed" (157–58).

As if to break an evil spell, Lucy turns to her hometown suitor, Harry Gordon, to look at her in the old way, with life. Like Stoker's Arthur Holmwood, Harry Gordon is the attractive and wealthy man who wished to marry Lucy, but flees not when he believes Lucy loves another man but when he believes she has had sex with him. With his "fine physical balance" (97) and his "physical force, [and] his big well-kept body" (112), Harry Gordon is a man of this world. Yet beneath the well-tended appearance and "jocular masks" there is real feeling (109). He is a complex and sympathetic figure—capable of showing both generosity and cruelty, of keeping others at a distance and of lowering his guard with Lucy. Lucy Gayheart's most vital human moments are with him, skating, attending an opera, visiting a museum. Unlike Sebastian, who draws her out of this world, Gordon draws her into it. But Gordon too seeks to possess Lucy, and his scenes with her are shot through with his assumptions of dominance. Even after his marriage to another woman, he is confident of his "ultimate mastery" over Lucy (217).

Lucy's struggle culminates on Christmas Eve. Lucy, who had in Chicago looked through her bedroom window with foreboding at the black night that threatened to drown her, now "was throbbing with excitement. . . . She put the blinds up high," and looked outward, "every nerve . . . quivering with a long-forgotten restlessness." Female sexuality, repressed when she is with Sebastian, reawakens, as "tonight, through the soft twilight, everything in her was reaching outward, straining forward" (183–84).[10] She feels again the yearnings she had sought to satisfy through Sebastian, but she now confronts her independence, asking "how could she go on alone?" The answer comes in terms of imagination directed outward, much as Thea reached toward ancient truths she was to find in Panther Canyon:

Suddenly something flashed into her mind, so clear that it must have come from without, from the breathless quiet. What if—what if Life itself were the sweetheart? It was like a lover waiting for her in distant cities—across the sea; drawing her, enticing her, weaving a spell over her. She opened the window softly and knelt down beside it to breathe the cold air. She felt the snowflakes melt in her hair, on her hot cheeks. Oh, now she knew! She must have it, she couldn't run away from it. She must go back into the world and get all she could of everything that had made him what he was. . . .

She crouched closer to the window and stretched out her arms to the storm, to whatever might lie behind it. Let it come! Let it all come back to her again! Let it betray her and mock her and break her heart, she must have it! (184–85)

The rather heavy irony of the action is that the world does "betray and mock her and break her heart" when Harry Gordon refuses to give her a ride. Fleeing her own emotions, she skates onto thin ice and drowns. The drowning climaxes the reversals that have run through this book, when suddenly the ordinary drops away. Unaware that the river had changed its bed, Lucy sets out on the ice "without looking or thinking"; even when she is "brought . . . to herself in a flash" upon hearing "a soft, splitting sound" and seeing "dark lines running in the ice about her," she is ignorant of her danger, for "it never occurred to her that this was the river itself." In dying as in living, Lucy is caught by forces of which she is ignorant, and over which she has no control: "She was groping cautiously with her feet when she felt herself gripped from underneath. Her skate had caught in the fork of a submerged tree, half-buried in sand by the spring flood" (198–99). On a narrative level, Lucy's death is, as Leon Edel noted, "as arbitrary as death can be."[11]

On a symbolic level, however, this ending is appropriate, even inevitable, for with it the central metaphor of drowning breaks into and dominates the narrative. The major emotion of the book is of being "gripped from underneath" by a submerged feeling of emptiness, in response to which characters cling briefly to something before they are pulled under. Sebastian's drowning forms a vortex into which others are swept. At the concert he reveals to Lucy "passion that drowns like black water" (31) and, at the funeral, "a wave of black despair" that seemed to carry "him and that black coffin up the aisle together" (54). With him Lucy feels herself "a twig or a leaf swept along on the current" (75); they cling to each other and the present, knowing they must lose it. In the end these feelings find final expression in literal drownings.

Only Harry Gordon survives, and in an epilogue Cather turns to him, suggesting the solace of age. Twenty-five years have passed, and Gordon has attended the funeral of his one remaining friend and the last member of the Gayheart family, Lucy's father. With Mr. Gayheart's death, Gordon realized, "a chapter [was] closed, and a once familiar name on the way to be forgotten." The Gayhearts are on the way to "complete oblivion" (207). The threat is that familiar to Cather's later books, seen in the annihilating wildernesses surrounding a rock in Canada, in Sebastian's emptiness upon realizing "his youth was forever and irrevocably gone," and it will reappear in Sapphira's terror following the funeral of her oldest servant.

Yet unlike Sebastian, Gordon has one unspoiled memory. Taking possession of the Gayheart house, Gordon enters Lucy's tomblike room, undisturbed since her death. Back outside, as if before a gravemarker, he pauses before her footsteps preserved in a slab of concrete sidewalk: "Nothing else seemed to bring her back so vividly into the living world for a moment. Sometimes, when he paused there, he caught for a flash the very feel of her" (227). The aesthetic sense is of resolution, for Gordon offers the calm of one who has served his sentence. He has been haunted by questions without answers, as by Lucy's ghostly "last cry on the wind" calling to him, has suffered remorse as if a penance, and has reached the long perspective of eternity, by which Lucy "has receded to the far horizon line, along with all the fine things of youth, which do not change" (221, 224).

But the footprints Gordon preserves are of a thirteen-year-old girl. The adult Lucy, the young woman pulsating with desire, no longer exists, even in memory. The horror of Lucy Gayheart's life was that the qualities that made her so attractive as a girl — her sensitivity, vitality, generosity, kindness — limit her capacity to grow up. Because she was, as her teacher comments, "too kind" to be an artist (the only independent life Cather offers to her major female characters), she would be admitted to the adult world only by yielding her vitality to another. The ghostly image of her, "a despairing little creature standing in the icy wind and lifting beseeching eyes" (224), recalls the ghost child Cathy Linton begging to be admitted to Wuthering Heights.

With *Lucy Gayheart* Cather takes her place in the long line of women writers who have explored the terrors that accompany female sexuality. The concern was not new in Cather's writing. She had used Christina Rossetti's verse from *Goblin Market* for the epigraph to her first volume of fiction, *The Troll Garden*:

We must not look at Goblin men,
  We must not buy their fruits;
Who knows upon what soil they fed
  Their hungry thirsty roots?

The Rossetti poem is, as Ellen Moers pointed out, replete with sexuality; girl children must beware of goblin men who would feed themselves thirstily upon them. [12] By using it to introduce her first volume of fiction, Cather introduces also a gallery of female characters who suffer because of their sexuality: Marie Shabata, Lena Lingard, Ántonia Shimerda Cuzak, Marian Forrester. But Cather was not so interested in sexuality per se as were her predecessors in the female Gothic Christina Rossetti and Emily Brontë. Not unexpectedly Willa Cather, a woman who neither married nor bore children, moved heterosexual sex and biological birth offstage. Even that most fertile of her women, Ántonia, is moved to Denver for the conception of her first child, and when she returns, having begun her period of fecundity, Jim Burden retreats, coming back to her only when, twenty years later, she is safely aged into an archetypal earth mother.

Cather does give major attention to another kind of passion and birth, what she called that of the "second self" and what we would call, perhaps, that of an authentic or individual self. This birth is much harder than the other one, Thea Kronborg's music teacher tells her; it is one each person has to bring about herself. In *Song of the Lark* Cather used female metaphors of conception, gestation, birth, and reproduction to celebrate such a birth; in *Lucy Gayheart* she used similarly female metaphors to tell a gothic story of abandonment. For Lucy is like a newborn seeking a parent, abandoned by those who could guide her: her mother died when she was six; her sister was temperamentally unsympathetic to her; the artist she loved left her; her hometown suitor rejected her pleas. To complicate matters, Lucy's newborn second self resided within a woman's body, announcing a sexuality for which she was unprepared. In creating Lucy, Cather was writing as a woman of the tragedy brought on a child by being female, and in doing so, she contributed to what Ellen Moers discussed as "the long and complex traditions of Female Gothic, where woman is examined with a woman's eye, woman as girl, as sister, as mother, as self." [13] As Elizabeth Sergeant recognized, "Perhaps only a woman writer, who has received a thousand confidences from women connected with the arts, could make so subtle a romance of an unequal human relationship doomed from the start." [14]

Lucy Gayheart is also about the universal experience of growing old. Cather framed her story of youth with aging characters facing death: at the beginning the older generation of Haverford recalls the dead Lucy; then Sebastian attends a funeral and recalls his dead boyhood friend; at the end Harry Gordon attends another funeral and recalls another youth. And though Cather focused her plot upon Lucy, she gave the emotional power of the book to Clement Sebastian and Harry Gordon. In discussing them, one is moved to use biography, always a temptation in reading Cather, a writer who heavily drew upon her own life. Parallels between character and creator are close, as if Cather gave to Sebastian her weariness over the present and to Gordon her pleasure in memories of the past. Certainly, Edith Lewis's description of the Park Avenue apartment they had taken shortly before Cather began her novel is remarkably similar to Sebastian's studio: comfortable, isolated, protected from former hardships, but also strangely suspended from life and detached from youthful creativity.[15]

Lucy Gayheart is an interesting book, for it illuminates themes that run through Cather's writing: tragedies of youth, complexities of sexuality, and despair over annihilation. I do not regard it as a successful book, however. Cather's return to youth with Lucy Gayheart is unconvincing, and as did Cather, I grow tired of the slight character. The novel is weakest in those sections focusing on Lucy, strongest in those presenting Sebastian and Gordon. Perhaps the weakness of the book can be described best by this split between narrative focus and emotional center, the one on Lucy, the other on Sebastian and Gordon. If so, it was a split Cather resolved in her subsequent writing. She concentrated upon the ambiguities of irresolution in *Sapphira and the Slave Girl,* her most fully realized Gothic novel.

16 *Sapphira and the Slave Girl:*
An American Gothic

"Also things began to grow scarce in Mansoul: now the things that her soul lusted after were departing from her."[1]

After completing *Lucy Gayheart,* Cather wrote little for almost three years. During much of 1935 she devoted herself to Isabelle McClung Hambourg, who was gravely ill. That winter the Hambourgs came to New York, where Isabelle saw doctors and received treatments, and where Cather assisted however she could. When Isabelle was hospitalized for three weeks, Cather visited her daily, and when the Hambourgs later traveled to Chicago on business, Cather accompanied them, helping to make the trip as comfortable as possible for Isabelle. Then, after the Hambourgs returned to Europe in August, Cather joined them in Paris, staying two months. It was the last time the two friends were together.[2]

In 1936 Cather wrote "The Old Beauty," an essay on Thomas Mann, and the preface for *Not Under Forty*—all fine pieces, but a slight output for her. And during most of 1937 she gave her time and energy to preparing the autograph edition of her writing, issued by Houghton Mifflin from 1937 to 1938, then completed in 1941. By autumn 1937 Cather was ready to begin a new novel.

Years earlier Cather had written of Jim Burden's returning to his birthplace, "having found out what a little circle man's experience is."[3] Now for her final novel Cather too returned to her beginnings. She made two trips to Winchester, Virginia, as an adult—first in 1913 with Isabelle McClung, then with Edith Lewis in 1938—but hers was not the feeling of coming home she gave to Jim. Though on both trips Cather felt great pleasure in the Virginia countryside, she felt estranged from the human community she found there. In 1913 she realized she no longer cared about the sacred peculiarities of the people and that the people she had once loved were all dead; in 1938 she found her childhood home, Willowside, in such disrepair that she did not reenter it.[4] There was, it seemed, no sympathetic person whose skin she could "get inside" to reach back into the past.

In 1938 other ties to the past were severed. Two of the people whom Cather loved most deeply—her brother, Douglass, and Isabelle Hambourg—died; and a hurricane destroyed the woods about Jaffrey, ruining for her a place she had visited for years. Finally, perhaps most importantly, World War II broke out. When the French army surrendered, Cather wrote in her "Line-a-day," "There seems to be no future at all for people of my generation."[5]

Against these catastrophes Cather worked with "a resoluteness, a sort of fixed determination which . . . was different from her ordinary working mood; as if she were bringing all her powers into play to save this, whatever else was lost. She often worked far beyond her strength. In the summers of 1938 and 1939," Edith Lewis recalled, "we stayed in New York through the heat until the end of July, because she did not want to interrupt what she was then doing. She finished the story at Grand Manan in September, 1940."[6]

The story was *Sapphira and the Slave Girl,* a book that has always startled Cather's readers. Starting with *O Pioneers!, My Ántonia, A Lost Lady,* and the other Nebraska novels, critics have identified Cather's major themes (the noble pioneer, the frontier, the creative imagination) and described her development (generally some version of an initial optimism over the frontier period followed by an elegiac lament for the pioneer past). From such a viewpoint Cather's last book seems an aberration which, if treated at all, is seen as an escape into a pre–Civil War southern setting, remote from Cather's major writing (that is, the plains writing). Moreover, the response it evokes is disturbingly unlike that of Cather's other books. We never experience with it that flash of recognition so characteristic of Cather's writing—that moment, when, reading *My Ántonia,* we feel, "Ah—that *is* Ántonia." When we put down *Sapphira and the Slave Girl,* it is with the sense that Sapphira Dodderidge has remained forbiddingly remote, a "chilly" character from whom we want to turn, yet one so powerful that we are unable to do so.

What we find in the criticism is a startling silence. There simply has not been much written about this book, as if, one critic wrote, readers have run out of steam when they reach it. Of the essays that have been published, one makes no attempt to deal with the novel critically,[7] and a second is, to my mind, unsatisfactory. Unlike Lavon Mattes Jobes, I do not find Sapphira a sympathetic character—at least not until her last scene, and then she is essentially changed from the Sapphira who intrigued me.[8] Other essays are solid and enlightening. The book is, as Merrill Maguire Skaggs writes, a narrative experiment in which Cather undercuts stereotypes of the southern lady; it contains the religious metaphors Richard Gianonne writes of, and his discussion of it as a threefold movement from "enslavement, through struggle to release" is useful. As Philip L. Gerber argues, it includes Cather's denunciation of capitalism; and as David Stouck writes, "it is a story of injustice and separation" which ends as "a romance of forgiveness."[9] But major questions remain concerning the power of Sapphira, the darkness of her action against Nancy, the disturbing effect of the novel, and its place in Cather's canon.

At first glance, *Sapphira and the Slave Girl,* set in 1856, does seem remote from Cather's earlier writing. The surface of the narrative has its own appeal, as E. K. Brown and Leon Edel note in their discussion of it as "a study of manners" in which "always there is the unspoken comment: was it not a gracious and wise way, would it not have been a pleasure to live in that place at that time?"[10] Cather remembered social conventions, gestures, and verbal nuances from the Virginia she knew and heard about in her childhood, and she described them in such rich detail that the novel resonates with "a culture's hum and buzz of implications," thus seeming to meet Lionel Trilling's famous definition of a novel of manners.[11] Details from the past weave through the book: the fichu Sapphira wears to church, the peacock feather flybrush that Sampson's Katie waves over the dining table, the shawl pin Henry Colbert uses. The narrator tells how ice cream is made in summer, and how rags are dyed, then woven into carpets; and she explains that any food carried in a gourd from the big kitchen to one of the cabins is not questioned, for "gourd vessels were invisible to good manners" (21). The effect is to heighten the sense of a past so distant it must be interpreted, a mannered world appealingly quaint and safely remote.

Yet this is also a world of unsettling contradictions, where a graceful façade of civilization covers actions of dark cruelty and where apparent clarity reveals ambiguity. To read this book is to move through layers of meaning, each layer appearing solid, then proving unsatisfactory and giving way to another: beneath the calm, mannered surface, Sapphira's attempt to bring about the rape of her slave girl is unmistakably evil, as is the fact of slavery itself. By making attempted rape the main action of the novel, Cather concentrated on the threat of violence she had merely suggested in previous books. To do so, she drew upon the Gothic tradition, placing within her study of manners the familiar plot of an innocent young woman trapped within a castle and sexually threatened by its villainous owner. Cather makes the conventions her own, of course: she transplants the castle to America, and she makes its owner female. But Gothic echoes remain, and they are the fiber from which the novel is made.

Sapphira Dodderidge Colbert is a literary cousin of the aristocratic hero-villain who lives in proud isolation, a law unto himself. In defiance of the role society would assign to her as a twenty-four-year-old unmarried woman, the aristocratic Sapphira Dodderidge built a large manor house in Back Creek Valley, married a miller, and moved with her husband and her score of slaves into a self-imposed exile. There, in further defiance — this time to the Back Creek community that was suspicious of slavery — she created a suspended world within which her power was unchallenged. Sapphira's control of that world reveals contradictions in her nature, for she acts with "shades of kindness and cruelty which seemed . . . purely whimsical" (219–20). In her is combined a baffling mixture of qualities: her courage, fortitude, and independence are heroic; at the same time, she is capricious, cold, even malevolent. Most of all, she is profoundly ambiguous. As her husband and daughter testify, others do not understand Sapphira. It is in her ambiguity that Sapphira is most clearly a literary cousin of the complex Gothic hero-villains, "impressively grandiose characters whose undoubted stature is compounded of dark aspirations and great force of character."[12]

Like a god, Sapphira presides over the Mill House, expressing contradictory impulses through her surrogates: through Till her impulse for order and through Martin that for chaos. Her home, too, is an extension of her nature, a Gothic setting adapted to the New World. As early as 1799 Charles Brockden Brown lamented the absence in America of castles, labyrinthian structures which could represent the recesses of the mind.[13] In American literature, castles were replaced by manor houses, both with the similar function of projecting their inhabitants' minds. The Mill House does so in several ways. In the contrast between its orderly façade and the "helter-skelter" private reality behind it, it contains contradictions between public and private dimensions of southern society—and those of its owner, Sapphira. Built on the Mount Vernon pattern familiar to all Virginians, it is a symbol of the southern caste system of which Sapphira is a product.

But this was a caste system that was dying in 1856, and the Mill House, despite the "air of settled comfort and stability" (41) of its parlor, has the qualities of a crypt. It is situated deep in a wooded valley, as though underground: around it the earth rises like walls, and within it there is, as Till says, the feeling of being "buried" (72). An atmosphere of death and decay hangs about it, in the cold and damp that permeate it and in the rains that seem incessant, making roads impassable and further isolating its inhabitants. Unless fires are lighted to keep their invasion at bay, disfiguring spots appear on the walls, reminders of the dissolution that threatens constantly.

Within the Mill House is entombed a vanishing society that remains in signs that no longer have meaning—linen and silver for parties not given and manners that "had little chance here" (69). It contains also Sapphira, a vestige of her former self, now confined to the wheelchair constructed for her by the coffin maker and attended by mournful Till, old Washington, and "shrivelled-up," mummy-like Jeff (33). In such a house Nancy is an anomaly, and Sapphira's action against her has symbolic meaning. Sapphira resents Nancy's innocence as age resents youth.

As Sapphira carries out her plan against Nancy, the house in which the girl is trapped becomes an ominous labyrinth, complete with stock Gothic elements—ancestral secrets; hints of incest; long, drafty, dark halls; creaking stairs. The action itself is strikingly close to the standard Gothic one, as evident from a synopsis: The master of a large manor house, living in proud and lonely exile from society, seeks the ruin of a beautiful and innocent young woman. The girl is brought to the manor house, where her would-be seducer is "after [her] night an' day" (216). She is especially afraid when, lying in her sleeveless chemise on her straw pallet at night, she can hear the creak of his stealthy barefoot steps on the stairs and passageways of the drafty manor: she knows that if she falls asleep, the villain will slip into her bed. She has only her wit to rely upon, for the servants of the manor are under the control of their master. Although she has been able to employ ruses to escape the rake's clutches, her eventual ruin seems inevitable. As she realizes the gravity of her situation, her desperation mounts until she looks on suicide as the only way she can protect her virtue. Fortunately, however, a rescuer intervenes, who under the cover of the dark of the moon helps her escape to safety.

This basic plot is so firmly presented that we respond to it as Gothic, though we may not consciously recognize it as such. Certainly, Cather avoids claptrap, and certainly, she embeds the conventional plot in an extremely loose, even casual narrative: Martin Colbert doesn't appear until halfway through the book, and at times we forget about him entirely as Cather digresses with stories within stories and characters unrelated to the main action. But this, too, is characteristic of the Gothic, the "proper plot" of which is "a series of intertwined stories held together by some loose unifying pattern,"[14] for the looseness enables the essential effect of suddenness or surprise.

And so we move from one layer to the next, past manners, characterization, and action to realize that in *Sapphira and the Slave Girl* Cather establishes an emotional pattern of disruption by which she explores the horror of estrangement and the psychology of evil. Here, where the grotesque constantly threatens to disrupt apparently normal situations, dark revelations are as central as sunny ones were to Cather's early novels. Like the young victim-heroine familiar to the Gothic novels, Nancy is caught in a world of bewildering transformations. She is the innocent victim of changes within her body, her developing sexuality that brings upon her the jealousy of her mistress and the pursuit of Martin. The familiar world about her has become nightmarish: the house that was her home has become threatening; the mistress who favored her has become cold and distant; the guest whom she welcomed has turned into her would-be rapist; the master who treated her with such kindness avoids her; even the cherry tree where she felt herself safely hidden turns into a trap when the man she believes just young and foolish violently turns upon her. Nancy's terror focuses upon the threat of rape by Martin, the action that links sexuality to questions of power and powerlessness in the manner of the Gothic. But her anxiety concerns her estrangement from all she had once depended upon.

Transformations threatening the other characters take different forms. The miller, Henry Colbert, is an enlightened person haunted by a demonic double, his "family inheritance" of carnal sense that is the "bad blood in the Colberts" (191–92). As Nancy feels an alien in her own home, so Henry fears losing himself and becoming his dark counterpart, whom he sees embodied in his licentious nephew, Martin. His horror is that "he had begun to see through Martin's eyes. Sometimes in his sleep that preoccupation with Martin, the sense of almost being Martin, came over him with a black spell" (209).

As befitting the complex hero-villain, Sapphira is more ambiguous than the other characters, an ambiguity Cather maintains by seldom revealing her character's thoughts. Yet she gives to Sapphira one revelation scene, important because it so fully expresses the anxiety that runs through the novel. Following the burial of her oldest servant, Sapphira retires to her room, where, alone, "her usual fortitude seemed to break up altogether. She reached for it, but it was not there. Strange alarms and suspicions began to race through her mind," and she begins to question her servants' loyalty, then her husband's, until, "scarcely breathing, overcome by dread," she almost loses consciousness. Finally, she breaks the spell by ringing the bell to call Nancy, whose "sleepy, startled voice" reestablishes the familiar: "It was over. Her shattered, treacherous house stood safe about her again. She was in her own room, wakened out of a dream of disaster" (105–7).

The irony is that Sapphira's "dream of disaster" is the reality, her sense of safety the illusion, for the threat that the familiar will fall away and reveal a grotesque reality is pervasive in Sapphira's world. By presenting seemingly casual digressions, then including in each a dark twist, Cather suggests there is no escape from the irrational, which without warning can break through the ordinary world we depend upon. Stories within stories present a past that disrupts an apparently serene present. Till appears as a highly competent housekeeper, a figure of calm and order; only later do we learn that in early childhood she saw her mother burn to death. Jezebel first appears as a venerable matriarch, a figure of wisdom and justice, and only later do we realize that she "saw her father brained and her four brothers cut down" (90) by the slave traders who captured her and brought her to America under the most brutal conditions.

Similarly, in idyllic digressions that offer an apparent release from the Mill House, the irrational threatens, usually in the form of underworld figures. When, for example, the Colberts' daughter, Rachel, leaves the valley to visit Mrs. Ringer on Timber Ridge, she believes she is leaving behind the troubling ambiguities of the Mill House and plans to enjoy herself in a simple world of natural good manners. But her visit is interrupted when she is called to an ugly scene of torture, in which she sees a young boy stripped to the waist and bound to a tree, about whom three men are lounging, one "laughing and cracking a lash of plaited cowhide thongs" (127). This is Buck, for whom the expression "a-actin' devilish" (129) takes on ominous significance: indeed, Cather introduces and closes his brief scene with numerous references to his "deviltry." Buck is one of those minor characters in Cather's writing that resonate with symbolic significance. With his mean, mocking laugh, his whip, and the "thick fleece of red hair on his chest and forearms" showing through his opened shirt, it is as though in Buck a demon reality is thrusting through the human façade.

The overall effect of these disruptions is that this novel, which seems to offer a retreat into the past, contains the distinctly modern search for meaning in an estranged world. Sapphira most fully illustrates the horror of an alienated life of empty forms. She lives in exile, of course, but in other, equally important ways, she is separated from transcendent values that liberate. Sapphira is the only one of Cather's major characters to lack a finely developed aesthetic sense. There is nothing in her even remotely resembling Alexandra Bergson's response to the beauty of the land, Thea Kronborg's to music, Ántonia Shimerda's to people, Myra Henshawe's to music and religion, Cécile Auclair's to domestic ritual. As Rachel recognizes, Sapphira is "entirely self-centered" (220). Rather than turning to culture, nature, or religion as a means by which she might be "dissolved into something complete and great,"[15] Sapphira uses each to establish and maintain her personal power. She uses manners as a camouflage: her laugh, her tone of voice, the topics she introduces in conversation and the letter she writes to Martin—all reflect her capacity for manipulation. She does drive out into nature when the wild laurel is in bloom, but we learn of these drives not that she perceived the beauty about her but only that she knew she looked to advantage when she stopped to visit with her neighbors. Even her religion seems hollow. In her annual Easter visit to her family, Sapphira "attended all the services of Christ Church," but in Cather's gallery of religious characters (recall Myra Henshawe's private talks with her priest and her solitary death, holding her crucifix; Fathers Latour and Vaillant's spiritual commitment; St. Peter's description of Easter services), Sapphira is decidedly superficial: "She was a comely figure in the congregation, clad in black silk and white fichu. . . . Her serene face and lively, shallow blue eyes smiled at old friends from under a black velvet bonnet, renewed or 'freshened' yearly by the town milliner. . . . No Dodderidge who ever sat in that pew showed her blood to better advantage" (28–29).

Looking for a saving human nature and finding none, we reach the next Gothic twist, for we realize that the character initially presented as a lady, then as a hero-villian, is a grotesque. Swollen until she she has become bloated, invalided so long she is wax-white, Sapphira is a nightmarish life-in-death figure. Only her eyes would not be affected by her disease, and Cather leads the reader to look to them for the living person imprisoned within the corpse-like shell: "But the eyes themselves were clear; a lively greenish blue," Cather writes, then adds the grotesque twist, "with no depth" (15). Her "shallow eyes," the characteristic most identified with Sapphira, suggest the inner blankness of a woman from whom a moral sense is missing.

This, then, is the woman who is, as her husband says, "the Master" of the Mill House. The house, the servants, their visitor—all are extensions of Sapphira and her undisputed power, a power as ambiguous as her nature. Initially her actions against Nancy seem motivated by jealousy, the understandable suspicions of a woman too long confined. Yet once again reversal occurs when Cather introduces quite another motive, that of diversion. Observing the conflict about her, Sapphira "laughed softly. It was almost as good as a play, she was thinking" (199). Her carelessness about the lives of those dependent upon her is perhaps the most chilling aspect of her action against Nancy, for there is in it the inhuman quality of a cat playing with a mouse that leads to "that surrealistically horrible recognition of a world of moral chaos where only power has meaning." [16]

Sapphira's power creates a whirlpool effect, a vortex of energy within which other characters seem helpless, and tension mounts over whether someone will oppose positive human values to the evil that is occurring. As Sapphira's husband, Henry is the one most suited to do so: he is painfully aware of Nancy's danger, yet he exhibits at best weakness, at worst sophistry. Upon learning of Martin's designs against Nancy, he declares, "I'll look after her" (191), then "shrank from seeing her at all" (193); his daughter's question, "Why don't you do something to save her?" (225) is a quietly sharp indictment of his struggle. When at last he provides the means for Nancy's escape, contradictions undermine the act: his money enables Nancy to escape rape, but in order to receive it, his daughter must act as a thief, at night reaching through an open window and taking the bills from his coat pocket. Other characters are willfully blind (believing "her first duty was to her mistress," Nancy's mother, Till, "shut her eyes to what was going on" [219]), ineffectual (Washington is too old to help Nancy), or unsympathetic (the cook Lizzie and her shiftless daughter, Bluebell, are vindictive against Nancy because of her earlier favoritism from Sapphira). Even the Reverend Fairhead, a man of God, is unable to hold his own against Sapphira and is banished from the Mill House, albeit under the polite guise of not being invited back.

But as the courageous lover helps the Gothic heroine to escape, so Rachel Blake, the abolitionist daughter of Sapphira and Henry, helps Nancy to leave the estranged world of the Mill House and join the human community. Their journey is an ascent from the underworld: Nancy is driven in a wagon of death, containing a coffin, past a tavern filled with drunken miscreants — figures of social disorder and misrule — then transported by a silent ferryman over a roaring river to the opposite shore, where she is met by a freed black preacher who speaks to her with "the voice of prophecy" (239) and welcomes her into a community of Friends, telling her "Dey ain't strangers where you're goin', honey" (238). And so Nancy passes out of Back Creek Valley, leaving behind Rachel calling farewell to the departing chaise.

Nancy's escape brings release from the Mill House. It does not, however, resolve contradictions within it. Rachel returns to her home, Sapphira orders her not to call again, and as Sapphira withdraws into proud isolation, silence descends. Here, too, *Sapphira and the Slave Girl* follows the Gothic pattern: the spectator/reader withdraws from the suspended world in which Frankenstein's monster disappears into the darkness, the body of Captain Ahab remains tied even in death to the white whale, and Sapphira continues to rule within the Mill House. Ambiguities are unresolved and the threat of the irrational continues, reified in a "dark autumn" during which rains come and disease spreads. Sapphira worsens, clearly dying; Rachel's two daughters become critically ill with diphtheria. It is as though without the youth and innocence of Nancy, the world that remains is helpless before death.

The eventual resumption of life is as inexplicable as was its suspension, more understandable in terms of an aesthetic impulse to reestablish harmony in the novel than in terms of character motivation or plot. The Reverend Fairhead, standing outside Rachel's house, witnesses the return of a divine presence to a world from which it had departed: he sees within the house an unearthly "white figure" drift through the kitchen and take nourishment, then recognizes it is the ill Mary, who had been forbidden by the doctor to take food or liquid. He is transfixed by the feeling that "there was something solemn in what he saw through the window, like a Communion service" (259). The act signals a reassertion of the sacred in a world that had been estranged from it, the communion an affirmation that Christ's body and blood are present again as an expression of divine life in community.

Following the rejoining of the divine is a rejoining with the human community. First sending help to her daughter, then inviting her to live at the Mill House, Sapphira becomes, in effect, another character: she is no longer a Promethean hero-villain or a grotesque, but instead a woman facing death who gathers her family about her. Though presumably more deformed than ever by advancing dropsy, Sapphira is no longer identified by the bloated body of a swollen corpse or the shallow eyes of moral vacancy. Her husband articulates the change in her, reflecting that her "composure which he had sometimes called heartlessness . . . now seemed to him strength" (268). Speaking for the first time of her death, Sapphira and Henry demonstrate compassion and love through a physical harmony absent from previous scenes: Sapphira "reached out and caught his hand," she "gripped his cold fingers" and "put her hand on her husband's drooping shoulder"; she "felt his tears wet on her skin." He in turn "reached out for her two hands and buried his face in her palms," then leaned "against her chair, his head on her knee" (265–67).

In an epilogue Cather completes the return to the human community by advancing twenty-five years and including herself as a child observing the reunion of Nancy and Till. Continuity replaces the static time and suspended reality at the heart of the book, and the familiar world is reestablished. But it is a familiar world behind which exists dark ambiguity, for Sapphira's contradictions remain unresolved and the evil of her act unexplained. And that is what distinguishes Gothic from romantic. As Robert Hume writes,

Gothic and romantic writing spring alike from a recognition of the insufficiency of reason or religious faith to explain and make comprehensible the complexities of life. We may distinguish between Gothic and romantic in terms of what they do within this situation. The imagination, Coleridge tells us, reveals its presence "in the balance or reconciliation of opposite or discordant qualities." Romantic writing reconciles the discordant elements it faces, resolving their apparent contradictions imaginatively in the creation of a higher order. Gothic writing . . . has no such answers and can only leave the "opposites" contradictory and paradoxical. [17]

In her response to epistemological ambiguities, Cather resembled her Old World predecessors. But *Sapphira and the Slave Girl* is an American Gothic, in which the irrational assumes distinctly New World forms. Cather drew upon pre–Civil War American history to present evil in the form of slavery, then developed her subject by ideas relevant to events preceding World War II. The fall of 1937, during which Cather began work on *Sapphira and the Slave Girl*, was a time of increasingly ominous tensions pointing to the war that Cather felt would be "the end of all." [18] One of Cather's most extended discussions of these tensions was in a letter she wrote to Sinclair Lewis in January 1938, when she was in the critical early stages of her new novel: writing at length of events in

Europe, Cather described conceptions of evil. She was concerned, she wrote, over Americans' gullibility and misplaced kindness, seen in evasive excuses for Stalin (that he must have good qualities) and Mussolini (that he did make Italy attractive for tourists), and she feared Americans would not wake up until mortally threatened. Americans tend to refuse to believe evil exists, she summarized—and that may be the problem. [19]

This is the idea Cather put at the heart of *Sapphira and the Slave Girl* and for which she used the Gothic, a form that expresses "the psychological problem of evil." [20] When we look beyond the antebellum Virginia setting, we realize that Cather's last novel, long dismissed as escapist, may well be the most directly political of all her writing. In its central tension over inaction of characters against the increasingly disturbing and, finally, evil action of a powerful central figure, Cather's novel unexpectedly resembles nothing so much as Thomas Mann's "Mario and the Magician." [21]

Finally, *Sapphira and the Slave Girl* has backward-looking implications. Our tendency is to use an author's early works to interpret later ones, yet to forget that her canon forms a whole, like the chapters in a single novel, in which the later parts illuminate their predecessors. For the moment, let us imagine that we read *Sapphira and the Slave Girl* first, rather than last, and then read the other books through the lens provided by it. Doing so enables us to respond far more fully to the threat of the irrational that runs through Cather's writing, and to recognize the long line of characters that are to a lesser or greater degree shades of Sapphira: Wick Cutter, Bayless Wheeler, Ivy Peters, Buck Scales—the list goes on. Indeed, there is no novel in her canon in which Cather did not draw upon Gothic conventions to present the possibility an ordinary reality may drop away to reveal unsuspected horrors. Usually a dark undercurrent to romantic optimism (Gothicism is a dominant impulse only in *Lucy Gayheart* and *Sapphira and the Slave Girl*), Cather's Gothicism works with her romanticism: though one ends in ambiguities and the other in resolution, both affirm the vitality of the imagination and emotion against the limitations of reason. In this affirmation Cather believed with Godfrey St. Peter that the real threat to people in a modern world is not the inexplicable but the prosaic, a world in which there are no mysteries: "The fact is, the human mind, the individual mind, has always been made more interesting by dwelling on the old riddles, even if it makes nothing of them. . . . As long as every man and woman. . . . was a principal in a gorgeous drama with God, glittering angels on one side and the shadows of evil coming and going on the other, life was a rich thing."[22]

In Pittsburgh, 1901 or 1902

Notes

Preface

1. *Nebraska State Journal*, 28 October 1894, reprinted in *The Kingdom of Art: Willa Cather's First Principles and Critical Statements, 1893–1896*, edited with commentary by Bernice Slote (Lincoln: University of Nebraska Press, 1966), 143. Hereafter cited as *The Kingdom of Art*.

2. *Lincoln Courier*, 2 November 1895, in *The Kingdom of Art*, 233.

3. "My First Novels [There Were Two]," in *Willa Cather on Writing: Critical Studies in Writing as an Art* (New York: Knopf, 1949), 94.

4. *The Kingdom of Art*, 31.

5. Edward A. Bloom and Lillian D. Bloom comment on Cather's romanticism in *Willa Cather's Gift of Sympathy* (Carbondale: Southern Illinois University Press, 1962). See, for example, the Blooms' comparison of Cather's romanticism to that of Hawthorne and James, all "defending that aspect of romanticism sometimes called moral realism" (25), their use of Coleridge's definition of a symbol to interpret Cather's symbolism (26), and their chapter "The Sympathetic Imagination" (153–96). And in *Willa Cather: Her Life and Art*, James Woodress places Cather "within the tradition of American romanticism" (1970; rpt. Lincoln: University of Nebraska Press, 1982), 159.

6. See, by Robert Langbaum, *The Poetry of Experience: The Dramatic Monologue in Modern Literary Tradition* (London: Chatto & Windus, 1957); *The Mysteries of Identity: A Theme in Modern Literature* (New York: Oxford University Press, 1977); and *The Modern Spirit: Essays on the Continuity of Nineteenth- and Twentieth-Century Literature* (New York: Oxford University Press, 1970). Also, Geoffrey Hartman, *Beyond Formalism* (New Haven: Yale University Press, 1970); M. H. Abrams, *The Mirror and the Lamp* (1953; rpt. New York: Norton, 1958); Harold Bloom, "The Internalization of Quest-Romance," in *Romanticism and Consciousness* (New York: Norton, 1970); Donald D. Stone, *The Romantic Impulse in Victorian Fiction* (Cambridge: Harvard University Press, 1980); Charles Schug, *The Romantic Genesis of the Modern Novel* (Pittsburgh: University of Pittsburgh Press, 1979). In an unpublished dissertation John Stoufer Zeigel points out varieties of romanticism in Cather's writing (romance, oriental ornamentation, subjective experience) and interprets Cather's career largely as a search for an escape from a modern wasteland. My approach to Cather's romanti-

cism is quite different: I stress, for example, the subjective imaginative experience in her writing more than does Zeigel, and I argue that her writing demonstrates a response to change rather than a retreat to a romantic past ("The Romanticism of Willa Cather," Claremont Graduate School, 1967).

7. David Stouck, *Willa Cather's Imagination* (Lincoln: University of Nebraska Press, 1975), 2.

8. In my definition here, I am indebted to Robert Langbaum's discussion, "Romanticism as a Modern Tradition," in *The Poetry of Experience*, 9–37. A note on terminology: I reserve "Romantic" and "Romanticism" with a capital *R* for the narrowly historical application of Romanticism, to refer to the literary period between 1798 and 1832 and to some writers within that period (e.g., Wordsworth, Coleridge, Shelley, Keats). I use "romantic" and "romanticism" with a small *r* to refer to the broader literary movement that began in the eighteenth century and extends in some forms and impulses to the present. Therefore, while I am arguing that Willa Cather was a romantic, I am not arguing that she was a Romantic, which by my usage would be a historical impossibility.

9. *My Ántonia* (1918; Boston: Houghton Mifflin, Sentry Edition, 1961), 352.

10. Charles Feidelson, Jr., *Symbolism and American Literature* (Chicago: University of Chicago Press, 1953), 56.

Chapter One: Beginnings

1. Edith Lewis, *Willa Cather Living: A Personal Record* (New York: Knopf, 1953), 17.

2. Interview, *Special Correspondence of the {Philadelphia} Record*, New York [1913], in *The Kingdom of Art*, 448.

3. *My Ántonia* (1918; Boston: Houghton Mifflin, Sentry Edition, 1961), 7.

4. Lewis, *Willa Cather Living*, 17.

5. Ferner Nuhn, *The Wind Blew from the East: A Study in the Orientation of American Culture* (1942; rpt. Port Washington, N.Y.: Kennikat Press, 1967), vii.

6. *The Kingdom of Art*, 31–112.

7. *Nebraska State Journal*, 1 March 1896, in *The Kingdom of Art*, 416.

8. *The Professor's House* (1925; New York: Random House, Vintage Books, 1973), 69. This is Cather's most famous statement of the idea, but it appears frequently in other writing, especially in her early essays.

9. *Nebraska State Journal*, 7 October 1894, in *The Kingdom of Art*, 178; *The World and the Parish: Willa Cather's Articles and Review, 1893–1902*, ed. William M. Curtin (Lincoln: University of Nebraska Press, 1970), 1:117.

10. *Nebraska State Journal*, 28 October 1894, in *The Kingdom of Art*, 143.

11. *Nebraska State Journal*, 23 November 1893, in *The Kingdom of Art*, 263.

12. *Nebraska State Journal,* 23 November 1893, 23 September 1894, 26 January 1896, and 1 March 1896; in *The Kingdom of Art,* 263, 407, 120, and 417.

13. "The shaping spirit of imagination" is Coleridge's phrase, in "Dejection: An Ode." Other quotations in this paragraph are from Lilian R. Furst, *Romanticism in Perspective: A Comparative Study of Aspects of the Romantic Movements in England, France, and Germany* (London: Macmillan; New York: St. Martin's Press, 1969), 44–46.

14. Robert Langbaum, *The Poetry of Experience* (London: Chatto & Windus, 1957), 22.

15. From *The Statesman's Manual,* in *Inquiring Spirit: A Coleridge Reader,* ed. Kathleen Coburn (1951; n.p.: Minerva Press, 1968), 104.

16. Langbaum, *The Poetry of Experience,* 27.

17. *Selections from Ralph Waldo Emerson,* ed. Stephen E. Whicher (Boston: Houghton Mifflin, 1960), 24.

18. *Nebraska State Journal,* 19 January 1896, in *The Kingdom of Art,* 351–52.

19. *Lincoln Courier,* 16 November 1895, in *The Kingdom of Art,* 222. Also note Cather's implicit approval of Poe's scorn for "the obtrusive learning of the Transcendentalist," *Lincoln Courier,* 12 October 1895, in *The Kingdom of Art,* 384.

20. *Nebraska State Journal,* 28 October 1894, in *The Kingdom of Art,* 143.

21. *Nebraska State Journal,* 10 March 1895, in *The Kingdom of Art,* 144–45.

22. Interview in *Special Correspondence in the {Philadelphia} Record,* 9 August [1913], in *The Kingdom of Art,* 449.

23. Elizabeth Shepley Sergeant, *Willa Cather: A Memoir* (1953; rpt. Lincoln: University of Nebraska Press, 1963), 111.

24. "The Best Stories of Sarah Orne Jewett," in *Willa Cather on Writing: Critical Studies on Writing as an Art* (New York: Knopf, 1949), 51.

25. See Robert Kiely's suggestive discussion of this problem in *The Romantic Novel in England* (Cambridge: Harvard University Press, 1972), esp. 1–26.

26. Quotations from the stories are from *Willa Cather's Collected Short Fiction, 1892–1912,* rev. ed., ed. Virginia Faulkner, intro. Mildred R. Bennett (Lincoln: University of Nebraska Press, 1970).

27. Langbaum, *The Poetry of Experience,* 20.

28. *Nebraska State Journal,* 2 February 1896, in *The Kingdom of Art,* 395–96.

29. *Willa Cather on Writing,* 41–42.

30. I have discussed these stories more fully in "Willa Cather's Plains Legacy: The Early Nebraska Stories," *Nebraska Humanist* 6 (Fall 1983): 48–52.

31. As a note to these paragraphs, I wish to call attention to a letter in the Pierpont Morgan Library from Willa Cather to E. Wagenknecht, 31 December

1938, in which Cather included "On the Divide" among stories she classified as wholly or partially spurious. Cather described "On the Divide" as a theme she wrote while at the university: a young professor touched up the story and had it printed without her knowledge; she was surprised that the professor attributed to a Swede farmer skill in wood carving.

Cather's letter reveals much about her attitude towards her early fiction, but for several reasons I do not consider it sufficient evidence to view these stories as spurious. While others (Cather's teacher and her friends) may have made minor changes in the stories, I continue to attribute them to Cather. First, stylistic differences do not distinguish the wood-carving passage from other sections of "On the Divide"; second, the other stories Cather disclaimed as spurious consistently bear the stamp of her hand ("Eric Hermannson's Soul," "Jack-A-Boy," "El Dorado," "The Professor's Commencement," and "The Treasure of Far Island"). Finally, in the last paragraphs of her letter Cather indirectly refers to the stories as hers. She argues that every writer has the right to cull those of his or her works that are not sound, to supervise that which he or she created. She considered it indelicate of others to call attention to her early work, something she would not do with Hemingway's early writing. And she argued that copyright laws give the writer the privilege of putting his flimsy pieces in his cellar and forgetting them.

Chapter Two: *The Troll Garden* and the Dangers of Art
1. Christina Georgina Rossetti, "Goblin Market," in *The Poetical Works,* with Memoir and Notes by William Michael Rossetti (1906; rpt. Hildesheim and New York: Georg Olms Verlag, 1970), 1.

2. *Nebraska State Journal,* 1 March 1896, in *The Kingdom of Art,* 417.

3. I am indebted to Helen Cather Southwick for informing me that Cather taught algebra during her first months of teaching at Central High School in Pittsburgh (personal correspondence). Ms. Southwick has reported on Willa Cather's life in Pittsburgh in "Willa Cather's Early Career: Origins of a Legend," *Western Pennsylvania Historical Magazine* 65 (April 1982): 85–98; see esp. 90.

4. James Woodress speculates that "five of the tales that were included in *The Troll Garden*" were among the stories Cather sent to S. S. McClure in April 1903, preliminary to her first meeting with him. "The Sculptor's Funeral" and "Paul's Case" were included, and probably "Flavia and Her Artists," "The Garden Lodge," and "The Marriage of Phaedra." "A Wagner Matinee" may have been among the group; it appeared in the February 1904 issue of *Everybody's Magazine.* "A Death in the Desert" had appeared in the January 1903 issue of *Scribner's.* See James Woodress, ed., *The Troll Garden* (Lincoln: University of Nebraska Press, 1983), xv–xvi.

5. Cather's *Troll Garden* stories are quoted from Woodress's edition, cited above. See Cather's 1895 extended discussion of "Goblin Market" as Rossetti's

"one perfect poem," *Nebraska State Journal*, 13 January 1895, in *The Kingdom of Art*, 346–49, more fully reproduced in *The World and the Parish: Willa Cather's Articles and Reviews, 1893–1902*, ed. William M. Curtin (Lincoln: University of Nebraska Press, 1970), 1:143–47.

6. Charles Kingsley, *The Roman and the Teuton*, vol. 10 of *The Works of Charles Kingsley* (London: Macmillan, 1884), 1–5. "The Roman and the Teuton" is a lecture that was first presented before Cambridge University and published in 1864. Bernice Slote first identified Cather's Kingsley quotation as from *The Roman and the Teuton*, and she included the text of Kingsley's story in *The Kingdom of Art*, 442–44.

7. Other critics have offered other interpretations of thematic contrasts among stories in *The Troll Garden*. E. K. Brown notes resemblances to James's juxtaposition of black magic and white magic in the stories of *The Two Magics*, and sees in Cather's *The Troll Garden* similarly juxtaposed strands between "the evil-working goblins and the industrious trolls." E. K. Brown, *Willa Cather: A Critical Biography*, completed by Leon Edel (New York: Knopf, 1953), 114–15. Bernice Slote argues that "we must consider the basic contrasts to be the Trolls inside and the Forest Children outside, the Romans and the Barbarians, Palace-Garden and Wood-Country, and the cyclic movements of decaying civilization and reconquering nature," in *The Kingdom of Art*, 95. Marilyn Arnold interprets the stories as dealing "with human values and relationships played against genuine art as an index of value," in *Willa Cather's Short Fiction* (Athens, Ohio: Ohio University Press, 1984), 45. And James Woodress relates the juxtapositions Cather made, "East against West, experience against innocence, civilization against primitivism," as tensions she infused into her *Troll Garden* stories, in Woodress, ed., *The Troll Garden*, xvii.

8. Ida H. Washington, *Dorothy Canfield Fisher: A Biography* (Shelburne, Vt.: New England Press, 1982), 29.

9. Woodress notes that Imogen was probably suggested by Dorothy Canfield. *The Troll Garden*, xix. To my knowledge, other critics have not written of parallels between Flavia Hamilton and Flavia Canfield, or between Arthur Hamilton and James Canfield.

10. In an extended discussion of *The Troll Garden*, Marilyn Arnold writes that "The Sculptor's Funeral" and "Paul's Case" as "two of the best pieces of fiction Cather ever wrote" and that the collection as a whole "demonstrates that for Cather a long and productive apprenticeship was over." Arnold, *Willa Cather's Short Fiction*, 43. While agreeing with much of what Arnold writes about these stories, I consider them part of Cather's apprentice period, even at their best rather self-consciously "made" pieces of fiction. Edward A. Bloom and Lillian D. Bloom suggest thematic continuities between stories in *The Troll Garden* and Cather's later fiction and interpret *The Troll Garden* as "primarily an extended colloquy between the artist as hero and a personified middle-class society as the villain," an early version of Cather's long interest in the artist as an

individual. See *Willa Cather's Gift of Sympathy* (Carbondale: Southern Illinois University Press, 1962), 117 et passim.

11. "The Enchanted Bluff" is quoted from *Willa Cather's Collected Short Fiction, 1892–1912,* rev. ed., ed. Virginia Faulkner, intro. Mildred R. Bennett (Lincoln: University of Nebraska Press, 1970).

Chapter Three: *Alexander's Bridge*

1. Sarah Orne Jewett to Willa Cather, 13 December 1908, *Letters of Sarah Orne Jewett,* ed. Annie Fields (Boston: Houghton Mifflin, 1911), 249–50.

2. James Woodress, *Willa Cather: Her Life and Art* (1970; Lincoln: University of Nebraska Press, 1980), 120.

3. L. Brent Bohlke discusses the circumstances concerning the volume, reports on a 1922 letter from Cather to Edwin H. Anderson in which she outlines details concerning the project, and concludes that this letter "necessitates the inclusion of that book within the Cather canon." "Willa Cather and *The Life of Mary Baker G. Eddy,*" *American Literature* 54 (May 1982): 288–94.

4. Willa Cather to Sarah Orne Jewett, 18 December 1908, Houghton Library, Harvard University.

The Goldsmith quotation is from "The Deserted Village," lines 93–94. The stanza from which the lines are taken reads as follows:

> In all my wanderings round this world of care,
> In all my griefs — and GOD has given my share —
> I still had hopes my latest hours to crown,
> Amidst these humble bowers to lay me down;
> To husband out life's taper at the close,
> And keep the flame from wasting by repose.
> I still had hopes, for pride attends us still,
> Amidst the swains to shew my book-learned skill,
> Around my fire an evening groupe to draw,
> And tell of all I felt, and all I saw;
> And, as an hare whom hounds and horns pursue,
> Pants to the place from whence at first she flew,
> I still had hopes, my long vexations past,
> Here to return — and die at home at last.

Collected Works of Oliver Goldsmith, ed. Arthur Friedman (Oxford: Clarendon Press, 1966), 4:290–91.

5. *Letters of Sarah Orne Jewett,* 249–50. Even Cather's original title for her novel seems a response to Mrs. Jewett, who had advised her, "When a woman writes in the man's character, — it must always, I believe, be something of a masquerade." Ibid., 246. Cather's first novel was originally titled *Alexander's Masquerade* and appeared as a three-part serial in *McClure's* from February through April 1912.

6. Bernice Slote, Introduction to *Alexander's Bridge* (Lincoln: University of Nebraska Press, 1977), viii, note.

7. *Alexander's Bridge,* new edition with a preface (Boston: Houghton Mifflin Co., 1922), vi.

8. *Alexander's Bridge* (1912; Lincoln: University of Nebraska Press, 1977). All references are to this text.

9. "My First Novels [There Were Two]," in *Willa Cather on Writing,* 91.

10. *Alexander's Bridge,* new ed. with a preface, vi–vii.

11. I am not disputing that Cather used historical prototypes for her novel. John P. Hinz has quite rightly linked *Alexander's Bridge* to a historical disaster. On 29 August 1907, Quebec Bridge collapsed over the St. Lawrence River, killing the chief engineer and others on the project. See Hinz, "The Real Alexander's Bridge," *American Literature* 21 (January 1950):473–76. Other literary and historical prototypes are possible. The Quebec Bridge collapse may have triggered in Cather memories of Kipling's "The Day's Work," and especially his story "The Bridge Builders," which she had reviewed for the *Pittsburgh Leader,* on 18 February 1899. In her review Cather summarized Kipling's story in terms that anticipate *Alexander's Bridge.* She saw "The Bridge Builders" as the story of a civil engineer who, in building a bridge over the Ganges, "built his life into the bridge." Moreover, Cather anticipated the conception of her character as an engineer-artist when she praised Kipling's celebration of energy as "the most wonderful and terrible and beautiful thing in the universe; the energy of great machines, of animals in their hunt for prey, of men in their hand-to-hand fight for a foothold in the world. He has found in this energy subject matter for art, whereas it has previously been considered the exclusive province of science." Quoted in *The World and the Parish: Willa Cather's Articles and Reviews, 1893–1902,* ed. William M. Curtin (Lincoln: University of Nebraska Press, 1970), 2:558.

More personally, Cather may have taken the name of her major character from another historical figure, Hartley Burr Alexander, a 1887 graduate of the University of Nebraska and from 1908 on the faculty of the Department of Philosophy. Unquestionably, Cather knew of Professor Alexander's teaching and writing. A volume of his book, *The Mid Earth Life,* inscribed "from Mrs. Hartley Burr Alexander, Lincoln, Nebraska," was part of the Cather family library.

Indeed, I believe that Cather may have used Professor Alexander as a model in other ways. Professor Alexander's actions while a member of Nebraska's philosophy department are remarkably similar to those of Godfrey St. Peter. Finally, Professor Alexander's book, *The Mid Earth Life* (Springfield, Mass.: H. R. Hunting, 1907), contains passages remarkably similar to passages in Cather's *Death Comes for the Archbishop.*

12. Dorothy Van Ghent, *Willa Cather,* University of Minnesota Pamphlets on American Writers no. 36 (Minneapolis: University of Minnesota Press, 1964).

13. *The Song of the Lark* (Boston: Houghton Mifflin, Sentry Edition, 1963), 466.

14. "The Bohemian Girl," *Willa Cather's Collected Short Fiction, 1892–1912,* rev. ed., ed. Virginia Faulkner, intro. Mildred R. Bennett (Lincoln: University of Nebraska Press, 1970). All references are to this text.

Chapter Four: *O Pioneers!*

1. *O Pioneers!* (1913; Boston: Houghton Mifflin, Sentry Edition, 1962), 116. All references are to this text.

2. "My First Novels [There Were Two]," in *Willa Cather on Writing,* 91–93.

3. Willa Cather to Elizabeth Shepley Sergeant, 5 July, 12 September, and 7 December 1912, Elizabeth Shepley Sergeant Papers, Pierpont Morgan Library.

4. Sergeant, *Willa Cather: A Memoir,* 86. Sergeant bases her account upon Cather's letters to her, now in the Pierpont Morgan Library.

5. With the title of her essay, "The Unity of Willa Cather's 'Two-Part Pastoral': Passion in *O Pioneers!,*" Sharon O'Brien draws attention to the pastoral mode; in her discussion, however, she focuses upon interpreting thematic unity of passion in the Alexandra and Marie-Emil stories rather than upon interpreting the novel within a pastoral tradition. *Studies in American Fiction* 6 (Autumn 1978): 157–69. In "Willa Cather and the Pastoral Tradition," John H. Randall III briefly discusses *O Pioneers!* but as a georgic, arguing that since "Willa Cather's novels contain no literal shepherds and shepherdesses, since she deals with a settled agricultural civilization—she is more in the tradition of Virgil's *Georgics* than of his *Eclogues.*" *Five Essays on Willa Cather: The Merrimack Symposium,* ed. John J. Murphy (North Andover, Mass.: Merrimack College, 1974), 81. I believe that Randall, by concentrating excessively on the "machinery" of pastoral, misses both the flexibility of the pastoral mode and the ways in which Cather adapted that tradition to the American scene.

6. William Empson, *Some Versions of Pastoral* (London: Chatto & Windus, 1935), 23; Renato Poggioli, "The Oaten Flute," *Harvard Library Bulletin* 11 (Spring 1957): 147; Leo Marx, *The Machine in the Garden: Technology and the Pastoral Ideal in America* (New York: Oxford University Press, 1964), 29; Raymond Williams, *The Country and the City* (New York: Oxford University Press, 1973), 22; and Harold E. Toliver, *Pastoral Forms and Attitudes* (Berkeley and Los Angeles: University of California Press, 1971), 5.

7. Virgil, *The Pastoral Poems: A Translation of the Eclogues,* trans. E. V. Rieu (Harmondsworth, Middlesex: Penguin, 1949). The eclogues concerned primarily with nature are I ("The Dispossessed"), IV ("The Golden Age Returns"), V ("Daphnis at Heaven's Gate"), VI ("The Song of Silenus"), and IX ("The Road to Town"); those concerned primarily with love are II ("The Passionate Shepherd to His Love"), III ("Are These Meliboeus' Sheep?"), VII ("The Sing-

ing Match"), VIII ("Damon and Alphesiboeus"), and X ("Gallus").

8. Early appearances of the Silenus/Ivar character are especially interesting. The hermit of "Lou, the Prophet" has characteristics Cather later gave to Ivar; in "Eric Hermannson's Soul" Cather describes an old man at the dance as "old Silenus," demonstrating that she was specifically aware of the Virgilian tradition she would later use for Ivar.

9. Toliver, *Pastoral Forms and Attitudes*, 9.

10. For a discussion of the cluster of metaphors that make up "the master symbol of the garden . . . all centering about the heroic figure of the idealized frontier farmer armed with that supreme agrarian weapon, the sacred plow," see Henry Nash Smith's "The Garden of the World and American Agrarianism," in *Virgin Land: The American West as Symbol and Myth* (Cambridge: Harvard University Press, 1950), 124ff.

11. Sergeant, *Willa Cather: A Memoir*, 92.

12. Marx, *The Machine in the Garden*, 343. See Marx's discussion of these contradictions on pp. 341–53 and elsewhere.

13. I am indebted here to Eleanor Winsor Leach's perceptive discussion, "Return from the Pastoral World," in her book, *Vergil's Eclogues: Landscapes of Experience* (Ithaca: Cornell University Press, 1974), 25–50.

14. Marx, *The Machine in the Garden*, 31.

Chapter Five: *The Song of the Lark*

1. *The Song of the Lark* (1915; Houghton Mifflin, Sentry Edition, 1963), 177. This edition contains revisions made by Cather in 1937. All references are to this text.

2. See "My First Novels [There Were Two]," in *Willa Cather on Writing*, 92–93.

3. Sergeant, *Willa Cather: A Memoir*, 92.

4. For a more extensive discussion of Cather's use of her childhood experiences in *The Song of the Lark*, see Mildred R. Bennett, *The World of Willa Cather* (1953; new ed. with notes and index, Lincoln: University of Nebraska Press, 1961).

5. Preface to *The Excursion*, 1814, in *Wordsworth's Literary Criticism*, ed. W.J.B. Owen (London: Routledge & Kegan Paul, 1974), 170–71.

6. From Cather's flyleaf dedication of Carrie Miner Sherwood's copy of *O Pioneers!*, included by Mildred R. Bennett in *The World of Willa Cather*, in illustrations following 222.

7. Carlyle, "The Everlasting No," in *Sartor Resartus: The Life and Opinions of Herr Teufelsdröckh*, ed. Charles Frederick Harrold (New York: Odyssey, 1937), 164. Indeed, the entire passage from Carlyle is remarkably similar to Cather's later description of Thea. Having sought work by which he would know himself, Teufelsdröckh realized he had been "strangely unprosperous" and that "the net-result of [his] Workings amounted as yet simply to—Nothing." He lived

in "a strange isolation. . . . The men and women around me, even speaking with me, were but Figures; I had, practically, forgotten that they were alive, that they were not merely automatic. In the midst of their crowded streets and assemblages, I walked solitary . . . savage also, as the tiger in his jungle" (163–64). Cather knew Carlyle well. Two of the books in her early library were *Sartor Resartus* (inscribed "Wm. Cather Jr." and "Wm W. Cather Jr.") and Ewald Flugel, *Thomas Carlyle's Moral and Religious Development* (New York: M. L. Holbrook & Co., 1891; inscribed "Willa Cather"). Both volumes are in the Cather Collection, Willa Cather Historical Center, Red Cloud, Nebraska. Cather's first significant published work was an essay on Thomas Carlyle, which appeared in the *Nebraska State Journal* and the *Hesperian* on 1 March 1891 (reprinted in *The Kingdom of Art,* 421–25).

8. "The Everlasting No," in *Sartor Resartus,* 168.

9. For a discussion of sexual passion in *The Song of the Lark* as "an integral, necessary part of growth toward artistic fulfillment," see Loretta Wasserman's essay, "The Lovely Storm: Sexual Initiation in Two Early Willa Cather Novels," *Studies in the Novel* 14 (Winter 1982): 348–58.

10. *Nebraska State Journal,* 7 October 1894, in *The Kingdom of Art,* 178–79.

11. David Stouck discusses *The Song of the Lark* as *Künstlerroman* in *Willa Cather's Imagination* (Lincoln: University of Nebraska Press, 1975), 183–98.

12. I am indebted to James Woodress for calling to my attention *Of Lena Geyer,* by Marcia Davenport (New York: Grosset & Dunlap, 1936), a *Bildungsroman* of an opera singer. Interestingly, Lena Geyer responds "passionately" to Cather's *My Ántonia,* identifying with its characters and sensitive to its beauty (380).

13. Portions of this discussion on Cather's use of female metaphors to present Thea's imaginative growth are adapted from my essay, "Willa Cather's Female Landscape," *Women's Studies* 11 (December 1984): 233–46.

Discussions of gender in Cather's writing, and especially of her treatment of women as artists, have become increasingly interesting in recent years. See Bernice Slote, "First Principles: The Kingdom of Art," in *The Kingdom of Art,* 31–112; Blanche H. Gelfant, "The Forgotten Reaping-Hook: Sex in *My Ántonia,*" *American Literature* 43 (March 1971): 60–82; Linda Pannill, "The Artist-Heroine in American Fiction, 1890–1920" (Ph.D. diss., University of North Carolina, Chapel Hill, 1975); Jane Rule, *Lesbian Images* (New York: Doubleday, 1975); Patricia Meyer Spacks, *The Female Imagination* (New York: Knopf, 1975); Ellen Moers, *Literary Women* (New York: Doubleday, 1976); Grace Stewart, *A New Mythos: The Novel of the Artist as Heroine, 1877–1977* (St. Albans, Vt.: Eden Press, 1979); Susan Gubar, "Blessings in Disguise: Cross-Dressing as Re-Dressing for Female Modernists," *Massachusetts Review* 22 (Autumn 1981); Carol Pearson and Katherine Pope, *The Female Hero in American and British Literature* (New York: Bowker, 1981); Sharon O'Brien, "Mothers,

Daughters, and the 'Art Necessity': Willa Cather and the Creative Process," in *American Novelists Revisited,* ed. Fritz Fleischmann (Boston: G. K. Hall, 1982), 265–98; Loretta Wasserman, "The Lovely Storm"; Linda Huff, *A Portrait of the Artist as a Young Woman* (New York: Ungar, 1983); Linda Pannill, "Willa Cather's Artist-Heroines," *Women's Studies* 11 (December 1984): 223–32.

14. Book Second, "School-time (continued)," lines 255–62, from *The Prelude of 1850 in Fourteen Books,* in *The Prelude, 1799, 1805, 1850: Authoritative Texts, Context, and Reception,* ed. Jonathan Wordsworth, M. H. Abrams, and Stephen Gill (New York: Norton, 1979).

15. Ellen Moers, *Literary Women: The Great Writers* (1976; Garden City, N.Y.: Doubleday, Anchor Books, 1977), 391–94.

16. *Nebraska State Journal,* 1 March 1896, in *The Kingdom of Art,* 417.

17. Willa Cather to Dorothy Canfield Fisher, 15 March 1916, Dorothy Canfield Fisher Collection, Guy Bailey Memorial Library, University of Vermont.

18. "My First Novels [There Were Two]," in *Willa Cather on Writing,* 96.

19. Robert Langbaum, *The Poetry of Experience: The Dramatic Monologue in Modern Literary Tradition* (London: Chatto & Windus, 1957), 48.

20. 1932 Preface to *The Song of the Lark,* vi.

Chapter Six: *My Ántonia*

1. *My Ántonia* (1918; Boston: Houghton Mifflin, Sentry Edition, 1961), 353. Unless otherwise indicated, all references are to this text.

2. Quoted by E. K. Brown, *Willa Cather: A Critical Biography,* completed by Leon Edel (New York: Knopf, 1953), 204–5.

3. James Woodress, *Willa Cather: Her Life and Art* (1970; Lincoln: University of Nebraska Press, 1982), 180.

4. David Stouck, *Willa Cather's Imagination* (Lincoln: University of Nebraska Press, 1975), 46–58; Paul A. Olson, "The Epic and Great Plains Literature," *Prairie Schooner* 55 (Spring/Summer 1981): 263–85; James E. Miller, Jr., "*My Ántonia* and the American Dream," *Prairie Schooner* 48 (Summer 1974): 112–23; Blanche H. Gelfant, "The Forgotten Reaping-Hook: Sex in *My Ántonia,*" *American Literature* 43 (March 1971): 60–82.

5. Brown, *Willa Cather: A Critical Biography,* 199.

6. Quotations in this and the following paragraph are to the 1918 introduction, *My Ántonia* (Boston: Houghton Mifflin, Cambridge: The Riverside Press, 1918), xii. Cather was to shorten her introduction for the 1926 edition, but she did not alter meaning in it.

7. For a discussion of *My Ántonia* as the story of "Jim Burden's success in converting [Ántonia] into a symbol of a way of life he approves of," see William J. Stuckey, "*My Ántonia:* A Rose for Miss Cather," *Studies in the Novel* 4 (Fall 1972): 473–83. Stuckey is quite right in stressing tension between Jim Bur-

den's "desire to convert Ántonia into a beautiful image of agrarian life and Ántonia's resistance to that conversion" (474).

8. William Wordsworth, *The Prelude of 1805,* Book First, line 305, in *The Prelude, 1799, 1805, 1850,* ed. Jonathan Wordsworth, M. H. Abrams, and Stephen Gill (New York: 1979).

9. For discussions of ways in which Cather drew upon life for *My Ántonia,* see Bennett, *The World of Willa Cather,* and Woodress, *Willa Cather: Her Life and Art.*

10. Wordsworth, *The Prelude of 1805,* Book First, line 305.

11. Coleridge, "On Poesy or Art," in *English Romantic Writers,* ed. David Perkins (New York: Harcourt, Brace, Jovanovich, 1967), 494.

12. John Keats to Benjamin Bailey, 22 November 1817, *The Complete Poetical Works and Letters of John Keats,* Cambridge Edition (Cambridge: The Riverside Press, 1899; distributed by Houghton Mifflin, Boston), 274.

13. This discussion on Cather's use of gender for narrative tension is adapted from my essay, "Willa Cather's Women," *Studies in American Fiction* 9 (Autumn 1981): 261–75.

14. Ellen Moers, *Literary Women* (1976; Garden City, N.Y.: Doubleday, Anchor Books, 1977), 350.

Chapter Seven: *One of Ours*

1. *One of Ours* (1922; New York: Knopf, 1979), 153. All references are to this text.

2. Willa Cather, "Nebraska," in *Further Adventures in Essay Reading,* ed. Thomas E. Rankin et al. (New York: Harcourt, Brace, 1928), 72, reprinted as "Nebraska: The End of the First Cycle," in *Roundup: A Nebraska Reader,* ed. Virginia Faulkner (Lincoln: University of Nebraska Press, 1957), 6.

3. Lewis, *Willa Cather Living,* 117.

4. Edith Lewis includes background details in *Willa Cather Living,* 117ff. Perhaps the most revealing sources for Cather's attitudes concerning *One of Ours* are her letters to Dorothy Canfield Fisher, in the Canfield-Fisher Collection, Guy Bailey Memorial Library, University of Vermont. These letters make apparent Cather's intense personal involvement with Claude as well as the emotional strain she felt over the book.

5. Lewis, *Willa Cather Living,* 122.

6. Eva Mahoney, "How Willa Cather Found Herself," *Omaha World-Herald,* 27 November 1921, magazine section.

7. *My Ántonia* (1918; Boston: Houghton Mifflin, Sentry Edition, 1961), 353, 18.

8. *Willa Cather on Writing,* 79–80.

9. Lewis, *Willa Cather Living,* 122.

10. Cather's description of writing *One of Ours* is from an interview by Latrobe Carroll, "Willa Sibert Cather," in *The Bookman* 53 (May 1921): 216. Earl

R. Wasserman has written: "What Wordsworth, Coleridge, Keats, and Shelley chose to confront more centrally and to a degree unprecedented in English literature is a nagging problem in their literary culture: How do subject and object meet in a meaningful relationship? By what means do we have a *significant* awareness of the world?" Wasserman, "The English Romantics: The Grounds of Knowledge," *Studies in Romanticism* 4 (Autumn 1964): 17–34, reprinted in *Romanticism: Points of View,* ed. Robert F. Gleckner and Gerald E. Enscoe, 2d ed. (Englewood Cliffs, N.J.: Prentice-Hall, 1970), 335.

11. Terms such as *naturalism* and *realism* have long been used for *One of Ours,* most recently by John J. Murphy, who argues that this novel is Willa Cather's "experiment in turn-of-the-century realism and naturalism." Murphy, *"One of Ours* as American Naturalism," *Great Plains Quarterly* 2 (Fall 1982): 234. I believe that *One of Ours* is within the romantic tradition of her other writing.

The naturalist upholds external reality as that which is real and seeks to be accurate to that reality, characteristically in an objective, even documentary style; the romanticist believes that external reality symbolizes or suggests ultimate truths and seeks to be accurate to an individual's experience or perceptions. The tragedy of *One of Ours* is not that it is the human condition to be struggling for survival in a world which operates by natural laws, but that Claude Wheeler *has* the potential for more and that his world *does* offer transcendent ideas. Claude had the bad luck to be born into a family temperamentally unsympathetic to him and to live in America during a period of mind-numbing materialism. Cather does not suggest, however, that such is the human condition. For although Claude is fooled, alternatives do exist: in the nature that murmurs truth to him; in the Erlichs, who live well; in Ernest Havel, who, like Cather's noble immigrant characters, has an Old World imagination; and in David Gerhardt, one of Cather's most sensitive artists. Such alternatives are those of the romanticist, not of the naturalist, and Cather is far indeed from Norris and Dreiser.

12. Charles Dickens, *Bleak House,* ed. George Ford and Sylvere Monod (New York: Norton, 1977), chap. 16 ("Tom-all-Alone's"), 198.

13. George O. Marshall, Jr., *A Tennyson Handbook* (New York: Twayne, 1963), 139–40. See also headnote to "The Marriage of Geraint," *Idylls of the King,* in *The Poems of Tennyson,* ed. Christopher Ricks (London: Longmans, Green, 1969), 1525–26. Subsequent references to "The Marriage of Geraint" and "Geraint and Enid" are to this edition and are included in the text.

14. Robert Langbaum, *The Poetry of Experience: The Dramatic Monologue in Modern Literary Tradition* (London: Chatto & Windus, 1957), 20. See my discussion of this point in Chapter 1 above.

15. For Cather's discussion of the revelatory scene in fiction, see "Defoe's *The Fortunate Mistress,"* in *Willa Cather on Writing,* 78–80.

16. Stephen Crane, "The Blue Hotel," in *The Portable Stephen Crane,* ed. Joseph Katz (1969; New York: Viking, Penguin Edition, 1977), 442.

17. This is Cather's title for book 5 of *One of Ours*.

18. Willa Cather to Mr. Johns, 17 November 1922, Clifton Waller Barrett Library, University of Virginia.

19. John R. Reed, *Perception and Design in Tennyson's "Idylls of the King,"* (Athens, Ohio: Ohio University Press, 1969), 90.

20. Eva Mahoney, "How Willa Cather Found Herself," *Omaha World-Herald*, 27 November 1921, magazine section.

21. *New York Times*, 10 September 1922, 14.

22. See Bernice Slote's discussion of Mencken's statements on Cather's writing in "Willa Cather," *Sixteen Modern American Authors: A Survey of Research and Criticism*, ed. Jackson R. Bryer (Durham, N.C.: Duke University Press, 1974), 40-41.

23. Edmund Wilson, *The Shores of Light: A Literary Chronicle of the Twenties and Thirties* (New York: Farrar, Straus and Young, 1952), 39, 40.

24. Ernest Hemingway to Edmund Wilson, 25 November [1923], ibid., 118.

25. Stanley Cooperman, "The War Lover: Claude (Willa Cather)," in *World War I and the American Novel* (Baltimore: John Hopkins Press, 1967), 129.

26. Sergeant, *Willa Cather: A Memoir*, 177.

27. "Willa Cather Discusses Writing and Short Story Courses," *Nebraska State Journal*, Saturday, 25 April 1925, 11.

Chapter Eight: *A Lost Lady*

1. *A Lost Lady* (1923; New York: Random House, Vintage Books, 1972), 79. All references are to this edition.

2. "The Novel Démeublé," in *Willa Cather on Writing*, 42-43.

3. Cather wrote of the genesis of her novel in a letter to Irene Miner Weisz, 6 January 1945, Newberry Library; the quotation is from an interview, "Willa Cather Discusses Writing and Short Story Courses," *Nebraska State Journal*, 25 April 1925, p. 11.

4. "Willa Cather Discusses Writing," 11.

5. Lewis, *Willa Cather Living*, 124.

6. "Willa Cather Discusses Writing," 11.

7. Ibid.

8. Lewis, *Willa Cather Living*, 124.

9. Bennett, *World of Willa Cather*, 70-75.

10. Ibid., 75.

11. Willa Cather to Carrie Miner Sherwood, 12 February [no year], Willa Cather Historical Center, Red Cloud, Nebraska.

12. For one of the best interpretations of *A Lost Lady* as social allegory, see John H. Randall III, *The Landscape and the Looking Glass: Willa Cather's Search for Values* (Boston: Houghton Mifflin, 1960), 74-202.

13. In an earlier essay I argued that *A Lost Lady* is not Cather's elegy for the pioneer past but rather her coming to terms with the question of "how to translate the best of the past into the present, despite essential changes between the times." "Willa Cather's *A Lost Lady:* The Paradoxes of Change," *Novel* 11 (Fall 1977): 51–62.

14. *My Ántonia* (1918; Boston: Houghton Mifflin, Sentry Edition, 1961), 352.

15. "Willa Cather Discusses Writing," 11.

16. Niel's response, coming from his deep longing for permanence in a world of change, is remarkably similar in motive and form to Keats's response to the objects of his odes. The odes characteristically begin with the observer feeling the impact of the object's fullness—for example, the Grecian urn's paradoxical combination of activity and immobility, of silence and expression:

> Thou still unravished bride of quietness
>> Thou foster child of silence and slow time,
> Sylvan historian, who canst thus express
>> A flowery tale more sweetly than our rhyme.

This initial sense of value is followed by the pain of separation from the object and an attempt to bridge that separation—to make the object give itself up to the observer. Tension builds between reason and imagination: the reason, an analyzing faculty, seeks to separate, divide, and categorize, while the imagination, a synthesizing faculty, seeks to perceive similarities, to unite, and to enter into. Increasingly intense questions addressed to the urn are frustrated by the object's self-sufficiency, and resolution comes only when the observer, ceasing his attempt to force the object to reveal its secrets allows himself to experience it in all its paradoxical fullness. It is at this point that the observer moves beyond the object as object and experiences it as a symbol; the experience forms the lyric climax of the ode. This experience is transitory, however, and so the observer drops back into separation—but a separation different from that at the poem's beginning, for he retains a memory of the symbolic richness he participated in.

17. Samuel T. Coleridge, *The Statesman's Manual* (London: Gale and Fenner, 1816), 37. Coleridge includes here his famous description of a symbol as "characterized by a translucence of the Special in the Individual or of the General in the Especial or of the Universal in the General. Above all the translucence of the Eternal through and in the Temporal." In *Willa Cather's Gift of Sympathy,* (Carbondale: Southern Illinois Press, 1962), 26, Edward A. Bloom and Lillian D. Bloom write, "The fundamental understanding of Cather's work is, indeed, dependent upon an understanding of her meaningful employment of a set of symbols, all of which are segments of the total theme"; they use Coleridge's definition to clarify Cather's symbolism.

18. Karl Kroeber, *Romantic Narrative Art* (Madison: University of Wisconsin Press, 1966), 53.

19. Recalling Mrs. Garber, Willa Cather compared memories of experiences and emotions to perfume, then went on to maintain that the memory has its own reality: "It is the difference between the remembered face and having that friend one day come thru the door. She is really no more yours than she has been right along in your memory" ("Willa Cather Discusses Writing," 11). Cather made a similar observation in her letter of 6 January 1945 (Newberry Library) to Irene Miner Weisz: When Cather wrote about the places and people she loved, they returned to her so vividly it was as if she had them all over again. They excited and warmed her, perhaps more than if they had actually been present.

20. In response to a draft of this essay, Patricia Yongue, of the University of Houston, commented on the paradox implicit in Niel's aestheticism: "There is aesthetic value . . . in Marian Forrester's expanding symbolic significance for Niel and for the reader. . . . Yet the same aesthetic process which gives Mrs. Forrester a dignity and makes her interesting as a symbol also limits her humanity and freedom. Insofar as Niel and the Captain . . . ask Marian to remain unchanged, they are asking her to be an object, an urn which depicts motion but does not move in terms of human growth and expansion. It is a request, of course, which she denies, and so she moves on to California and finally to South America" (personal correspondence, 16 October 1981). For Yongue's general treatment of this "allegiance to an aristocratic ideal which often serves as a fundamental component in the dynamics of [Cather's] fiction," see her two-part essay, "Willa Cather's Aristocrats," *Southern Humanities Review* (1980), 14:43–56 and 15:111–25. For my own general treatment of the relationship between Cather's narrators and the objects they describe, see "Willa Cather's Women," *Studies in American Fiction* 9 (Autumn 1981):261–75.

21. Robert Langbaum, *The Poetry of Experience* (London: Chatto and Windus, 1957), 26.

22. Kroeber, *Romantic Narrative Art,* 58.

Chapter Nine: *The Professor's House*
1. *The Professor's House* (1925; New York: Random House, Vintage Books, 1973), 265. All references are to this text.

2. Lewis, *Willa Cather Living,* 136.

3. Willa Cather to Dorothy Canfield Fisher, 8 April 1923, Canfield-Fisher Collection, Guy Bailey Memorial Library, University of Vermont.

4. "Prefatory Note," in *Not Under Forty* (1936; New York: Knopf, 1953), v.

5. E. K. Brown, *Willa Cather: A Critical Biography,* completed by Leon Edel (New York: Knopf, 1953), 240–45. Brown uses formalist criticism to interpret Cather's house symbolism, and he presents his argument most fully in *Rhythm in the Novel* (Toronto: University of Toronto Press, 1951), 71–78. For an interpretation of house symbolism from a psychological approach, see Leon

Edel, "Willa Cather's *The Professor's House:* An Inquiry into the Use of Psychology in Literary Criticism," *Literature and Psychology* 4 (February 1954): 69–79, reprinted in *Literary Biography* (London: Rupert Hart-Davis, 1957), 61–80; reprinted also as "A Cave of One's Own," in *Stuff of Sleep and Dreams: Experiments in Literary Psychology* (New York: Harper & Row, 1982), 216–40.

6. Stephen Tennant, "The Room Beyond: A Foreword on Willa Cather," in *Willa Cather on Writing,* v.

7. In his comments on *The Professor's House* as a novel of "letting go with the heart," James E. Miller, Jr., stresses the importance of this passage, then says, "I have seen no discussion . . . that has come to terms with it." Miller, "Willa Cather Today," *Great Plains Quarterly* 4 (Fall 1984): 270–77.

8. Robert Frost, "Stopping by Woods on a Snowy Evening," in *Complete Poems of Robert Frost* (New York: Holt, Rinehart and Winston, 1967), 275.

9. Robert Langbaum, *The Modern Spirit: Essays on the Continuity of Nineteenth- and Twentieth-Century Literature* (New York: Oxford University Press, 1970), 102, 106. Though he does not mention Cather or her book, Langbaum provides a superb introduction to *The Professor's House* in his book *The Modern Spirit,* and especially in his chapters titled "The New Nature Poetry" (101–26) and "The Mysteries of Identity: A Theme in Modern Literature" (164–84). I am indebted to his argument in the following paragraphs of my discussion.

10. Langbaum, *The Modern Spirit,* 109.

11. Ibid.

12. Ibid., 171.

13. Because any discussion of archetype today evokes Jungian connotations, I wish to clarify that I am arguing that Cather turned to an archetypal imagination in the general sense rather than in any specifically Jungian one. As I shall discuss later, while Cather was not antagonistic to Jungian ideas *per se,* I believe her appeal to an archetypal imagination is independent of "the truth or falsity of Jung's special theories of the collective unconscious and of whether its 'primordial images' are transmitted by inheritance." Philip Wheelwright, *The Burning Fountain: A Study in the Language of Symbolism,* rev. ed. (Bloomington: Indiana University Press, 1968), 33, 54–55. Wheelwright's entire chapter "Four Ways of Imagination" (32–55) is useful as background for Cather.

14. W. B. Yeats, "Crossways: The Song of the Happy Shepherd," in *The Collected Poems of W. B. Yeats,* definitive edition, with the author's final revisions (New York: Macmillan, 1956), 7–8.

15. Gaston Bachelard, *The Poetics of Reverie,* trans. Daniel Russell (1960; New York: Orion, 1969), 173–75.

16. Leon Edel, for example, argues that *The Professor's House* is seriously flawed because it consists of "two inconclusive fragments," because "nothing in the book really explains" St. Peter's deep depression, and because St. Peter's "wish to die is at no point sufficiently motivated by the facts." Edel, *Stuff of Sleep*

and Dreams, 223, or in other reprints of this essay as cited in n. 5, above.

17. Blurb on the back cover of *The Professor's House,* Vintage Books edition (1973). It is significant, I believe, that Cather referred to Lawrence as the most gifted writer of his generation. Letter to Carrie Miner Sherwood, 4 August [1932], Willa Cather Historical Center, Red Cloud, Nebraska.

18. C. G. Jung, *Modern Man in Search of a Soul,* trans. W. S. Dell and Cary F. Baynes (1933; Harcourt, Brace & World, n.d.), 11. For a discussion of the word *dream* as used by symbolists, see Hazard Adams, *Philosophy of the Literary Symbolic* (Tallahassee: University Presses of Florida, 1983), esp. chap. 6, "The Modern Dream," 154–76.

19. Willa Cather, "Miss Jewett," in *Not Under Forty,* 93.

20. Willa Cather to Dorothy Canfield Fisher, 21 June 1922, Canfield-Fisher Collection, Guy Bailey Memorial Library, University of Vermont.

21. Sergeant, *Willa Cather: A Memoir,* 239.

22. Willa Cather to Dorothy Canfield Fisher, 27 February [1925], Canfield-Fisher Collection, Guy Bailey Memorial Library, University of Vermont.

23. Joseph Collins, *The Doctor Looks at Literature: Psychological Studies of Life and Letters* (New York: George H. Doran Co., 1923), 15–16.

24. Ibid., 16.

Chapter Ten: *My Mortal Enemy*

1. *My Mortal Enemy* (1926; New York: Random House, Vintage Books, 1961), 96. Subsequent references are to this text.

2. Lewis, *Willa Cather Living,* 138.

3. E. K. Brown, *Willa Cather: A Critical Biography,* completed by Leon Edel (New York: Knopf, 1953), 250; Dorothy Tuck McFarland, *Willa Cather* (New York: Frederick Ungar, 1972), 88.

4. C. Hugh Holman, *A Handbook to Literature,* 4th ed., based on the original edition by William Flint Thrall and Addison Hibbard (Indianapolis: Bobbs-Merrill, 1980), 410–11.

5. *Pittsburgh Leader,* 8 July 1899, in *The World and the Parish: Willa Cather's Articles and Reviews, 1893–1902,* ed. William M. Curtin (Lincoln: University of Nebraska Press, 1970), 2:698–99.

6. *The Professor's House* (1925; New York: Random House, Vintage Books, 1973), 94. All references are to this text.

7. As is indicated in Chapter 15, *"Lucy Gayhart:* A Female Gothic," I consider the relationship between Clement Sebastian and Lucy Gayheart something quite different.

8. Elsewhere I discuss *My Mortal Enemy* as a female *Bildungsroman* of awakening: see "The Novel of Awakening," *Genre* 12 (Fall 1979):313–32, reprinted in *The Voyage In: Fictions of Female Development,* ed. Elizabeth Abel, Marianne Hirsch, and Elizabeth Langland (Hanover, N.H.: Published for

Dartmouth College by University Press of New England, 1983), 49 – 68.

9. For a fuller discussion of changes in Nellie Birdseye, see my essay "Narrative Technique in *My Mortal Enemy*," *Journal of Narrative Technique* 8 (Spring 1978): 141–49.

10. *A Lost Lady* (1923; New York: Random House, Vintage Books, 1972), 55.

11. I am using the most general definition of tragedy. See, for example, the explanation of tragedy by Holman in *A Handbook to Literature*, 4th ed.

Chapter Eleven: *Death Comes for the Archbishop*

1. *Death Comes for the Archbishop* (1927; New York: Random House, Vintage Books, 1971), 50. All references are to this text.

2. Earl R. Wasserman, "The English Romantics: The Grounds of Knowledge," *Studies in Romanticism* 4 (Autumn 1964): 17 – 34, reprinted in *Romanticism: Points of View*, ed. Robert F. Gleckner and Gerald E. Enscoe, 2d ed. (Englewood Cliffs, N.J.: Prentice-Hall, 1970), 335.

3. *Denver Times*, 31 January 1916, first reprinted in Susan J. Rosowski and Bernice Slote, "Willa Cather's 1916 Mesa Verde Essay: The Genesis of *The Professor's House*," *Prairie Schooner* 58 (Winter 1984): 81–92.

4. *The Song of the Lark* (1915; Houghton Mifflin, Sentry Edition, 1963), 373. Cather wrote that Thea held "conceptions in her mind" that had "almost nothing to do with words" (373).

5. *The Professor's House* (1925; New York: Random House, Vintage Books, 1973), 219.

6. Ibid., 221.

7. "On *Death Comes for the Archbishop*," in *Willa Cather on Writing*, 5.

8. Lewis, *Willa Cather Living*, 139.

9. *The Song of the Lark*, 378.

10. "On *Death Comes for the Archbishop*," in *Willa Cather on Writing*, 10.

11. For one of the classic treatments of symbolism and a superb background to *Death Comes for the Archbishop*, see Susanne K. Langer, *Philosophy in a New Key: A Study in the Symbolism of Reason, Rite, and Art* (Cambridge: Harvard University Press, 1942).

12. "On *Death Comes for the Archbishop*," in *Willa Cather on Writing*, 11.

13. In a perceptive essay, Glen A. Love argues that in novels from *Alexander's Bridge* through *The Professor's House* Cather attempts to adapt western additions to modern experiences. Love sees in these books Cather's "hope to define the social role of the archetypal new American, the scientist-inventor, in terms that would not sully his individual striving." In so doing, he raises important questions concerning Cather's western themes, especially that of creative individualism as expressed through science and technology. He does not, however, consider any novel written after 1925. Glen A. Love, "The Cowboy in the Laboratory," in *New Americans: The Westerner and the Modern Experience in the*

American Novel (Lewisburg, Pa.: Bucknell University Press, 1982), 107–69; quotation from p. 162.

14. Charles G. Herbermann et al., eds. *The Catholic Encyclopedia* (1913), 9:397.

15. Anders Nygren, *Agape and Eros,* trans. Philip S. Watson (1953; rpt. New York: Harper & Row, 1969), 91; Alan Richardson, ed., *A Dictionary of Christian Theology* (London: SCM Press, 1969), 200.

16. David Daiches, *Willa Cather: A Critical Introduction* (1951; rpt. Westport, Conn.: Greenwood Press, 1971), 113.

17. *The Catholic Encyclopedia,* 9:398.

18. Herbert Read notes that as self-styled Cubists increased in numbers, there emerged "this tendency, which may be implicit in the mechanistic bias of our modern civilization, is an expression, perhaps unconscious, of the will to substitute for the principle of *composition after nature,* the principle of *autonomous structure.*" *A Concise History of Modern Painting* (New York: Praeger, 1959), 82–84.

19. Angus Fletcher, *Allegory: The Theory of a Symbolic Mode* (Ithaca, N.Y.: Cornell University Press, 1964), 187.

20. Ibid., 195. In *Some Versions of Pastoral* (London: Chatto & Windus, 1935), William Empson argued that double plots suggest magical relationships.

21. "On *Death Comes for the Archbishop,*" in *Willa Cather on Writing,* 9.

22. *The Catholic Encyclopedia,* 8:262.

23. Père Delehaye, as quoted in "Foreword," *The Golden Legend of Jacobus de Voragine,* trans. Granger Ryan and Helmut Ripperger, pt. 1 (London: Longmans, Green, 1941), x.

24. For a discussion of Cather's style in the manner of Puvis de Chavannes, by which "the field is homogeneous; everything is equal in a kind of optical democracy," see Clinton Keeler, "Narrative without Accent: Willa Cather and Puvis de Chavannes," *American Quarterly* 17 (Spring 1965): 119–26.

25. Susanne K. Langer, "Life-Symbols: The Roots of Sacrament," in *Philosophy in a New Key,* 155.

26. "On *Death Comes for the Archbishop,*" in *Willa Cather on Writing,* 5–6.

27. *One of Ours* (1922; New York: Knopf, 1979), 45; *The Professor's House,* 67–69, 221.

28. Susanne K. Langer, "The Fabric of Meaning," in *Philosophy in a New Key,* 287.

29. "On *Death Comes for the Archbishop,*" in *Willa Cather on Writing,* 10.

Chapter Twelve: *Shadows on the Rock*

1. *Shadows on the Rock* (1931; New York: Random House, Vintage Books, 1971), 198. All references are to this text.

2. Sergeant, *Willa Cather: A Memoir*, 226.

3. Ibid., 226–27.

4. Lewis, *Willa Cather Living*, 152.

5. Ibid., 156–57.

6. Ibid., 157; Sergeant, *Willa Cather: A Memoir*, 240.

7. "On *Shadows on the Rock*," *Willa Cather on Writing*, 15, 16.

8. "On the Divide," *Willa Cather's Collected Short Fiction, 1882–1912*, rev. ed., ed. Virginia Faulkner, intro. Mildred R. Bennett (1965; Lincoln: University of Nebraska Press, 1970), 493–504.

9. "On *Shadows on the Rock*," *Willa Cather on Writing*, 16.

10. In an undated letter to Dorothy Canfield Fisher, now in Guy Bailey Memorial Library, University of Vermont, Cather compared writing *Shadows on the Rock* to working on a tapestry.

11. Rhythms characterize thematic and structural relationships. For a detailed description of the structural plan of *Shadows on the Rock*, by which Cather has introduced and woven together major themes (wilderness, order, self-denial, maturity, national identity, family), see John J. Murphy, "The Art of *Shadows on the Rock*," *Prairie Schooner* 50 (Spring 1976): 37–51.

12. For an extended discussion of differing ways in which Cather reconciled past to present, see Sargent Bush, Jr., "*Shadows on the Rock* and Willa Cather's View of the Past," *Queen's Quarterly* 76 (Summer 1969): 269–85.

13. *Death Comes for the Archbishop* (1927; New York: Knopf, 1980), 97–98.

14. Ad de Vries, *Dictionary of Symbols and Imagery* (Amsterdam: North-Holland, 1974), 187. Other relevant symbolic meanings of fire are almost endless: it is symbolic of the essence of life and has powers of purification; it is related to the hearth to symbolize "hospitality, humane warmth; the centre of home . . . immortality." It is, as Cather wrote in "On *Shadows on the Rock*," a "sacred fire."

15. See the discussion of saints' lives in Chapter 11, above.

16. See discussions of the Virgin Mary in Ferm, *An Encyclopedia of Religion* (1945), 814; Hastings, *Encyclopaedia of Religion and Ethics* (1927); Herbermann et al., *The Catholic Encyclopedia* (1913).

17. Ferm, *An Encyclopedia of Religion*, 628.

18. In a perceptive interpretation David Stouck argues that *Shadows on the Rock* contains "a drama of innocence and guilt," and that life in Quebec has a "special holy and penitential nature." The idea of penance is, of course, related to that of purification. Stouck, *Willa Cather's Imagination* (Lincoln: University of Nebraska Press, 1975), 149–67.

19. *Special Correspondence of the {Philadelphia} Record*, New York, August 9 [1913], reprinted in *The Kingdom of Art*, 446–49.

20. "On *Shadows on the Rock*," *Willa Cather on Writing*, 16.

Chapter Thirteen: *Obscure Destinies*

1. *Obscure Destinies* (1932; New York: Random House, Vintage Books, 1974). All references are to this text.

2. For identification of models Cather used for characters in *Obscure Destinies,* see Bennett, *The World of Willa Cather.*

3. In this letter Cather was writing specifically about "Two Friends," but her point is a general one. Willa Cather to Carrie Miner Sherwood, 27 January 1934, Willa Cather Historical Center, Red Cloud, Nebraska.

4. *My Ántonia* (1918; Boston: Houghton Mifflin, Sentry Edition, 1961), 18.

5. "Song of Myself," stanza 50, 9th ed. (1891–92) of *Leaves of Grass,* in *Complete Poetry and Selected Prose,* ed. James E. Miller, Jr. (Boston: Houghton Mifflin, Riverside Editions, 1959), 67.

6. *O Pioneers!* (1913; Boston: Houghton Mifflin, Sentry Edition, 1962), 309.

7. "Song of Myself," stanza 52.

8. "Katherine Mansfield," in *Willa Cather on Writing,* 108.

9. For a fuller discussion of the sequence of female narrators in this story, see Susan J. Rosowski, "Willa Cather's Women," *Studies in American Fiction* 9 (Autumn 1981): 261–75.

10. "Katherine Mansfield," in *Willa Cather on Writing,* 108–10. Again, Cather's comments on Mansfield's stories seem a gloss to "Old Mrs. Harris":

One realizes that even in harmonious families there is this double life: the group life, which is the one we can observe in our neighbour's household, and, underneath, another—secret and passionate and intense—which is the real life that stamps the faces and gives character to the voices of our friends. Always in his mind each member of these social units is escaping, running away, trying to break the net which circumstances and his own affections have woven about him. One realizes that human relationships are the tragic necessity of human life; that they can never be wholly satisfactory, that every ego is half the time greedily seeking them, and half the time pulling away from them. In those simple relationships of loving husband and wife, affectionate sisters, children and grandmother, there are innumerable shades of sweetness and anguish which make up the pattern of our lives day by day, though they are not down in the list of subjects from which the conventional novelist works.

11. Willa Cather to Carrie Miner Sherwood, 27 January 1934.

12. For a discussion of the relationships between Cather's writing and the Populist movement of the early 1890s, see Robert W. Cherny, "Willa Cather and the Populists," *Great Plains Quarterly* 3 (Fall 1983): 206–18.

Chapter Fourteen: The Shadows of Evil

1. *The Professor's House* (1925; New York: Random House, Vintage Books, 1973), 68. Subsequent references are included in the text.

2. *My Ántonia* (1918; Boston: Houghton Mifflin Company, Sentry Edition, 1961), 353.

3. G. Richard Thompson, "Gothic Fiction of the Romantic Age: Context and Mode," in *Romantic Gothic Tales, 1790–1840* (Perennial Library Edition; New York: Harper & Row, 1979), 9. As a term to be defined, *Gothicism* is almost as elusive as *romanticism*. Recent critics agree, however, that the Gothic "is basically a mode of perception, rather than a set of things perceived." Patricia Merivale, "The Esthetics of Perversion: Gothic Artifice in Henry James and Witold Gombrowicz," *PMLA* 93 (October 1978): 992. In an excellent chapter, "The Gothic Alternative," Peter L. Thorslev, Jr., ranks "the Gothic or the grotesque universe with the organic," largely because "whatever it may have been in its origins, the literary convention of the Gothic became for the Romantics symbolic, and the universe so symbolized was fully as real as the organic, and diametrically opposed to it. The Gothic in literature represented a pessimistic protest to the optimism either of mechanistic science or of organic faith." Thorslev, *Romantic Contraries: Freedom versus Destiny* (New Haven: Yale University Press, 1984), 126–41.

4. For a discussion of the effect of alienation and estrangement, see Wolfgang Kayser's classic study, *Das Groteske: Seine Gestaltung in Malerei und Dichtung* (Oldenburg: Gerhard Stalling, 1957), translated by Ulrich Weisstein as *The Grotesque in Art and Literature* (Bloomington: Indiana University Press, 1963; rpt. New York: McGraw-Hill, 1968). For a discussion of Gothic fiction as a grotesque mode, see Maximillian E. Novak, "Gothic Fiction and the Grotesque," Novel 13 (Fall 1979): 50–67.

5. *Willa Cather's Collected Short Fiction, 1892–1912*, rev. ed., ed. Virginia Faulkner, intro. Mildred R. Bennett (Lincoln: University of Nebraska Press, 1970). Quotations from the short stories are from this edition.

6. David Punter, *The Literature of Terror: A History of Gothic Fictions from 1765 to the Present Day* (London: Longman, 1980), 11.

7. Ellen Moers, *Literary Women: The Great Writers* (Garden City, N.Y.: Doubleday, Anchor Books, 1977), 163.

8. See Kayser, "An Attempt to Define the Nature of the Grotesque," in *The Grotesque in Art and Literature*, 179–89.

9. The term "intellectual exorcism" is from Richard Chase's *The American Novel and Its Tradition* (Garden City, N.Y.: Doubleday, Anchor Books, 1957), 145.

10. Novak, "Gothic Fiction and the Grotesque," 58.

11. *My Mortal Enemy* (1926; New York: Random House, Vintage Books, 1961), 54. All references are to this text.

12. "On *Death Comes for the Archbishop*," in *Willa Cather on Writing*, 11.

13. *Death Comes for the Archbishop* (1927; New York: Random House, Vintage Books, 1971), 127. All references are to this text.

Chapter Fifteen: *Lucy Gayheart*

1. *Lucy Gayheart* (1935; New York: Random House, Vintage Books, 1976), 32. All references are to this text.

2. E. K. Brown, *Willa Cather: A Critical Biography,* completed by Leon Edel (New York: Knopf, 1953), 294–95.

3. Lewis, *Willa Cather Living,* 174.

4. Ibid., 174–75. Lewis writes that Cather's right wrist was inflamed, but James Woodress notes that Cather's letters in 1934 specify the left that was inflamed, sprained, and in splints, though the right hand too was overworked, so she was not writing at all (personal correspondence).

5. Lewis, *Willa Cather Living,* 177.

6. Brown, *Willa Cather,* 298. For models of Lucy Gayheart, see Bennett, *The World of Willa Cather,* 42, 217, and James Woodress, *Willa Cather: Her Life and Art* (1970; Lincoln: University of Nebraska Press, 1982), 250. Cather writes of Sadie Becker in a letter to Carrie Miner Sherwood, 28 June 1939, Willa Cather Historical Center, Red Cloud, Nebraska.

7. Portions of this discussion of "The Joy of Nelly Deane" are adapted from my essay, "Willa Cather's Female Landscapes," *Women's Studies* 11 (December 1984): 233–46.

8. "The Joy of Nelly Deane," in *Willa Cather's Collected Short Fiction, 1892–1912,* rev. ed., ed. Virginia Faulkner, intro. Mildred R. Bennett (Lincoln: University of Nebraska Press, 1970), 55–68. All references are to this text.

9. In "Lucy's Case: An Interpretation of *Lucy Gayheart,*" *Markham Review* 9 (Winter 1980): 27, John J. Murphy comments that there is "something almost Draculan" about scenes in which Sebastian embraces Lucy.

10. I disagree with those critics who interpret Lucy's scenes with Sebastian as erotic; to my mind, they suggest not the active passion of Cather's vibrant female characters but a disturbing passivity.

11. Leon Edel, *Willa Cather: The Paradox of Success* (Washington: Library of Congress, 1960), reprinted in *Willa Cather and Her Critics,* ed. James Schroeter (Ithaca: Cornell University Press, 1967), 266.

12. Ellen Moers, *Literary Women: The Great Writers* (Garden City, N.Y.: Doubleday, Anchor Books, 1977), 153–60. Moers notes that "perhaps the last generation to grow up with *Goblin Market* was that of Willa Cather" (153). James Woodress remarks about the sexual politics seen by modern feminists in Rossetti's poem, and adds: "The conscious or unconscious sexual-religious meaning must have been apparent to Cather, who was herself fighting her way to literary success in a male-dominated world." *The Troll Garden* (Lincoln: University of Nebraska Press, 1983), xvii.

13. Moers, *Literary Women*, 166.

14. Sergeant, *Willa Cather: A Memoir*, 255.

15. As a final note, I refer the reader to an essay on *Lucy Gayheart*, published after I had completed this chapter. In "Movement and Melody: The Disembodiment of Lucy Gayheart," Blanche H. Gelfant argues that Cather "revealed her anxieties about the end(s) of writing" in *Lucy Gayheart*, using "the language of love story romance [to testify to] the elusive ideals of the Romantic imagination," while also demonstrating its destructive potential, for "Lucy's desire for disembodiment must presage disaster." Gelfant, "Movement and Melody: The Disembodiment of Lucy Gayheart," in *Women Writing in America: Voice in Collage* (Hanover, N.H.: Published for Dartmouth College by the University Press of New England, 1984), 111–43. I would suggest only that Cather reveals her anxieties about the destructive potential of creativity primarily through the effect of Sebastian upon Lucy, and that the power of the novel results from Cather's using youth's point of view to tell of an aging artist's struggle to cling to youthful creativity. At a time when Cather was returning to childhood memories for her own writing (to Red Cloud for *Obscure Destinies* and to Virginia ones for *Sapphira and the Slave Girl*), she wrote of what it is to be youth, fed upon by age.

Chapter Sixteen: *Sapphira and the Slave Girl*

1. *Sapphira and the Slave Girl* (1940; New York: Random House, Vintage Books, 1975), 210. Cather is quoting John Bunyan's *Holy War*. All references to *Sapphira and the Slave Girl* are to this edition.

2. Lewis, *Willa Cather Living*, 178–79.

3. *My Ántonia* (1918; Boston: Houghton Mifflin, Sentry Edition, 1961), 372.

4. See Willa Cather to Elizabeth Shepley Sergeant, letters in Pierpont Morgan Library, and reported by James Woodress, *Willa Cather: Her Life and Art* (1970; Lincoln: University of Nebraska Press, 1982), 260–61. See also Lewis, *Willa Cather Living*, 181–82.

5. Lewis, *Willa Cather Living*, 184.

6. Ibid.

7. Paul C. Wermuth, "Willa Cather's Virginia Novel," *Virginia Cavalcade* 7 (Spring 1958): 4–7.

8. Lavon Mattes Jobes, "Willa Cather's Last Novel," *University Review* 34 (October 1967): 77–80.

9. Merrill Maguire Skaggs, "Willa Cather's Experimental Southern Novel," *Mississippi Quarterly* 35 (Winter 1981–82): 3–14; Richard Giannone, "Willa Cather and the Unfinished Novel of Deliverance," *Prairie Schooner* 52 (Spring 1978): 25–46; Philip L. Gerber, *Willa Cather*, Twayne's United States Authors Series (Indianapolis: Bobbs-Merrill, 1975), 131–33; David Stouck,

Willa Cather's Imagination (Lincoln: University of Nebraska Press, 1975), 225–32.

10. E. K. Brown, *Willa Cather: A Critical Biography,* completed by Leon Edel (New York: Knopf, 1953), 311–12. More recently, Marilyn Arnold has argued that in *Sapphira* Cather was "an escapist," making "the patterns of escape" central to the book. "Cather's Last Stand," *Research Studies* 43 (December 1975): 245–52. While I agree with Arnold that patterns of escape run through *Sapphira,* I interpret Cather's treatment of them as her indictment of escapism rather than as her own escapism.

11. Lionel Trilling, "Manners, Morals, and the Novel," in *The Liberal Imagination: Essays on Literature and Society* (New York: Viking, 1950), 206.

12. Robert D. Hume, "Gothic versus Romantic: A Reevaluation of the Gothic Novel," *PMLA* 84 (March 1969): 287.

13. Prefatory letter with *Edgar Huntly; or, Memories of a Sleep-Walker* (1799; Philadelphia: David McKay, 1887), 4.

14. Maximillian E. Novak, "Gothic Fiction and the Grotesque," *Novel* 13 (Fall 1979): 54; see also 66 et passim.

15. *My Ántonia,* 18.

16. James E. Keech, "The Survival of the Gothic Response," *Studies in the Novel* 6 (Summer 1974): 136.

17. Hume, "Gothic versus Romantic," 290.

18. Brown, *Willa Cather,* 309.

19. Willa Cather to Sinclair Lewis, 14 January 1938, Beinecke Library, Yale University.

20. Hume, "Gothic versus Romantic," 287.

21. In 1935–36 Italy conquered Ethiopia, then intervened in Spain and formed an increasingly close association with Nazi Germany; in 1936 Cather wrote of 1922, the year of Mussolini's "march on Rome," as the time when "the world broke in two" (preface to *Not Under Forty*); in 1937 Cather began work on *Sapphira and the Slave Girl,* which would appear in 1940, the year France fell and the Vichy regime was installed.

22. *The Professor's House* (1925; New York: Random House, Vintage Books, 1973), 68.

Index

Mencken, H. L., 109

Merivale, Patricia: on the Gothic, 269 n. 3

Miller, James E., Jr.: on *My Ántonia*, 75

Milmine, Georgine, *The Life of Mary Baker Eddy and the History of Christian Science:* Cather's role in writing, 33

Miner family: as the Harlings in *My Ántonia*, 78

Moers, Ellen: on the Female Gothic, 213, 229–30, 270 n. 12; on *The Song of the Lark*, 70

Murphy, John P.: on Draculan embrace in *Lucy Gayheart*, 270 n. 9; on *One of Ours*, 259 n. 11

Music: Dvorak's *From the New World* source of heroine's ecstasy in *The Song of the Lark*, 64; humanizing effect on narrator of "A Wagner Matinee," 27–28; in *My Ántonia*, 82–83; "valid romanticism" inspired by aria in *My Mortal Enemy*, 149

My Ántonia, 74, 75–91, 95, 96, 103, 114, 130, 144, 154, 161, 189, 233; Ántonia as archetypal woman, 86; Ántonia as mediator between man and nature, 79; autobiographical elements in, 78; child's view of outside world, 81; circular movement of, 77; dialectic pattern of, 12; different critical interpretations of, 75; episode of Peter and Pavel in, 80–81; exorcism in, 214–15; Gothic elements in, 213–15; image of plow in, 83; lyrical structure of, 76; miraculous in, 78; music in, 82–83; narrator's mythmaking in, 12, 89–90,

207; particularity of, 78; reversal of roles in, 90–91

"My First Novels [There Were Two]": Cather on writing *O Pioneers!*, 45

My Mortal Enemy, 143, 144–45; awakening in, 146, 153, 264–65 n. 8; characters' rejection of sentimental romanticism, xii; contrasting scenes in, 153; conventions stripped away in, 154; death in, 152–53; dialectic pattern of, 12; false gods in, 150–51; Gothic elements in, 217; narrator of, 154–55; revelation scenes in, 149; structure of, 146; theme of romantic love, 146

Myth: Ántonia as New World Earth Mother, 12, 130; Arthurian legend echoed in *One of Ours*, 99; Claude's belief in New World myths, 105–6; mythic aspect of Alexandra, 62; New World Eden, 54, 57, 130; New World Golden Age, 48, 52, 61; romantic version of the Fall in *The Professor's House*, xii, 131; Sleeping Beauty, 148, 150; use of myth in early stories to humanize plains, 16

"Namesake, The," 13, 33

Naturalism: rejected as mode of *One of Ours*, 259 n. 11

Nebraska: Cather on critical response to, ix; Cather's paradoxical feeling for in *The Song of the Lark*, 74; challenge of plains in early stories, 15; the "Divide," 51, 177; escape from in "The Bohemian Girl," 39–41; imaginative return to in *Lucy Gayheart*, 220;